Loving yourself

The Mastery of Being Your Own Person

SHERRIE CAMPBELL, PH.D.

authorHOUSE®

AuthorHouse™
1663 Liberty Drive
Bloomington, IN 47403
www.authorhouse.com
Phone: 1-800-839-8640

Published by AuthorHouse 1/2/2013

ISBN: 978-1-4772-8932-7 (sc)
ISBN: 978-1-4772-8933-4 (hc)
ISBN: 978-1-4772-8934-1 (e)

Library of Congress Control Number: 2012921432

Acknowledgments

*To my daughter London,
you are my inspiration
for everything I do in my life.
I love you.*

*Thank you to Marc.
My vulnerability is safe with you.
You have saved my life
and shown me the true meaning
of love and acceptance.*

*Thank you to my parents
for this amazing journey.*

*Thank you to SARK,
my beloved mentor,
I love you!*

To Chris, Kathryn and Tracy.

To He and She

Table of Contents

Introduction: Welcome to the journey into Loving Your Self............1

Three Part Journey...5

Traveling the Story: The River of Old Programming

Finding the Meaning in the Suffering

Living What You Have Learned: The Crystal Palace

Part I: Traveling the Story: The River of Old Programming
The Old Program is made up of all the faulty things we learned to think about Ourselves.....................................7

Ingredients for your Journey..9

*Eye-Sight: False beliefs about who you are.................9

*In-Sight: Sight within or intuition...................................9

*Life Class Lessons: Lessons in uncovering and understanding...9

*Extra-Credit Advantages: Healing reading to put you at an advantage..10

*Differentiating Opportunities: Just suppose... you could change your life..11

*Permission to feel: Bring your emotions......................11

*Open Mind: Container for new information.............12

*Willingness to Grow: Effort and perseverance..........13

*Forward Moving Questions: Curiosity for solutions....13

*Journal and Pen: Document your travels...................13

*Self-Acceptance: Loving all of who you are, flaws included...14

*Patience: Endurance to withstand the uncomfortable...15

*Time: The bringer of solutions.......................................15

*Courage: What is used to dismantle fear...................15

*Love: Always a necessity..15

The Voyage through Emotional Landscapes 16

*The Land of the Omen: Inner knowings, signs and signals 16

*The Land of the Unexpected: Abuse and shame 31

*The Land of the All Alone: Loneliness and isolation . 45

*The Land of the Human Angels: The power of recognition 59

*The Land of the Unstable: No one to depend upon.73

*The Land of the Unbelievable: Self-absorbed parents 87

*The Land of Insecurity: Feelings of not being good enough 99

*The Land of Authority: Anger and rebellion............ 110

*The Land of Help: Therapy 125

*The Land of He and She: Family and belonging.....140

*The Land of the Lost: Having no direction................150

*The Land of the Bad Man: Parental infidelity 162

*The Land of Secrets: Exposing family secrets 174

*The Land of Searching for Meaning: Making sense of emotional pain 187

*The Land of Surrender: Letting go 199

*The Land of Books: Paper parents 213

*The Land of Fear: Personal evolvement 225

*The Land of Femininity: Emotional depth and body image acceptance 239

*The Land of the Individuated: Independence 258

*The Land of the Unique: Freedom of full expression 271

Part Two: Finding the Meaning in the Suffering 287

*Growth and meaning come through surpassing fears 289

*Alchemy as your transformational process to deeper meaning 291

*Emotions are vehicles for meaning 292

*Pain is opportunity 293

*Letting go 295
*Asking questions leads to meaning..........................296
*Life is a series of classes 298
*Time provides the space to find meaning 300
*Be true to your Self 301

Part Three: The Crystal Palace: Living what we have learned.... 305
The Internal Operation: Welcome to your inner Self 307
The Crystal Palace 309

The Cellar: A New Beginning 309
*Loving yourself at the cellular level 310
*Cleansing by looking at our life in review.................311
*Working through resistance..312
*Putting yourself back together 313
*Seeing the good 315
*Healing has its own timing 317
*Getting to know yourself.. 320
The Ground Floor: Getting Grounded........................324
*The Kitchen: Examining your in-sights 325
*The Office: Staying on track and measuring success 344
*The Living Room: Learning to live 346
*Windows: Seeing inward and outward, light 347
*The Front Door: Standing your ground with boundaries... 348

The Second Floor: Rest, Cleanse, Rejuvenate...........351
*The Bathroom: Prepare, release and cleanse 352
*The Bedroom: Rest and rejuvenate......................... 354
*The Self-Preservation Room: Finding resolve........... 355

The Third Floor: Perspective and Understanding 357
*The lesson of perspective: the ability to see the bigger picture.. 357
*Looking down: how to deal with love and

relationships 358

*The Porch: Your chosen family........................362

*The Yard: Your social circle............................ 363

*The Fence: People in your life who need boundaries.. 363

*Looking out: Unlimited Possibilities............................ 365

*Looking up: Endings followed by new beginnings. 365

Elevator and Stairs: The Process of Evolution............367

*The way you move through life.................................372

*Synergy between the Cellar and Third Floor 376

BOOK Foreword

BY SARK

WOULD you LIKE TO experience MORE well BEING, SHIFT easily during STRESS points and upgrade your CAPACITIES for self-love and CARE?

THIS BOOK will MAGNIFICENTLY SUPPORT you in doing so.

We've All Been TAUGHT and TOLD to love ourselves "AS THY NEIGHBOR," yet we are not encouraged to ever TALK ABOUT it!

If we do TALK ABOUT it, it's MOST often Misunderstood AS NARCISSISM, self ABSORPTION or JUST plain selfishness.

THIS Means THAT THERE Are Few open dialogues or EXAMPLES of self-loving people, Living self-loving Lives. WHICH Means THAT Dr. SHERRIE CAMPBELL'S BOOK, Loving Yourself; The Mastery of Being Your Own Person is A MUCH needed and spectacular Guide TO CREATING A PRACTICAL, WORKABLE system For you To Be Able To expand your self-love Systems and CAPACITIES.

THE MORE truly self-loving people THERE Are, THE MORE THE WORLD Benefits. It's THE self-loving people WHO create positive SHIFTS in THE WORLD.

I wish for everyone in this world to live like a "full cup" of self-love, sharing the overflow. And when you feel half empty, turn to this book to fill yourself back up—from the inside. Filling yourself up from the inside and not looking to outside circumstances to fill you, means that your process will be sustainable.

This book is innovative and can really shift your perspective. I know this because I learn best by experience, example and practice—and this book delivers significant opportunities for all three.

The systems and processes in the book will blend beautifully with your own, and can transform your self-love abilities significantly.

Having worked with Sherrie and her writing as a mentor for a number of years, I can tell you that she lives what she teaches and practices what she believes, and her book reflects that beautifully.

Among the many other treasures in this book, you will learn through insight and eyesight, life class lessons, extra credit advantages and differentiating opportunities (where you are supported and shown more about doing things your way—and the value of that.)

You will be guided in, and given permission for, all of your feelings, and skillfull ways to be with them. You'll experience many additional opportunities to grow and change throughout this book and beyond.

As part of this book, she has created a profound system to support the ways you learn and live. It is called the Crystal Palace The Differentiating Formula. It is all about a wise way to live the teachings in this book and expand your perspectives and perceptions beyond where you have taken them before.

Within this book, Dr. Sherrie Campbell is sharing a true "Happy Life Map" and ongoing processes to support your unique self.

I could write a whole book in response to what I feel and think about this book— I invite you to experience it for yourself. You'll experience the nourishment, joy and wisdom that live on these pages and then, in your world.

Joy·fully,
Susan (aka SARK)
Author, Artist, Succulent Wild Woman
planetSARK.com

Introduction

I am inviting you to journey with me. The journey you are being invited on is the human journey through your conditioning or old programming into a deeper and more solid relationship with yourself. It is an emotional journey, and my only request of you as my reader is to give yourself permission to feel and to bring an open mind to learn. You will not be traveling alone. You will be traveling with me. We will journey together. We will not be traveling through the outer world; we will be traveling through the inner world.

This book tells how I was able to heal my life. It can serve as a template for you to heal yours. The story is authentic, autobiographical, and vulnerable. When I wrote the first draft of this piece of work, I had no intention to publish. The poetry part of the book was written in twelve days. I experienced an opening within me; all of a sudden my life began to make sense. For many years, I did not really know what to do with it, although I sensed a miracle had come through me onto the paper. I am grateful I kept it in its original form, as it allowed me more time to grow and more time to make some pivotal mistakes that would add the self-help sections of the book. In this book I teach what I have learned. ***Your first lesson is that mistakes are your self-created learning experiences.***

On this journey, you will be transported out of your world and into a new world, a world of emotion, traveling, learning, feeling, falling, getting up, experiencing, expelling, growing, repressing, developing and gathering insights from broken pieces. You will travel through childhood all the way through to adulthood with guidance, insights and lessons being offered all the way through. The purpose of the book is to help you to develop a confident, fulfilling relationship with yourself. Having this type of connection with your Self is the key to a happy and successful life. This book will teach you how to free yourself of all the false beliefs you have developed about yourself and develop a more differentiated Self, created solely by you.

To differentiate is to become your own person. Direct guidance will be offered to you in how to differentiate in each section of the book. You are not an extension of those who raised you. You are here to be a complete and different unique 'other.' Nature does not repeat itself. There is only one of you, there will always be only one of you, and you have a responsibility to take advantage of this gift. Why? Because you are a gift. The journey is learning how to see yourself as a gift, to express your gifts and to give your gifts to the world. You are needed in this world for your contribution, or you wouldn't be here. We all have purpose.

We are all rare diamonds. Coming out of childhood and other poisonous relationships, our diamonds become covered in dirt and tar. As you grow, identify, and individuate, you clean this diamond off one facet at a time. This is called cleansing. As we cleanse, we create a shine. It is our shine that begins to attract miracles to us. When we shine, the good stuff in life begins to happen. Let me prepare you, however; cleansing is not accomplished in a moment. Cleansing is accomplished over time with much diligence, organization, and hard work. When we cleanse, we often need to use elbow grease so get ready to work, to self-examine, and to learn. As this process takes place, your rarity will begin to surface, and your shine will begin to light the world you live in.

You will learn that each and every one of us is most lovable when we are being 100% ourselves. Many of us are people who are acting like we think people want us to act. We are changing to be what we think others want us to change to be more lovable. We are taking on the ideas of others in terms of who we think we should be and in doing so the majority of people suffer from an 'I Am Not Good Enough' perspective. This is the great human emotional affliction. Well, let me tell you, we are all good enough. This book will guide you and challenge you to rip away and change the outdated beliefs you hold about yourself. This book will act as your guide to show you how to deal with the most maimed parts of you. It will also help you to see what parts of you, ***you*** *would like to change. It will guide you through your feelings, help you to ask yourself the right questions so you can heal, and it will teach* *you to separate real from false so you can choose to throw away the outdated beliefs that no longer serve you.*

As I share my story with you, you will see you are not alone. We can all identify with the feeling world because we all feel emotions the same way. Emotions are the universal language. We can relate to each other, when we put ourselves in the feeling shoes of another. We all know what it is like to feel sad, so we can all identify with that emotion in another. This identification process is what allows us to develop the deepest bonds with each other. We are the most emotional creatures on our planet. You will learn how to deal with all your emotions in this book. I am vulnerable in sharing mine, and this will help you to be vulnerable in looking at yours.

There are gifts to being vulnerable with ourselves. In our vulnerabilities, we have to practice loving ourselves. If we love ourselves in all our glory and with all of our flaws, we will be able to relate to people in much deeper ways. In loving ourselves, we become more aware, and awareness transcends into our personal and closest relationships. All healthy relationships we have in the world are born out of the love we have within ourselves. Loving ourselves is action oriented. It is a commitment we need to make each moment of each day. Being vulnerable is the doorway into Self-love. Let us use our vulnerabilities to open the door to our inner worlds. Before the door opens, we will first look at what it really means to love ourselves.

What does it mean to love your Self? I have always found that statement to be direct in its message but to contain no direction on how to do so. This journey is about the hows in the idea of loving your Self. Self is separate to indicate the inner you. The inner you is your emotional/intuitive world. It is the world inside of you which is not seen by others. It is your private experience. Most of us have been conditioned to see loving ourselves as something we should feel guilty about: If we give our Self too much attention, we are somehow being self-indulgent. Further, we have received the message that if we entertain Self-love we should only give ourselves a certain quota of love or else we are being narcissistic.

What I have personally learned through my journey is that I have to love my Self. The love for my Self is the only love I have any direct control over. If I do not have this love I will not be able to fully enjoy my life experience. I live with me, so it is in my best interest that I love me. In order to accomplish this type of relationship, I have to really know my Self. I have to know my inner world. I have to know and be in understanding and acceptance of all that I feel. My inner world is not a world I can avoid and still find true happiness in my life. The more I know myself and what it takes to be in a relationship with my inner world, the deeper my life experience becomes and also the more comfortable.

To love something requires us to give that something attention. We cannot love a child too much. We can give a child too many things, but we can never give a child too much love. This is also true of the love we are going to develop with ourselves. This book is the journey into that relationship. You will be guided through the inner world and will be provided clear direction into learning to love your Self. You will learn about your inner world, as you are guided through mine. This book is somewhat of a template for you to use to access your own inner world. It is this inner world where your uniqueness resides. Your goal is to bring this inner world out of the darkness and into the light.

If you are reading this book, then be assured you are ready to heal and to accept change. You are ready to feel, ready to grow and ready to become the new form of yourself. Welcome to the journey, we are about to take together. The book will end with a "uniqueness operating system" that is especially for you. I saved the best for last. You will leave this journey wiser, with new information, and the inspiration to heal your life.

Come...let's journey together.

Three part journey:

Part I: Traveling the Story: The River of Old Programming

Part II: Finding the Meaning in the Suffering

Part III: Living What You Learned: The Crystal Palace

Part I
Traveling the Story
The River of Old Programming

Ingredients for your journey:

Before you begin any sort of travel, you must pack all the necessities to take care of your needs while you are gone. The following is a list of the necessary items of understanding you will need to travel on this journey:

Eye-sight is how you were taught to see yourself, love yourself, and feel about yourself from your adult conditioners and other relationships. When you are looking at life only through your **eyes,** you are limited in your perception. Your eye-sight is a reflection of the distortion you were raised in. Your adult conditioners have the most powerful impact upon you, because it is through them that you see your first reflection. You see yourself in the other before you are able to see yourself from the "I" point of view. As an infant you are totally dependent upon the outside world to meet your emotional and physical needs. Throughout this book, eye-sight is reflective of your faulty conditioning. You were taught to see yourself other than you really are.

In-sight is reflective of your healing. This is seeing life through your **heart**, your intuition, and your own discovered truths. This is your sixth sense. When you have in-sights you are having a knowing from within that you are different and more magnificent then what was mirrored to you as a child. In-sights are what you gain in self-examination. They are ah-ha moments.

Life class lessons are your *home*-work. A separate Self is your true home. So you will do *home-work*: work on the Self. Each section of the book has explanations and learning opportunities. It is my belief that one of the best ways to learn is through asking questions. In each section, I show a sample answer to the question being asked to help generate your own thought process. It is not my intent for you to answer them. It is my intent to get you thinking and wondering and integrating how you came to be the *you* you have become.

You have permission to examine these lessons in any way that is best for your learning. You can glance over them, you can come up with your own questions, you can think deeply about them, you can write about them, but whatever you do, I want you to, at least, think about them and observe the emotions which surface. Even if the emotion of resistance surfaces... observe it. This is important information. Whatever you resist, will persist.

The questions are useful to you, as they serve to guide you deep into your own story through relating to mine. This allows you to develop a more clear understanding of who you are, to note the things you would like to improve, and to notice what you love and do not love about yourself. When you ask the evolving questions, you will receive the answers which help you to make sense of your feelings and circumstances. The questions are designed to undo the faulty conditioning you endured. The purpose of the life class lessons is to get your attention away from your suffering and onto what you have the opportunity to learn.

Anyone who is focused on gaining understanding in their life is bound to succeed in personal growth.

Extra Credit Advantages:

Healing reading for home-work

Reading opportunities will be offered all along the journey. I will offer personal flexibility in how books can be read as well. The books I have chosen have all served a different purpose in my life. For example, some books I have read over and over. Others, I learned from but didn't feel compelled to finish.

Not finishing a book should not be confused with quitting. Rather, I simply got what I needed, so there was no reason to read the rest. Sometimes, I open a book to a random page to pull some sort of message for me to contemplate for that day or week. Sometimes I read part of a book's knowledge, but did not feel ready for the rest. Time travels on, and I might be inspired to finish what I started at a new place in my life.

I look for what resonates with me, my process, my direction and my emotions. I would like you to do the same and to approach these reading opportunities with the same amount of flexibility.

I have read many books but more importantly, I have studied them. There is a difference between passively reading and studying in order to make the material applicable to everyday change opportunities. The way to have an extra credit advantage in your growth is to read with the intention of changing. This means you practice what you read and find opportunities to apply your new behaviors to your daily life. As you do so, you are connecting new neurons to new neurons creating new behaviors, thus creating a new life. If you do not apply what you read, the information is dead. The point of the journey is to become more and more alive! I am offering extra credit to put you at an advantage as a seeker.

Differentiating Opportunities: *Just suppose your life could be whatever you dream...*When you differentiate, you are separating from the old eye-sights and running toward the new. It doesn't matter what happens along the way in your journey because you can overcome any and all obstacles, especially your old conditioning. What is important is that with each differentiating opportunity, you are getting closer and closer to your real Self. As long as you keep getting closer, your belief in your ability to heal will grow, and you will feel it is more realistic and attainable. Your energy and determination will increase with each step along the journey. You will see how to be open to all positive possibilities for yourself and your life. If you have picked up this book, guess what? You are ready to grow and master being yourself. You are ready to do things your own way! It is living the art of possibility.

Supplies:

Permission to Feel:

When feelings come up, we tend to feel uncomfortable. When we feel uncomfortable, the natural response is to resist. When we resist our natural emotions, we place ourselves in an unnatural emotional state which works against our natural flow. As you read this, give yourself permission to feel. Feel whatever it is that comes up and observe it as an area of interest. You do not have to hold it in. This is a safe place to let it all out, the good, the bad, and the ugly. No one is watching after all...so why not just give yourself the freedom to feel. In this journey, you do not have to be controlling of your emotions.

The feeling/emotional part of this story is told through poetry. The poetry is not obscure or confusing with hidden meanings or secrets to decode. Rather, it is direct and raw. It is the expression of experienced feelings. Not written for audience or approval, it was simply released in its pure and uninterrupted raw expression. I could have edited it to make the reader more comfortable. But then it would not have been my authentic story. It would have been a story glossed over so as to not make waves.

The poetry element should be read in the same space in which one would watch a movie. It is story-telling, and has the potential to draw you into the story of your own life and the emotions your life contains. You will be in the boat floating down the river of the story being told. The river reflects the way emotions create the currents and flow of any life journey. Emotions are liquid. They are unstable, always in motion, and they take us from one place in life to the next. So, just observe, escape into the story.

After each poem, you will stop and rest along the river banks and get clear with explanations, lessons, and new directions for you to apply to your own life story. The explanations will offer you clear direction on your path just like a compass will give you your direction. In this way, you will never feel lost.

<u>Open Mind:</u>
A mind, which is closed, is a mind not open to new information. A mind not open to new information is a mind which cannot change or evolve. To this journey bring an open mind. Be open to new questions, to new ideas, expanded thinking and new ways to live your life. Let your memories and emotions

unfold. Be open to them. *If you are open to them, then you can make sense of them.*

Willingness to Grow:
The signature purpose of life is to grow and expand into the newer and newer levels of who you already are. You must be willing to grow because it takes effort and commitment. When you are truly willing, the miracles begin to come, so let yourself *become a willing miracle creator in action!*

Forward Moving Questions:
Once you are open and willing, you can begin the life classes with commitment and interest. The life class lessons will help you find the roots of your issues and help you move from the place of *what happened to you* to *what can you do about what happened to you.* You are moving in one direction in life as dictated by the element of time and that is forward. Forward moving questions keep you in the natural flow of your life and out of resisting and creating friction.

Journal and Pen (optional but highly suggested):
These are here for you to document your travels through your inner world. Some of the most successful people throughout history have kept journals. The act of writing is organizing and solidifying. Writing accesses your left brain, which is analytical and rational. When your left brain is entertained and/or distracted, your creative right brain is free to feel, intuit, and create. The right brain opens up the unexpected solutions. What a gift to become your own best problem solver. This is just one treasure obtained through writing.

Journal writing is *transformational.* Writing engages in you the process of working through something. The simple act of writing thoughts and feelings down immediately calms an unsettled mind and heart.

Taking the time to write your feelings down helps you *know yourself more deeply.* Because writing provides the space and time to be raw and uninhibited in your experiences, it aids in *clarifying the truth of what you feel.* When you know your truth you know exactly who you are.

Because writing helps access clarity in what you think and feel, it helps you to *resolve your challenges in your relationships.* When you write about your conflicts or misunderstandings with others, you get out of your own head and put yourself onto the paper in the form of a conversation. You are able to clarify your feelings and point of view and to examine how you think the other may be feeling. This is the best way to enter into an actual conversation. When you enter a conversation with clarity, you are more able to keep your life in a place of stability. Once you expel your emotions through writing them out, you may find a real conversation isn't necessary. You worked it through on your own.

You can document growth over time by noting your patterns of behavior and your solutions to past problems. This way, when you are facing an issue that seems insurmountable, you can go through past journals and see how you have dealt with previous problems and this will guide you into solving the new.

In engaging in this type of writing, you will have a deeper experience of this book and it will allow you to get the most out of it. It is as powerful as any talk therapy and it all comes from within, which means you can heal and stand on your own. Journaling and having a therapist is doubly powerful because in this instance there is a team of transformational experiences helping you to make sense of your life. I ask all my patients to keep journals, and we often go over their writing in session. This way I teach them to be their own best allies.

<u>Self-Acceptance:</u>
Surrendering to a process and not needing it or yourself to be different is what acceptance brings to your healing. This is about acknowledging the facts of a situation or yourself and then deciding what you would like to do about it. Understanding where you are in any given situation in your life will help you to see what your limits are, how far you have come and where you would like to go. If you can accept your circumstances, you have clear vision to create change.

Patience:

Patience is a state of endurance under difficult conditions. It is the ability to stay steadfast without acting out in a negative way. Patience promotes maturity because you have to delay your gratification which includes quitting. It keeps you focused on the long term, bigger picture. Having patience is the key to solving all problems.

Time:

There is no need to rush through this journey or to rush through your own healing. When it comes to healing, examining, and growing, time is the conduit that brings us to all the solutions up ahead. There are no "have to's" on any journey to healing. There is enough time.

Courage:

Courage dismantles fear. Courage represents your ability to confront fear, pain, danger, uncertainty, and/or intimidation. Healing is usually a fear-based process, so pack your courage along with you and let it stand up whenever necessary. Courage is the path to confidence. As we are courageous, we become open to new possibilities. When we fill ourselves full of possibility, we gain courage.

Love:

Bring love on this journey. Love is the key to healing of any kind.

Now that you have been educated on the essentials and you have your list covered and packed, we are ready to journey. I am so excited, let the story begin....

The Voyage through Emotional Landscapes

Omen is perhaps one of my favorite words. Omens are signs. An Omen is believed to foretell the future, often signifying the initiation of change. What I had to change was my faulty belief system. This would be the biggest change in Self-love I could make.

Omen

I asked for an omen,
and here I sit,
a pen in hand,
in appearance
reminiscent of an ice pick.

I am going inside
to chip away,
on a journey to uncover
my icy, cold, inner decay.

The aspects I shaved off out of shame...
I want to reclaim them
and give them a name.
I no longer want to hide the pain.

I have learned it is never really hidden.
When it gets triggered,
I am unexpectedly frostbitten.

So, here I am,
pen in hand,
traveling into this
cold, strange familiar land.

My bones,
they ache from the cold
as my pain begins to unfold.
I can feel it and sense it;
there is a unique smell to it.

The smell
is stinging
the inside of my nose.

It is so dark in here.
Nothing is clear.
I feel afraid.

It is no wonder I pushed
these memories away.
I could not live with
this ache in my bones
day to day.

It was survival for me.
Down here, so many
memories and faces of me.
At one time ashamed of them,
I cut them off from my inner vision.
Each pain is now yearning
for resurrection.

I am down here alone.
I do not know where to go.
It is so slippery and bitingly cold.
Afraid I will fall,
I feel so small.

Aware of the pain,
I am about to see.
A boat appears;
it is here to guide me.

I am so freezing,
so unbelievably cold.
I fear I will stop breathing.

Panic sets in,
my chest begins
uncontrollably heaving.
I feel the tears forming,
I am resisting.

I climb in the boat;
it starts down the river.
So overwhelmed,
I'm afraid I will splinter.

I feel the presence
of all aspects of her.
She is haunting me,
hunting me…
she wants me to help her.

It is just so cold,
the pain so deep,
I feel out of control;
I begin to weep.

I need some light.
I cannot see.
It is so dark in here;
it is paralyzing.

I see a memory.
She is so small,
this infant; she is preverbal.

She senses the stress,
her parents a mess,
too young to create a healthy nest.

My parents were not happy.
No chance for the creation of a family,
between them so much immaturity.

Me, just arrived from heaven,
my body absorbing this novel haven.
My senses so fresh and alive,
from what I could feel,
I sensed this life was going to be a ride.

I chose difficult this time.

I became aware the boat had stopped

waiting for the reclaiming
of the me at this spot.

Back to reality,
the cold biting at my sanity.
The boat moved on.
The memory made me clear.

I started this life
alone and in fear.
I felt this so powerfully.
No wonder my soul
had such deep misery.
Too much for me then,
I was just a baby.

This was my beginning.

In the Omen resides the beginning of Self-awareness. As I sat with my pen and journal, my life's movie began to play. I was on the precipice between the old and the new. When you visit here, you will actively re-experience the pain of the vision of the beginning of your conditioning. You will be able to see where the old program began. As you journeyed this section of the river you have gazed at the scenery through the lens of the Omen, so now it is time to get out of the boat and discover.

The natives of this place pay close attention to times of change and they will teach you to read and trust the Omens in your life. The people here are healers and those who can intuit. As you exit the boat, you will learn of their culture. Here, in this land, all change begins. The place of the Omen is somewhat haunting as you are not in the new and no longer in the old. It is the place of signs and signals that change is coming. It is consumed with anticipation anxiety as you are unsure of what is to come. The Omen people say you will have to change your inner world in order to change or affect your outer world. You will begin to see, as you walk around, how your sense of worth initially got lost. Hold the Omens close and follow their direction. There will be wisdom here. This wisdom is sure to show you the faulty way in which you were taught to see the world and your distorted views of yourself. The people of this world let you know it is faulty eye-sight.

Eye-Sight

Life, in a strange way, is divinely open to possibility. Through all the treachery you experience, you travel in life with a "passenger consciousness." When you are an infant, you are the most vulnerable. You are essentially born a fetus. Unlike other creatures, the human being cannot walk on its first day of life. You are at the complete mercy of your caregivers. Yet, in utero, you begin to develop the emotional programming which serves as your eye-sight. You feel and learn the emotions of your mother and the environment she is living in. You are flooded with her emotional state.

Each person takes in their mother on the *cellular* level. This is how deep the first conditioning experience is. If, when she was pregnant, she felt scared, upset or anxious, your body knew it. Your cells absorbed it. Your body was awash in her every emotional experience. If she felt happy, content and secure, your body also knew this. In this way your very cells contain the conditioning impact of your mother and her emotional experiences. I learned from my very beginning, life was going to be an emergency. Stress was the first emotional experience I had. My cells absorbed all her stress as *my* stress. Her life was not in a stable place when she was pregnant with me. The eye-sight or belief I was born into was life was not safe. Worry would be a conditioned emotional state placed upon me. I was conditioned not to trust from conception.

When you are an infant or young child, your thoughts and emotions are experienced in the now; they are packaged away, and later in life, those emotions and memories are consolidated into past/present understanding. As you age, you can look back at those packaged life experiences. You can examine them and see how they impacted you as a whole person, how you see the world, how you love, how you trust and how you navigate your life. You can see you have broken pieces from how you came through your childhood.

I had an opening in consciousness where I began to see my past life unfolding in front of me as memories. I could see all my broken pieces and how they were impacting me from an observer's vantage point. I had, a need, an instinct, to go inside myself and revisit those emotions I so resiliently survived as a child with a *now* consciousness. They were survived but not healed.

The calling in life is to be whole and to be whole, you have to recognize and look at what is broken and impacting you as an adult. It is like clearing cobwebs. If your broken pieces are ignored, they will continue to poison you, your relationships, your jobs, and your view on life. You will get into a relationship and become someone you no longer like. If you do not know from where that originates, you will continue on that pattern. My worry and lack of trust in life, learned as far back as infancy created a person who drove intimacy away. At our core we are emotional beings. The emotions are meant to be examined. It is where "being conscious" originates. It starts within. In the poem, *Omen,* I started the journey of becoming conscious.

In-Sight: My reactions to the world and relationships are based upon conditioned thoughts and beliefs which have nothing to do with me.

Reflections:

The genetic material of emotions is powerful. Think about it. Your body has an electromagnetic frequency all around it, fifteen feet in all directions. This is your 'buzz.' What some call the aura is this exact frequency I am talking about. Scientists call it the Electromagnetic Frequency or EMF. Scientists have discovered that everything has a frequency down to every individual cell in your body. This frequency is your individual energy, and your energy is full of information. It is how you *feel* to other people.

You store your emotions in this frequency. Positive emotions create a brain chemical called dopamine, which is expansive, elated, joyful and feeling good. Negative emotions produce neuropeptides which are suppressive, depressive, and feeling bad. Your emotions are *felt* by the other, as the glial cells in their brains pick up on the energy you are emitting. The EMF is your electrical energy flow. When your emotions change – like switching radio stations – so does your frequency. The genetic material of the emotions has a conditioning impact on the other. Just as the energy around the cell determines cell function, the energy around the infant/child that determines the child's emotional functioning.

As you absorb these emotions, you make the mistakes that match them. You make similar mistakes or live similar life patterns to those of your parents. Anxiety and emergency were the emotions flooding my emotional system. I learned life was scary and could not be trusted. I learned to *survive* life instead of *live* life.

These subconscious patterns become your life-approach habits. Life-approach habits are fixed and based in control. Control, or the clutching of life, will always bring pain. Once you experience enough pain you have the opportunity to see your mistakes as opportunities to exhume faulty learning. We need to go in and cleanse our Cells (Selves).

You do not come into the world feeling unworthy. Your conditioning creates who you are <u>not</u>. At your essence, you are not insecure, less than, ugly, a burden, in the way, or not good enough. These are the false-self.

How do you know if you are lovable? By how your parents loved you. Since the very earliest part of your life is preverbal, meaning you have not yet developed your ability to communicate in words to form an attachment, everything about your existence depended upon the emotional interactions you received. If you did not have someone to reflect your emotions to you, then you did not have access to knowing who you were. You need your caregivers to mirror your existence back to you. This is how you develop the beginnings of a *Self*. Or if your needs were met with impatience, frustration, and anger, you learned you were not lovable. Essentially, the child's understanding of the world comes directly from the parents. If the parents fail to provide a secure emotionally healthy emotional environment, a sense of fear will develop in the child.

If security and trust were present, an interpersonal bond between you and your caregivers would have developed. This bond would be based in love and trust. You would feel the safety of being able to depend on someone. This interpersonal bond is the foundation for all other relationships. You learn of your worth in the interpersonal bond between parent and child. Such a connection is crucial. *Parents who are shut down emotionally cannot reflect and support the emotions of their children.*

When I look at my parents, the first thing that stands out is they were too young to be raising children. They were lost. When you are conditioned, you become lost too. Lost people get us lost. If your parents were lost people, they had no chance of parenting you to be found. Young people, who have children, often operate out of ownership over the child: "This is my child." They exert control over the child.

My parents had hardly finished being parented themselves. They were still looking for their answers, still searching for their clues and thus were parenting with very little life experience. They hadn't defined themselves and so had no chance to define me as an individual. I have examined the emotional Self of each parent and am able to see that in many ways having a child interfered in their own personal development long into adulthood. *Their intention was never to harm me; their immaturity allowed them to do so.*

All are born worthy and perfect. As you study the positive and negative traits of your parents, you will understand the development of your emotional programming. Tracing these emotions that had become constant companions of mine has been liberating. I know these responses are natural, but learned. *If these automatic responses can be learned, they can be unlearned.* To be conscious means to be in constant awareness of automatic thoughts which trigger automatic, unnatural, emotional reactions. Once we have this awareness, we can run interference on what has been automatic. Automatic reactions are immature reactions. When you react automatically, you have not taken the time to think. When I get into an automatic panic state I now know there is no real threat. The only threat is my own automatic panic emotion because it distorts my world view. When my world view is distorted, it is difficult to find positive solutions because the distortion disconnects me from reality.

When you have panic, you will feel a loss of power, like the defenseless infant. Now, when I experience panic, I remind myself that nothing has power; *anxiety is fear projected forward in my imagination*. In theory, panic is simple. It is thought distortion. When we get into situations that scare us, our imaginations take over filling our minds with endless horrifying stories/outcomes. Once you spiral down this path it is difficult to reign in the thoughts that create the panic emotions. At this point you are disconnected from the *thinking* parts of your brain. There is nothing more isolating than being disconnected from your own mind.

I have learned the only things that have power are *my thoughts* about the thing that has power. I will always have the opportunity to change what I think. That simple reminder helps to orient my mind to the now. I can more easily move from reacting to responding. To do this, I wait out the emotional waves of panic and fear until they subside. Waiting when you are feeling reactive is grueling. When you are reactive, you are in a fight or flight scenario, wanting to do *anything* to make your fears go away. Waiting is the only thing that can orient the mind back into reality. Reality supersedes distortion, and waiting is the most effective way to get clear. This waiting is how I decondition the automatic response I was taught by my parents. Once it subsides I am better able to respond with a clear, rational, truthful response and regain my power.

Life Class Lesson:

Anxiety was the big conditioning agent in my household and I learned this to be my own fixed state. What exactly is anxiety?

It is not fear, really. It is fear projected forward onto unknown situations which have not yet occurred. An actual fear has to do with something which is right in front of you, posing a real threat or danger. Anxiety is a form of fear for certain. It is more like dread about something 'out there' which seems foreboding, and which may not even be out there. Anxiety is more in your head than in reality.

When you live in this fixed state you are constantly on guard and geared for any possible threat or threats which could exist in your world. Anxiety can be so bad that even when you are told there is no real threat you still always feel on edge/tense and can have a difficult time calming your chaotic internal world. This can sadly ruin your life and be the unconscious emotion in the driver's seat. All people experience anxiety which makes this an important class.

Let's start the life class journey. Asking questions is like creating a map. It helps you find the origins of your emotional habits. It helps you get to know yourself and the emotions which surface with each question. The questions are designed to trigger feelings because if you can understand how you feel, then you can understand who you are and how you take in the world.

**What did your parents teach you about your value or lovability?*

**What were the negatives of each parent?*

**How did those negative qualities impact your view of your Self?*

**Where did you learn anxiety?* Example: I learned anxiety mostly from my mother. Even to this day I experience my mom to be an incredibly anxious person who cannot sit still for more than five minutes and cannot live life without a concrete plan centered around being on time to everything. This rigidity extends to eating times and bed times. Everything always felt rushed and her tone was usually one of frustration and 'hurry up or else.' I was never sure what the 'or else' would be, but she made it seem like utter catastrophe.

**How do you handle anxiety?*

**Do you live life as if it were an emergency?*

**Can you not react when feeling anxiety and work on staying connected to the thinking part of your brain?*

**How would you do this? Writing, talking your anxiety over with someone uninvolved who can get you back to thinking instead of reacting?*

**Who are those people you can count on for this?*

**Are you shut down emotionally?*

**Were your parents shut down emotionally?* Example: To be emotionally shut-down means to be unavailable, to be too consumed with your own emotions, experiences, feelings, wants, and needs to make room for anyone else's. My parents were both this way. When I desired to express my feelings, the conversation always turned to my parents talking about themselves. This was especially true of my mother.

My Dad, when I was young, was incredibly shut down in that he was struggling day to day with his own demons and often acting them out on us. He would also leave for extended periods of time with no explanation or predictable time of return. He was in and out of our lives according to *his* emotional needs. When you have children, your children's emotional needs should supersede your own. He just couldn't seem to get his life together. He was focused on him, and it was always his choice to leave his children. He was abandoned young, as was my mom.

However, neither parent was completely shut down emotionally. There were many parts of my childhood that were fun, loving, outdoors, and full of laughter and joy. *People are not usually totally impaired emotionally: they simply have areas of deep impairment.* I have many positive memories of both parents and have become emotionally closer to both as life has progressed. I was always financially provided for, and my Mom has been my savior in some really desperate times for which I felt so loved. My mom is someone I consider generous, a lot of fun, and an extremely hard worker. Emotions and understanding were not her place of availability the majority of the time. However, both parents were physically affectionate, and this was one part of my childhood I treasure.

So why do the negative aspects of our parents stand out the most? I think *we internalize our parents at their worst.* Their "worst" is what creates your scars, your ideas of limiting beliefs, and your low self-esteem. It is these scars and not your happy times that are the most imprinting, because pain hurts. You remember what hurts in order to protect yourself from further damage. It is these hurts, however, that have been my greatest gifts because it is in the process of undoing and re-learning from which all growth sprouts. You can be birthed out of your pains, if you can use them for growth and change. In many ways, parents teach you who you do not want to be and what parts of them you do want to be. They teach you what you need through what you lacked due to their limits. This is invaluable information.

**What are you doing to wake up?* Example: Waking up is coming out of the illusion that you are somehow substandard into the belief that you just may have some magnificence within to build upon. Waking up is about coming to terms with the need to supply for your Self the love you needed from your parents and/or other relationships. It is coming into the idea that you need to have a healthy love for your Self. Once this idea is established, you can make the choice to de-condition your Self from your past.

Doing is key in this question. If I do not *do* for me then I am not likely to find others to do for me either. *Waking up is about deciding to take responsibility for your life and any and all feelings.* Once you take responsibility for your feelings, you will be much better at handling them. If you look at your feelings, examine them, and understand them, you can then talk about them with a level of clarity and maturity which can help you solve your own problems. When you are irresponsible with your feelings and you are reacting/being defensive, you create more problems.

**How can you take responsibility for automatic responses and understand that now they are yours, regardless of where you learned them? How can you choose to be different?*

**What can you do today to practice a different and more mature response?*

**Can you see yourself as the owner and chooser of your current experience and look to see how you can respond differently than what you have been taught*

Extra Credit Advantage

Healing reading home-work:

Drama of the Gifted Child (Alice Miller): This book is one of my all-time favorites. In this book, Alice talks directly about the conditioning we go through as children. She very directly explains how we start to shave off essential aspects of who we are each time we are told no as children. We shave these parts off in an effort to maintain love, approval, food, home and shelter. It clearly articulates how we learned to hide our own feelings, memories, and needs in order to win parental love and affection. This book is a life changing read. I have read it several times.

The Biology of Transcendence: A Blueprint of the Human Spirit (Joseph Chilton Pierce): Wow what a read! This book explains how the brain takes in and adapts to conditioning from in utero onward. It was life altering to fully understand the power our conditioners have upon us and what a responsibility it is for each person to undo this faulty learning. In this book, you will learn how your brain actually takes in the outside world and creates habits of behavior based upon survival and how to change these patterns which no longer serve you in your life. If you're interested in the brain, this is one of the most readable books you will come across. It's fascinating, spiritual, and mind blowing.

Children of the Self-Absorbed (Nina Brown): This book evoked deep emotion within me. It made me angry but also led me into a new understanding. It discusses the roots of low self-esteem developed in children raised by emotionally unavailable parents. It gives direction into how we learn not to see ourselves as important, as we are always riding along in the shadow of the parent who is focused on him/herself and wants everyone else to focus upon them as well.

The Biology of Belief: Unleashing the Power of Consciousness, Matter, & Miracles (Bruce H. Lipton): This book is written by a pioneer. This author is not mainstream, and this knowledge provided about the biology of our cells and our brains is epic. You cannot read this book and leave the experience unchanged in some way. This is a book I will read and re-read.

Differentiating Opportunity:

Life is uncertain because you can never fully predict or control what has not yet happened or what is currently happening. When you are conditioned into anxiety, it is impossible to enjoy life. Just suppose you could approach life from an "I Wonder" space, knowing that life is an uncertain and exciting journey and you will do the best to face life as it comes to you. Just suppose you could feel excitement about it rather than anxiety. Really, all you have to do in life is take every novel experience one step at a time. When you look too far forward, things seem insurmountable. If you break life down and take only the steps each moment requires, you are sure to succeed! This new way of thinking is differentiating.

To differentiate means to see your Self as separate. Differentiating requires us to think new thoughts and to try new unexplored things. It is worth it to differentiate so you can begin to live the life that you dream of, guided by your *own* influence. When you live out your own dreams, life becomes worth living. Your dreams become an authentic expression of who you really are. Differentiating is the drive for independence and uniqueness. It is about becoming your *own* expression.

All people are born dependent. The more dependent you

are, the more undifferentiated. The first feeling of separation occurs the day you are born. When you are in utero, you are connected and safe within another person. Then the bottom falls out, literally. What you learn in infancy is the first imprinting of your false-self.

It is the task of each person to separate – to differentiate – from their source relationships and find their independence. This is how we become individualized. If, as you age, you choose to keep the unhealthy responses you learned from your parents, you become an unrealized Self. Remember, you are a unique and separate person, and the rights to your life experience belong to you. You get to choose. If you do not like what you have chosen for your life, choose again! This is the journey. Welcome!

I am back in the boat
being swept away.
Sad for the me
in that last display.

Aware of the cold,
my clothes now feeling damp,
I sit and shiver
not wanting to camp.
I want to keep moving.
My heart so heavy,
inside me a feeling of intense anxiety.

Up ahead,
I sense another memory
of the me that is there.
This time, I am a little girl.
I am all of seven.

As you enter back into to the boat and leave the world of the Omens, I want you to re-enter the movie as if you just released the pause button and allow the emotions of your inner world to engage in the story. In each poem/ place you visit, you leave with the treasure of an in-sight. This is like a souvenir to remind you of where you have been and what you have learned. This is the gift of analyzing your internal world. The souvenirs are your in-sights. Your in-sights are your compasses for new behaviors. Put this treasure aside as you are traveling again into a new land.

You will be arriving at the place of the Unexpected. You will gain the gift of viewing how the Unexpected operate. Each emotion has its own culture and character, and it is worth traveling here because you will be faced with the Unexpected in life. When the Unexpected happens to you, you experience a complete disequilibrium to your inner world. When the Unexpected occurs, you immediately get into your basic survival coping mechanisms to get through the situation. Allow yourself to bring up memories of how the Unexpected in your life has created disequilibrium for you as you read.

Unexpectedly

On a weekend visit
to see him,
something unexpectedly
happened.

He was tickling me.
I was in ecstasy,
laughing and squirming
uncontrollably.

Then…unexpectedly,
he was furious at me.
He began yelling and cursing.

He said I had kicked his face.
I felt so ashamed,
I didn't know.
My brain too slow to understand,
just two seconds ago
I was giggling in happy land.

I looked into his eyes;
he was so mad.
Feeling scared,
I wanted to be fair.

I told him he could hit me.

His fist hit my face.
My head flew back,
my brain too far behind
to realize
I had been attacked.

My head lunging forward now
I looked into his eyes.
His face, ten steps behind his fist,
wore a look of surprise.

I felt the pain
in my eyes and nose.
Unexpectedly,
my dad had thrown blows.
Before I knew it,
I was bleeding.
The warmth and taste of blood,
such a shocking feeling.
My Dad, reeling,
leapt up to start cleaning.

So in shock,
I did not cry.
The blood dripping from my face,
I was paralyzed with fright.

He came back from the kitchen
with some ice in a towel.
Inside me,
my heart wanted to howl.

I did not make a sound.
I realized my Dad
was wound.

After he put the ice on my face,
he went down the hall
and cried in shame.

I got up from the couch
to check things out.
His door would not open,
I was locked out.

I gently knocked.
I could hear him cry.
I knew it was my fault,
I wanted to die.

I felt so bad;
I had made him so mad.
I promised him I would not tell.

At seven,
this experience was hell.

I felt so responsible.
When I got tickled
I squirmed and wiggled.
Arms and legs flailing,
I loved to giggle.

I swear
I didn't mean to hit him.
I promise
I will never
wiggle so hard again.

This was what I learned at seven.

Breathe for just a moment and sit with and embrace the Unexpected. As you glanced into this landscape, you saw the impact of shock and the after effects of shame that any type of abuse creates. The waters were rough, and the emotions cold. This is what the land of the Unexpected is like. It is unpredictable in its climate, and irregular in its landscape. The people here are emotionally out of control. You may feel heavy hearted as you pause the movie. It is okay. It is okay to feel these feelings. This is how it feels when the Unexpected happens, no matter how or in what form it shows up. When the unexpected occurs, you are somewhat silenced in the sheer awe of the disaster at hand. Pull over to the bank to get out and take a slight rest. There is no need to travel on quite yet. You must get out to gain the intelligence of the Unexpected and to see how you can use this place to grow, so just pause for one minute. Gather yourself together and take your time to learn about this place and of its people. The inhabitants here are stuck in shame, and they will try to inject into you the false belief that you were responsible for the shame created by the Unexpected. You must learn the ways to undo this induced eye-sight so you can heal.

Eye-Sight

Life is unpredictable. As a child, you live in an alert state of basic survival. You look to the grounding of your parents to bring you a sense of normalcy. You are at the mercy of their emotional health and well-being, or you are at the mercy of their lack of emotional health. You depend upon your parents to provide safety, nurturing and guidance. It is horrifying for a child to have the experience of a parent being emotionally out of control. It rips away the child's stability.

When you are emotionally and or physically violated by a parent, your psyche will get caught off guard. You will slip into fight or flight survival mechanisms and do whatever you can to take care of the feelings of the adult who violated you. This is where you learn codependency and people pleasing. In *Unexpectedly,* I was violated, and I took on the role of the nurturing parent to the immature parent who violated me. It is amazing how children can be so nurturing in an effort to find stability. It is adapted behavior for survival. The problem is that you learn to nurture the wrong people as you grow. I was conditioned with the eye-sight that I was the problem and my parents' happiness was my responsibility.

We can all identify times in life when we develop the attachment habits of codependency and people pleasing. Being violated on any level by a parent has a strong impact on the self-worth of any child. We all want to feel good so we do whatever we have to even if that means taking the blame as the victim. These moments, if not healed, can impact us for the rest of our lives, as will be evidenced in the relationships we choose.

The impact of childhood trauma creates your *core wounds.* Core wounds are the stories you learn to tell yourself about who you are. For example, the belief in being always wrong is a core wound; the belief in being not good enough is a core wound. They are alive at your core because they were imprinting emotional experiences which began to occur in the first seven years of life and well beyond. To avoid feeling these core wounds, you develop adaptive strategies. As you learn to please those who are abusive, you set a pattern in motion where you do this with bullies, bad boyfriends/ girlfriends, husbands/wives, bad friends etc. Each time you engage in people pleasing, you give away a little piece of your self-worth to the other. Your energy becomes infused with a non-deserving frequency, which becomes the powerful attractor for abusive people to continue coming into your life. This non-deserving frequency is the core wound in action, and it often shows itself in how you move, your posture, your tone of voice, the speed with which you speak, your facial expressions etc. This is easily detected by your bullying counterparts, and thus, you begin this cycle over and over again. I found I had trouble trusting people in general. This would take me years to undo.

In-Sight: Each time, I am people-pleasing I am giving a little part of me away.

Reflections:

At the age of seven, children are becoming more aware of themselves as separate individuals. Their main question at this age is "how can I be good?" They want a feeling of competence or success. At seven, children work hard at being good, responsible and doing things right. On this day, I had kicked him on accident, so to be good and do the right thing, I told him he could hit me. At this age, children have a good understanding of cause and effect, and I wanted to make things fair. I knew I did something bad when I wiggled too hard because of the effect it had on him. I thought if I was fair he would not be mad anymore. Moral values were developing within my psyche.

Self-confidence is another primary development at this age. We either feel a sense of confidence in the new ways we are developing, or we feel inferior. I would leave this age in my life feeling inferior. I felt so small and so afraid on this day. I was in shock and wanted normalcy. I felt relief at making him feel better because he wasn't mad anymore. His mad was scary, and I never wanted to make him mad like that again.

As I carried all the blame that day, my self-confidence did not grow. I felt flawed and defective at my natural response to being tickled. It was frightening how something could start off so fun with my Dad and end so horribly.

I learned to repress myself. It became my responsibility to clean up the messes the adults made in my life. The adults in my life showed very little concern for how their messes were impacting my life. I do not feel they were even aware they were having an impact on my life or my self-esteem. On this day, I am not sure if my Dad was crying because he assaulted me or if he was crying because he was mad at himself. He *went away* and cried by *himself*. He did not come to me and cry with me or validate me. He cried for him, for his lack of control, and his bad behavior. I was abandoned that day. I needed him. I needed him to say sorry, to acknowledge that what he did was terribly wrong. I needed him to hug me and kiss away my tears. I needed him to not make me scared of him, to cuddle me, and to reassure me he would never lose control like that again. Instead, he was pathetic about himself. I felt bad for him. On that day, I carried his shame. This would not be the last time I saw my Dad lose control. I saw him be violent on cars, other people, etc.

It is the responsibility of parents to keep their children safe and to use their authority to guide, educate, nurture, prepare and teach them how to navigate life. If a parent does not protect the child from harm, the child will not learn how to protect themselves from harm. It is the natural instinct of a child to love the parent because the parent is the authority, so children naturally love unconditionally to maintain security. If you learn early on that you are not worthy, it sets an emotional and mental conditioning pattern into motion. *When you live out of a lack of worth, you give other people worth they do not deserve. You view everyone as more worthy.*

I was already being conditioned to put others first. I learned I had little to no importance if I was not somehow making a contribution to someone else's life. People-pleasing is a high risk to one's health. It puts undue pressure and stress on the pleaser. I would essentially make myself sick and exhausted from doing too much to get others to like me. I had depression early on from having to suppress my grief. My sadness was not okay because it mirrored back to my parents that they were imperfect. My anger was not okay because it came in conflict with their needs for themselves. The eye-sight I was developing at this time was the pressure to not be my Self. I was being conditioned to be the need-meeter of my conditioners. If my emotions interfered with their wants, I would carry the shame.

At its core, people-pleasing is about the loss of selfhood and the complete development of a false-self. The false-self condition is created to cover up the feeling of being imperfect and defective inside. If you can please others and make them happy, then you must be good. You learn that safety and happiness are totally dependent on the outside world and in catering to this we limit ourselves in the development of an inner world. Joel Covits quotes: "She learned to her dismay that she only felt loved when she wasn't being herself." This was my experience.

I completely lost my ability to say no. The ability to say no comes from the natural emotion of anger. It is natural to feel anger. Saying yes when you want to say no triggers a feeling and then represses it. Unfortunately, all my repressed emotions were becoming threats to me. Repression becomes like compression, pressure. Keeping others happy is a pressure. Learning to say no when I needed to say no would not come for many years.

In-Sight: It is important to say no, to set limits, to realize you have choices, to realize your Self has to come first.

Life Class Lesson:

The purpose of this lesson is to get you in touch with the faulty belief that you are somehow responsible for other peoples' happiness. When you live with this responsibility, it is a burden and an illusion. You are not capable of being the sole source of another person's well-being. This can be difficult to understand when as a child this was your strategy to maintain love, security and bonding. When people-pleasing becomes a habit as an adult, you end up pleasing someone else and slowing killing yourself. It is an incredibly destructive way to live. As you please, you waste so much time and energy trying to figure out what to do or how to act to keep other people happy. I first started doing this on the day I was hit.

How do you know if you are a people pleaser? If you are motivated in relationships by a sense of guilt, duty, or obligation, you have pleasing attributes. When you operate this way, you sacrifice doing for yourself and instead, you do what you believe you are obligated to do or what you think you are supposed to do in order to make other people happy. You set your own needs for comfort and happiness aside and prioritize what others want ahead of you. When you operate from this place, you essentially do not see your feelings or needs as important as the needs of other people.

Because you are operating out of duty, making decisions becomes uncomfortable. Making decisions can make you feel selfish because it may provoke the way another person feels. Your decisions may frustrate or disappoint someone else, so you avoid your truth and become a peace-maker instead.

There is no path to happiness when you feel drained from giving out and do not receive enough of your *own* time and attention. In uncovering the beginnings of this faulty belief, you can start to learn how to take care of yourself first. *When you learn to put yourself first, you develop a sense of Self. When you put others first, you lose your Self.*

**As a child, did you feel responsible for your parent's happiness?*

**If you were being ill-behaved, did your parents oppress you?*

**Were you allowed to say no?*

**When did you learn not to say no?*

**Are you able to say no now?* Example: Saying no now is much easier than it has ever been in my life, but I have had years to practice and decondition for this new habit. I used to experience absolute discomfort and guilt at the thought of saying no. I felt badly about myself if I felt my saying no would upset or disappoint someone else. The last thing I wanted was to upset another person. As a child, I hated cleaning up the emotional messes of my parents. By not saying no, I never had any mess to clean up, but I became a mess inside.

I began to notice that others had no problem saying no to me, and that began to feel hurtful. I had gotten myself into a place of imbalance with my inability to say no being at the core of the problem. *The coping skill that made me safe as a child harmed me as an adult.*

**If not, what are your fears?*

**What are the causes of your fears of saying no?*

**Are you afraid of anticipated consequences?*

**Are you afraid to make others mad?*

**Are you afraid someone may come back at you with even more conflict?*

**Are you afraid of loss or abandonment?*

**Make a list of these fears and let them go.*

**How do you feel people-pleasing poisons you long term?* Example: It does not at all aid me long term. As I am out pleasing other people, I am losing track of my Self, my desires, my needs, my wants and my dreams. I have learned the hard way I cannot be a fully expressed or functional human being if I see it is my *duty* to make *other* people happy. If I put all my work and effort into someone else, I will drain my Self dry. I will set up the expectation in the other that I "have to" do everything for them so whatever I give will become a demand, and I will be deeply unhappy and unfulfilled.

One thing I have learned is that many people who give too much are seen as weak by others. I believe that to be true. When you cannot stand on your own two feet and put your needs, your life, and your comforts first, you stand no chance of having a healthy life, a happy relationship with another or a sense of peace and fulfillment. I have learned the hard way that there are no healthy benefits to people-pleasing. It's best to take personal responsibility for this pattern in your life now.

**How does it aid you short term?* Example: This, for me, is a simple answer. It reduces the opportunity for conflict. Phew. When I avoid something I get caught in the *approach/ avoidance conflict.* What this means is when I am thinking about confronting something and I am in the approach to it, I feel good. I am generating my response and preparing, but once it is time to face it first-hand, I avoid it. This keeps me stuck. It will continue to happen until I face the challenge. The more I avoid the harder and more frequent, the life pop quizzes will come.

Extra Credit Advantage

Healing reading for home-work.

When Pleasing You is Killing Me (Dr. Les Carter): This is not a book I actually read. I was enticed by the cover and the title resonated deeply with me. The cover has bright yellow writing and at the bottom of the page is a black bomb about to go off. The yellow writing symbolizes the energy of life and happiness, and the black bomb (negativity) is ready to kill the life energy. When I opened the pages, I found that it was a workbook, and I was not in that head space, but the title alone was so powerful that I placed it upright on my bed side table facing me, just so I could wake up and remind myself that pleasing other people was only killing me. What a fantastic reminder.

The Verbally Abusive Relationship (Patricia Evans): As an adult, I attracted a lot of wrong people/relationships into my life, male and female, and I was unable to recognize when a relationship was unhealthy. Unhealthy was my "normal" due to my childhood, and so I kept falling into one bad experience after another. This book went deeper than just verbal abuse. It helped me recognize abusive patterns as a whole which helped me to better recognize when abuse, whether covert or overt, was occurring in my life.

Why Does He Do That? (Lundy Bancroft): This book opened my eyes wide to abusive patterns of all types. It helped me see abusive patterns, including my own patterns, which got me stuck in unhealthy relationships. When we are violated as children, we learn to attract abuse until we can recognize it, shift it, change it, and work to be done with it. This book delves deeply into defining the character of abusive people and their abilities or inabilities to grow.

Differentiating Opportunity:

If you were able say no when you needed to say no, how different would your life be? Imagine the confidence you would have in taking ownership of your own life. Saying no is one way to take ownership of your direction in life. When we differentiate, we challenge ourselves to think in new ways. Just suppose you had a shift in belief and focus, and you placed attention on your own life. Just suppose you could break your fears of being rejected which would alleviate your need to please. How much stronger of an individual you would become! Just suppose you committed to you to the same level and degree to which you commit to the other. You might start to really love your Self. How fun!

Why do you please? You please out of fear. You learned your fears as a child. Your fears become the fears that your parents taught you. Since you are a unique and different person, these fears are now yours, regardless of where you learned them. What is one step you can take to be responsible for your own fears?

In not saying no, I learned to be deceptive. People-pleasing is a form of deception because you are not being authentic in your relationships. You are not living your truth. If you are deceptive, you have to unlearn or decondition the safety of being deceptive and face the challenge of telling your truth before you can really know the Self. You have to differentiate. Today, start saying no when you want to say no, and see yourself as a truth-teller. Face the challenge of the other person's response. Get back to putting what you feel first, and operate from that place.

To decondition the false-self, sometimes you even have to figure out what you are feeling. So that would be the first step. *When you can see a negative trait as yours by choice, you can choose to transform it.* This makes changing worthwhile because in saying no and/or yes according to your genuine wants, needs and desires, you begin live authentically according to your likes and dislikes. Imagine how much more free you would be in your relationships and your life simply by using your yes's and no's as authentically as possible. You are here to be free to be yourself. Never forget that.

Sitting and quivering in the boat
with this moment at seven reclaimed,
my perception has changed.

I was aware
of my father's inner rage.
I learned that
being around him,
I was not always safe.

In the boat, my vision blurred,
as I felt his fist hit me.
I was again punctured.

With this memory,
the temperature dropped.
My chest so cold from the air,
I began to cough.
I am just so cold.
I want this journey to stop.

The next memory ahead,
brings up feelings
of despair and misery.

Shivering now and wondering,
will this journey be
never ending?

The boat slowly moves on.

Oh my gosh,
I see me again.
I am nine years old,
almost ten.

The cold, it is killing me.
I can barely focus on what I see.
I see her,
She…

Hold the previous in-sight securely in your consciousness as you re-enter the river of transformation. All rivers have their own haphazard flow, just as do each of the life experiences you have lived. In this next scene, you are going to enter the emotions of a little girl who feels All Alone. She lives in the land of the lonely. In this land, one feels without love. Because you have also experienced this feeling, you will be open to relating to the emotions being illuminated.

This particular emotion has a darker culture. It is difficult to inhabit this environment. There is not a lot of light here. Allow your Self to remember and re-experience your own aloneness, so you can enliven and awaken to these emotions. As we travel, we are all feeling these emotions together and we are all traveling these landscapes together. No one is watching, so you can release any shame or discomfort and allow your Self to absorb the principles this All Alone feeling has to teach. You can leave with a lesson. Each experience that evokes empathy, invites you to be empathic with yourself. If you can have empathy for your own experiences, you are loving your Self.

All Alone

She is all alone
at nine years old.

Her mom had asked her
not to hate her that day.
She told this little girl,
"mommy has to go away."

Until then,
she had never been
without her mom,
until this fateful day.
"Why mommy
do you have to go away?"

"Please,
I promise
I will behave."

"What will happen to me
if you do not stay?"

The little girl....
so unclear.

She was consumed
with inner fear.
Her life had changed dramatically.
She was overwhelmed with
inner tragedy.

All alone with her pain,
she cried each night.
She was terrified,
not sure how to fight.

She was desperate
as she cried,
her vulnerability exposed
and denied.

Her sadness
is so deep,
it chills her bones.
It aches so bad,
she is consumed with defeat.

So much fear and anxiety.
This child cannot sleep.
She just wants her mom
to come home and
pet her cheek.

How could her mom
abandon her
and leave her
in such terrible need?

So many emotions
in her heart.
Each day was so
difficult to start.

The new school,
too much to bear.
This little girl was
too overwhelmed to care.

Inside, she always felt sick.
The ache inside
was like being stabbed
deeply with a sharp stick.
She did not want to live.
The emotions in her life
were just too thick.

At nine years old,
she cried and cried.
She told her mom,
"If you don't come home,
I am going to die."

With empty words,
she was reassured,
but it didn't work.

This little girl
continued to go backward.

With no coping skills
to survive,
this little girl
was no longer alive.
She was dead inside.

The only thing she had
was being alone
in her bed
where she could disappear
into her own head.

This child
began to live in fantasy.
Thank God for
Little House on the Prairie.

In fantasy,
she pretended to have a family.

Love is as necessary for your health as air and water. Love is the breath of the Universe, and we are all meant to have love. We all deserve love, and we all need love. As you traveled by this land, you got to observe the despair of feeling All Alone. It has a thick mist all around it, because when you are lonely you cannot see your lovability. This is a place of great separation between people and very little to no connection to oneself. It is quiet here, but the smells and thickness of the mist make it clear that sadness and despair are the rulers of this countryside.

Each of us has experienced feeling All Alone, so step out, journal and pen in hand, and see if you can uncover the secret teachings of loneliness. You will first learn to see through the distortion of your incorrect vision as caused by the thick mist hiding your lovability. The natives are awaiting your arrival so they can teach you about healing your loneliness. Feeling lonely, you will learn, begins with thinking you are not worthy. This first thought changes the lens you see through.

Eye-Sight

Consistency and stability are the most important qualities children require. It is common in divorced families to have a child spend all or most of their time with one parent, while seeing the other on a scheduled pattern. This is a consistent structure the child can depend upon. When I was little, I lived primarily with my mother. That was where *home* was. *Home* is about safety and having a place of permanence in the world. This is how children experience *Home*.

There is a huge gap in the way that children and adults take in the world. When an adult changes and shifts the structure on a child, the adult can see the change is not forever, but the child cannot. *All Alone* demonstrates the devastating impact a disruption in the structure can cause. I experienced abandonment and rejection. I slipped into a deep state of insecurity and depression. I turned to fantasy to escape my fears and anxieties about my safety and security. I lived with the conditioned eye-sight that I was disposable.

Children feel emotions as deeply as adults, but children do not have the mind set to understand that things will get better or back to normal. Children are shoved into intense emotional experiences that feel like they will go on forever. Emotional pain can be unbearable to children. Rejected, abandoned children often move through the world with a "who will love me consciousness" trying to find their value in the other, rather than a "who deserves me consciousness," where they know their value and are discerning of who is let into their emotional space.

Hurt is organic. It is raw, painful, scary, and pure. Low self-esteem can become the consistent organic state in which you learn to live. Once a pure belief of "I am not good enough" is established, it becomes the lens or eye-sight through which the world is experienced. I was never asked how I was feeling about my life as a little girl. There was no escape from these feelings, and no one to talk to. My emotions became a living entity within me. My frequency was low.

Parents can divorce and still provide form and structure for their children. Form and structure is created through love, rules, conversation, honesty, and providing a sense of predictability for changing circumstances through communication. You can tell the child about the changes to come and prepare them. My parents simply did what they wanted, when they wanted to do it, and I was not informed. To not inform a child of impending life changes is to devalue that child.

In-Sight: A child's life needs form and structure.

Reflections:

One of the most basic needs children have is structure. Children ensure their survival strategies by having a sense of boundaries which encapsulate their lives and give them form. When you have a predictable comfort of knowing where the structure is, who you can count on, and a general feeling of what life is like, you are able to use your energy more efficiently. Without any limits or boundaries, the child becomes easily confused and emotional.

External structure helps to develop internal structure. If the outside world is chaotic, the inside world will be chaotic. When you have structure, you have direction. You have a sense of being *human*. You have understanding and order to depend upon. If you are not provided this, you live in the world of the unknown and become identified with your insecure emotions. Without structure, there can be only a limited bond between parent and child.

Grief is a natural emotion. It arises within you when you have to say good-bye to someone or something you are not ready to say goodbye to. When my mom left, my whole world and predictable structure went with her. My full time life with her was all I knew. I had to change homes, rooms, parents, friends, the loss of my step-father, schools, loss of my sport, and adjust to an entire new life.

My adjustment would include my mother's new boyfriend, who I did not know existed. One day, he was just in my life, no adjustment time, no conversation that touched on my feelings about it. At nine-years-old, I was old enough to have and understand the 'new boyfriend' conversation. The first time I met him was on my mother-daughter birthday celebration. The birthday was no longer about me; it was about her being able to see him.

When my mother left, my entire life axis was taken away. The grief I felt was profound. I lost respect for my mother and already had no respect for my father. My love for them would return, but not the respect. They had abandoned me.

I was not able to express my sadness. My sadness was a burden and an annoyance to my parents. Their desire was to move on with their lives and my feelings got in their way. I told them both with all my tears that this was not working for me, that I could not handle it. The message I got was "toughen up, get over it."

If you are able to express your sadness freely, you can work through it efficiently and with security. If on the other hand, your sadness is a burden to others, you learn to repress. Repressed sadness turns into depression. I was failing school and not adjusting well to my new peers. I felt sick to my stomach. My sick stomach caused me to miss a lot of school. I then got punished for not getting good grades. This is when loneliness took over. I enjoyed being alone as a child. Being alone is about space and I loved being in my own space. Feeling lonely was different. *Lonely was to be without love.*

If children are not allowed the expression of their emotions, the emotions become an alienated or cut-off part of the child's Self. Then, when the child experiences that emotion, they experience the emotion as shameful. In my case, each time I felt sad, I felt ashamed that I had annoyed my parents. I, therefore, had to internalize my sadness and disown it. But there was no way for me to rid myself of my sadness. I just stopped expressing it to my parents, and I felt like I always had an upset stomach. My sadness transferred from an emotion into a physical symptom. My stomach aches were acceptable to my parents because they had nothing to do with the physical symptoms.

I was lonely for my mother, for my previous stability and safety. I was lonely for my old school, my sport, my old friends, my little girl room, my step-father, my house, my dogs, my old neighborhood, my consistency and my sense of security. I was so empty that I used to pray at night that God would take me in my sleep. Each morning, when I woke up, still there, I further lost my faith in God. My brother was still apparently thriving, which increased the frustration with me. I sometimes heard him yelling in his sleep.

When you are abandoned emotionally, you lose sight of yourself. Because my parents were not consistent with me, I did not learn to be consistent for my Self. You learn you are valuable when people care about what you say. Family members began to label me as "too sensitive." This would haunt me for years to come.

In reality, was I too sensitive or was I intuitive? Biologists have found that this too sensitive trait reflects a certain type of survival strategy. I have always been a deep thinker, largely impacted by the subtleties of behavior and my environment. I picked up on nuances that others did not notice.

These things would make me anxious and acutely aware of other people and their perceptions of me. I could pick up on someone's bad mood or annoyance from a quick facial expression or mood change. I have learned that I am more right brained. I have a heightened sense of arousal, my nervous system is easily activated, and I am able to quickly synthesize information. When I was young, this was not seen as a gift. I was made to feel that something was *wrong* with me rather than something was *right* with me. This was my conditioned eye-sight, the way I was taught to view my Self.

To be intuitive is to experience thoughts and preferences that pass through the mind without much reflection. Intuition, like being too sensitive, is right brained. I could *feel* my world; I did not *think* about my world. I have always been this way, and for most of my life was told my feelings were wrong, and thus, I began to feel I was wrong. As I was made to feel like I was an annoyance, I was conditioned further and further away from my natural feelings. I began to question and feel frustrated with myself just like my parents. My false-self developed a lot during this period of my life. I was pushed even further away from my natural worth.

Sensitive or intuitive people are deeply impacted by the emotions and moods of the people around them. They are deeply impacted by everything in their environments from noise, light, temperature, and movement. I still experience this today, and now, I see it as a gift. If you identify with being too sensitive, let me tell you, you have an innate sense about life and people. It is a gift. There is nothing wrong with you except that other people who are less sensitive will feel violated by your *knowing* of them. Whenever you are told you are too sensitive, I would pose this question back "Am I too sensitive or do I just see through you?"

Life Class Lesson:

I want you to take a moment to contemplate the emotions of sadness and loss. If you were conditioned to feel shame around your emotions, you can take this opportunity to look at the fact that the emotions are naturally occurring experiences triggered each moment by any given stimulus. Let's be honest, your negative feelings feel really bad. You can feel trapped inside of them. When you have an overpowering emotion, it can feel as if there is no escape, and this is the reason that many choose to end their lives. The emotions can be uncomfortable, unrelenting, and scary.

You cannot get rid of the emotions; you are supposed to have them. They are here to teach and guide you and yet, you get conditioned to be ashamed of something beyond your control. Adding shame to the already uncomfortable nature of negative emotions, makes them even harder to carry. Try to see your emotions as messengers, for instance, your sadness is a messenger. It is telling you something extremely important about yourself. If you are sad, you need to look at why. Once you find the why, you need to look at the core of that answer. If you are sad, you usually are feeling some kind of loss. It could be the loss of the feeling of control, the loss of something valuable to you, the loss of stability, the loss of direction, the loss of reputation. It could be anything. Sadness is just there to tell you that you are feeling the emptiness of something important to you.

For this lesson, let's get rid of the shame around sadness and look at this emotion with respect and humility. It is a necessary and important part of life to be sad. Let's answer the questions around it with no inhibitions. If you can understand how you were conditioned regarding your emotions, how shame was instilled, and by whom, you have the opportunity to unlearn that old program. You will start to reawaken the natural emotional self within. If you feel nothing, there is nothing to know about you.

**What were you forced to say good-bye to before you were ready?*

**How were you supported or not supported through those losses?*

**Have you ever been told you were "too sensitive?"* Example: I was constantly told in some form or another that I was too sensitive. If the message did not come directly through words, it came through non-verbal behaviors such as eye-rolling, sighing in exasperation at my feelings or telling me things like "well, I don't know what to tell you." This treatment was rejecting, infuriating, and created an immense amount of self-doubt within me that would end up making me feel anger. My unexpressed sadness fueled my anger. It still can trigger anger to look back and see how my emotions were parented. I was too sensitive, and the sensitivity chip was missing in both my parents.

My father did not take financial or emotional responsibility for us, and much of the time, he behaved as if we owed him something. My mother was too nervous and consumed with her own life to give us what we needed emotionally, but my mom was the more consistent parent of the two. It must have been hard for them to have a child who was attuned enough to see through them and to experience the full capacity of what they lacked emotionally. What they lacked, I now know they could not give.

** How did being told you were too sensitive impact you?*

**If you were told you were too sensitive, did you lose trust in the sharing of your emotions for the fear of criticism?*

**If so, what did you do with the emotions?*

**Are you too sensitive, or are you intuitive?*

**How would you know the difference?* Example: Intuitions are quiet and consistent. My intuition never changed as a little girl. I knew to the depths of my soul that my parents were totally off balance. They were both agenda oriented and not relationship oriented, as they put their adult needs far before the needs of their children. This knowing was fixed, and it never changed. When times were good, I was always aware that it was partly because I was going along with their desires. They forced their will on me rather than giving me the space to allow me to be me.

Being too sensitive would come up when I tried to communicate a need of my own that may have been in conflict with their agenda. Things would then backlash, and I would be criticized in some form. I could get overly emotional out of sheer frustration, and I would use those emotions to make noise in an effort to be heard. However, driving my noise or my too sensitive nature was that gut feeling that things were not as they should be. Children should come first to their parents, not the other way around. It was ass backwards in my world. This was the core issue: them first and children second, many times lower down the totem pole.

**Make a list of you quiet consistent emotions you can remember having through childhood.*

Extra Credit Advantage:

Healing reading for home-work

The Highly Sensitive Person: How to Thrive When the World Overwhelms You (Elaine N. Aron, Ph.D.): This book showed me I was not some crazy sensitive freak of nature who was over reactive and emotionally out of control. In this book, I felt normal, like I actually had a gift instead of this horrible deficit. This book helped me see how to use my sensitivity to its full advantage. I feel proud to be a highly sensitive person now that I understand this is how I am built and supposed to be. I have not finished this book, but I practice much of what I learned here on a daily basis. I will revisit it once I have perfected what I have learned so far. Then I will go back for more.

Conversations with God and Uncommon Dialogue (Neal Donald Walsh): Neal's books are some of the most inspiring I have ever touched. In one of his books, there is a discussion of the emotions. It is written in such simple and direct language that it melted through my psyche with ease of understanding. I learned that our emotions are natural. Sadness is natural. It is natural for everyone. I learned about what happens if we repress our sadness and the destruction it causes. I learned sadness has a purpose. This specific part of the book was all I needed to understand the emotional times in my life.

Toxic Parents (Susan Forward): This is a great read that covers all types and levels of parenting. I did not identify with all the extreme cases, but I did identify with much of the information on parents who are self-focused and who use guilt and manipulation to gain power of their children. I also identified with the addiction part because one of my parents was pretty heavily into drugs when I was little. I do not believe drugs or drug addicts should be anywhere near children. This book doesn't leave anything out, and some of the most powerful chapters discuss confrontation and reclaiming your life. I have confronted both parents and have had to focus not on their response but on my bravery to confront. I did not confront to change them. I confronted to heal me. If my healing was dependent upon their responses, I would still not be fully healed. My healing comes in having the courage to stand up for myself in the ways they never honored me.

Differentiating Opportunity:

Just suppose sadness is a gift, that sadness's whole purpose is to heal and cleanse your inner world. If you allow your emotions their rightful place in your life, you would move through them more efficiently onto the next place the emotions are designed to take you. You are here to feel, to live, and to experience. To heal your emotional pain, you have to call it into your conscious awareness and take the time to look at the emotions. Just suppose your negative emotions are the omens to let you know when there is something within you which has the need to be released and healed.

Sadly, most of you were conditioned to believe that you were somehow flawed due to your feelings. You were not given the permission to feel them because they were not okay. It was even less okay to feel the really strong emotions that threatened your conditioners when you expressed how you were feeling. Your emotions triggered unconscious wounds in them, and they did whatever they could to influence you to bury your own feelings. However, you are emotional by design. Just suppose you started embracing your emotions today. Just suppose you cared enough about yourself to spend quality time looking within. Just suppose from this you could find there is an infinite source of emotional support and wisdom that is always available to you from within. Just suppose your emotions can guide you to the places, things and relationships which make you feel good and away from those places which are not a fit for you. You are feeling 'something' every second of every day. Just suppose you were able to embrace who you are designed to be how much more free, honest and magnificent your life would be.

Your sadness is yours, regardless of who caused it for you. Your sadness's make you unique and reveal something unique about you and the way you respond to the world. Own your sadness, and see what you can do to better understand and nurture it. Study your sadness, and let it teach you something about your life. It will tell you when you like and when you do not like something about life. This is incredible knowledge for decision making.

Sitting in the boat,
I see the me then.
She cries so deep.
I re-experience the pain,
my bones feel weak.

I cannot look anymore,
this vision too hard to repeat.
She is just so sad,
I want to scream.

Shaking and teeth chattering,
moving so slow,
my muscles have frozen.
I climb out of this boat.

I walk toward her.
I breathe the memory in
to absorb her.
My lungs are filled with icy cold air.
This memory filling me with despair.

I want to reclaim her.
To love her,
would be her answered prayer.

Having this memory,
I experienced her sadness.
Amazed that the me then
did not lose it to madness.

Filled with sadness
from this memory I saw,
I felt angry fate had created
this memory at all.

It was this memory when my life changed.
From here on out,
I was never the same.

Alone.....
I realized both my parents
were insane.

In the boat,
I could hardly breathe.
This memory
brought me to my knees.
I sit in silence as the boat moves on.

I am so cold,
my thoughts so clouded
being warm again,
I cannot imagine.

The sadness has now
wrapped me in its canvas.
I pray to God,
I, the me now,
does not lose it
to madness.

The journey
sensing my misery
gives the me at nine
a little reprieve.
My journey sent
an angel to me.

The next destination is about meeting evolved people. When you arrive here, you will see this is a place of Hope. Hope is an emotion which makes you feel a sense of relief and a sense of security. When you travel through here, you will see this place has light. Its inhabitants are practicing faith and feeling a sense that the future of their culture will be okay after all. The people here look like angels. Hope is the omen that you are never really alone, but that sometimes you don't know this until you are at your bottom. Whenever you hit a bottom in life, it seems that if you are open and pure of heart, a miracle will come.

In this instance, my miracle came in one very special night from a complete stranger. Push play again and feel the boat moving underneath you and take in this next learning experience. At the end, you will again gain another souvenir in-sight. With each new in-sight you are enlivening your inner world. You are awaking into a deeper love and compassion for who you are and all you have been through. As you are reading, allow the memories of the miracle people in your life to come into your awareness. These are the people, who gave you hope along your journey. These people are instrumental teachers of love.

Human Angel

She came to me one night.
She had heard me cry.
She said she understood,
her Dad had recently died.

As she talked,
she cried.
I was mesmerized.
She did not know it,
but at that moment
she was saving my life.

She knew my pain.
She did not ignore me
with contempt, frustration, or disdain.

Alone in the dark,
I yearned for comfort.
She wiped my tears.
With her there,
I felt no fear.

My human angel.

My Dad
downstairs drunk.
My mom,
off living with the latest hunk.

Seeing I had no one who cared,
she let me know I was not alone.

She lay beside me.
I can still feel
her long blonde hair.

She talked to me
and told me how
life could be unfair.

Her voice so soft,
she wiped my tears.
In these moments,
I was not lost.
I fell asleep with her there,
her hugging me
and petting my hair.

She promised that
life would get better...
that I would find
people who would care.

My human angel.

In the morning,
she was gone,
the memory of her
still so strong.

In one moment,
she parented me.
Each night after,
I would make believe
I could hear her breathe.
Pretending she was next to me
put me at ease.

This human angel was sent to me.
For one moment, I was saved.
For this moment,
I know I was graced.

As you passed by, looking into the land of the Angels, a little light shone. The people in this culture are here to nurture the broken spirited. They wait for the moment that the spirit is just about to break, and then, these special people appear to nurture you before you give up. They are gifts. As the boat pulls over to the bank, you can see these people, and you can feel their hearts. They have had life's pain, and they heal you through their own understanding of their suffering. These angels have become wise enough from their pain to relate to another who is in pain. There is so much to learn here. The angels will teach you of your own angelic nature. Here, you will learn how you can let your pains make a difference in the life of someone else. It is time to get out of the boat and nurture your soul in the presence of the Angels. You will take their wisdom and let it heal your broken views of the world and people. It will change your eye-sight.

Eye-Sight

When you are at your lowest low, the magic in life will bring the exact right person/place/experience to lift you up. There is a silent, ethereal message that says "you are not alone, you are always safe." In *Human Angel*, a stranger entered into my loneliness and despair, and loved me in a way I desperately needed. A friend of my father's, she spoke softly and quietly as she cuddled me in my bed and wiped away the tracks of my tears. What she did was simple. She lifted me up, she saw me and she loved me. I felt hope. Remembering still brings tears to my eyes.

To be seen, loved, and understood are the basic needs of each person, regardless of age or life experience. You learn your value in childhood. You either learn you are of value, or you learn you are not of value. You learn of your importance. You learn your place in the world of love. Sometimes, you learn you have no place in the world of love. This one woman, in this one moment, sat me at the table of love and nurtured my broken heart. I needed her.

How do you know if you are lovable? Answer: by how your parents loved you. My eye-sight was that I was unlovable.

This is how I was conditioned to see my Self. I had never felt so deeply lovable until this moment with this stranger. The woman identified my pain as the same as her pain, my loss as the same as her loss, my despair as the same as her despair. Basic human emotions are universal, and this woman was in touch with hers enough to be in touch with mine. I felt shock at her love and compassion for me. I wanted to bathe in her sensitivity toward me. I could feel her essence. For that moment, I could breathe.

In-Sight: We all feel emotions the same way. The way I feel pain and loss is the same way that another feels pain and loss. When we connect in our pain, we feel "seen."

Reflections:

In my room at that house, I had two sets of bunk beds. On the set I slept in, I made the bottom bunk my bed and draped blankets all around so I had a cave to hide in. This night, I chose to sleep unprotected up on the top bunk. I see this as symbolic of not pretending or hiding my emotions. On this night, I let it all hang out. I let my real Self be public, heard, and open. I remember purely sobbing. My Dad was downstairs with a man and a woman. They had gotten home late. There was no babysitter. He had left me alone, and I was only nine-years-old. I was grieving the security of the life I had had with my mother. I allowed myself to be open and vulnerable. I wanted my pain to be known.

I heard the female voice say "Jesus Christ isn't anyone going to go up and take care of that child?" The night this woman came into my room still remains one of the most profound moments of my life. I was able to cry freely, to express and expel my natural emotions of loss and abandonment. She provided the space and permission for me to have my feelings. As she let me be in my essence and let me experience my emotions, I was able to rid myself of them. I was finally able to let them out without condemnation, annoyance or frustration from someone...at least for this moment.

This woman allowed me to be *human*, to have limits to what I could handle emotionally. She mirrored those limits back to me as being normal and natural. She didn't make me feel ashamed that I wasn't handling this transition better. What an amazing feeling for someone to allow me to just be human. She loved me in such an insightful manner. She made me feel I could be loved and should be loved for just being me. She showed me acceptance rather than impatience. She showed me I was a priority rather than in the way of her needs. She showed me I was a *real person*. Thank God for her.

My little body was trembling with emotion. My face was soaked with my tears. I was sad. I was angry and lonely. She did not resist, fight, or ignore my sadness. She served as a container. She let me stop resisting. She let me fall apart. When it all came out, I was no longer trembling, my body no longer shaking. I was still. I needed this release. I needed this beautiful woman, her caress, her voice, her long hair, her story, her tears, and her hugs and kisses. What this woman provided took very little time, a listening ear and compassion. She saw me, she listened to me, she understood me, and she held me. She let me know I was not alone. She loved me. For the first time, I experienced that *love is always the answer to healing of any kind.*

This woman responded to me with compassion, identification, and softness. She created an open space where I could finally surrender to these feelings and let them go. In this moment, I learned that *the left-over state of genuinely expelled emotion is love and a sense of peace.* There is never violence or bad feelings after we are allowed to express without inhibition or the fear of another's reaction.

After that night, I figured out how to do what she did for me for myself on a smaller scale. I used my imagination and pretended she was there with me, talking to myself as if I were her telling me it would all be okay. These imaginings or visualizations helped me survive the rest of the time I stayed at my Dad's. I also used the characters from the *Little House on the Prairie* books as my imaginary family. These books provided me a pretend family with cohesion and structure, and I would listen to Ma and Pa. They brought me comfort.

Later in life, I would see the power of thought is where happiness lies. As I grew, I took care of my feelings through writing in a journal. It was how I validated my *too sensitive* perceptions. We often desire to have our feelings validated by those we feel created them, which can be a losing battle. Not that there aren't those phenomenal people who are capable, but most, due to their defenses, are not.

Learning that your feelings are always correct for you can provide you with the reassurance you need by allowing you to stay true to your feelings without having to prove yourself. On this one night I found there was a language outside of right and wrong, and good and bad. That night I experienced emotions had their own language. I learned emotions are the sight within or in-sight.

Giving of one's time is an essential aspect of the work of love. Parents need to be there for the child. Another working aspect of love is listening. Children are clear about what they need and will tell their parents in one way or another. Parents need to listen. To listen to your children requires a fair amount of emotional maturity which my parents did not have, but what this woman did have. This woman had the emotional maturity to give to me what my parents could not, time and attention.

This was my first experience of being understood emotionally. To communicate means to commune, to come together. The way you experience sadness is the same way I experience the emotion of sadness. The way you feel fear is the same way I feel fear. The same things may not trigger these emotions in us, but the way they are felt is the same. You can only come together or commune on what you *feel*. When you feel you have related with another, you feel close to them, you feel as if you have deepened a connection. Trust is developed because you were able to be seen, loved and understood by someone else. *The emotions are never looking for agreement but rather are searching for understanding.* Only thoughts are looking for agreement.

Her most precious offering was her gift of listening. She listened patiently and intently to my words and my feelings, both expressed and unexpressed. She was walking that mile in my shoes, and it felt so incredible that I did not want to stop expressing. This night, she allowed me to empty my whole heart, all my fears, all my sadness, loneliness and pain. I was able to release all of it. Her listening was pure, non-judgmental and steadfast. She created this empathic space where I was not only free to express, but simultaneously, I felt understood and validated. She did not provide me any solutions, advice, or answers – just love, encouragement and a safe container. What her focused listening did for me was powerful beyond measure. It was the first time I felt that what I felt and had to say made sense.

Feeling understood immediately shifted my emotional experience from feeling invisible into feeling visible. I went from feeling exasperated to feeling hopeful, from feel totally contracted to feeling expanded and from feeling lonely to lovable. This woman related to me from her own experience: she was sad with me from her own experience. She understood me from her own experience. We came together that night. I was not alone, and neither was she.

Life Class Lesson:

In this lesson, you are going to examine what it is like when you know you have been genuinely heard, loved, and understood. In order to have this experience, the person doing the listening has to really hear you. The person, who can hear you, will understand you. When someone understands you, they can have empathy and love for you. To be heard is the first step in any successful communication. If you are genuinely heard, it means the other has taken you in. When someone can listen to you just for the sake of hearing your story and your sadness, it makes the interactive space comfortable. You can see this person has walked a mile in your shoes and has empathy for the feelings that mile created. When you feel this way, you get the feeling of acceptance. Someone accepted the facts about your story and did not reject you. You were allowed to have the normal feelings that would be the natural result of the story told.

It is not often in life that you are genuinely heard. While most people listen they are more focused on the conversation in their own head, then they are really hearing you. Listening to really hear requires total focus from the other person. If you were not listened to as a child, you can become someone who also never learns to listen. Listening is an art. It is something that is active and not passive. It is having the flexibility to give time and attention to someone else.

I can also tell you that the better a listener you become, the more fulfilling your life will be. I imagine the woman, who helped me that night, got as much as I did or more out of the experience. Nothing makes you feel better about yourself than helping a person truly in need. That night was healing for me, and it was healing for her. What she gave to me was probably what she had needed at some time in her life for herself.

**Who is the first person to really see you?*

**How did this person change your belief about yourself?* Example: As this person affirmed that my feelings were the natural response to my difficult circumstances, she helped me stop fighting my feelings and begin to accept them. She normalized me. She made me feel "of course you are sad" like this was what I should be feeling, and this made me feel peace inside. I felt reassured there was nothing wrong with me or my feelings. She made me feel safe, normal, and not alone. It was beautiful. This was something my parents were totally incapable of providing me. My parents could not listen, because they were too focused on defending. She changed my belief about myself in that moment because she made me feel important and valuable. This is why it is still such a powerful memory for me.

**What did this person do, say, and be to make you feel whole and loved?*

**How has your life been permanently impacted by this person?*

**What did you learn about life and love from this person and/or people?*

**How have you embodied that learning within yourself?*

**Do you allow yourself to be human without contempt for yourself?* Example: This has been a difficult one for me to master. I have always had contempt for my feelings or emotions because they were not pleasing to the people in my life. I used to feel such deep levels of frustration that I could not be accepting like my brother or the way my parents wanted me to be. Because others did not like my feelings I learned that my feelings were *wrong*.

So, here I was feeling like I was feeling all the wrong things, mad that I had no control over these feelings and diminished for having them. This placed me into deep internal conflict and feelings of total despair. This woman, on this night, was the first experience of someone *not* having contempt for my feelings, and I believe it is largely why the memory is so incredibly powerful. The brilliant thing is she knew exactly what I needed because she was okay with her own feelings. She could relate to me. I believe that this night has been instrumental throughout my life. I use this night as a model for how to take care of myself and how to relate to others. I use it every day as a therapist. I allow my daughter her feelings, and I love her the way I was loved that night.

**In what ways has your pain helped you to identify with the pain of the other?*

**How has your pain been unique to you simply because you are a unique person?* Example: We all have our own deck of life cards. We are all here having a human experience, and much of that experience is determined by our pain. Our painful feelings are universal, as we all feel this emotion the same way. But what brings us our pain is what makes us unique. We all have unique tests to pass, mistakes to make, responsibilities to own, and changes to transform. Not one of us is exactly like the other, and so in this way, we all travel our journey alone but we, at the same time, can relate to others' journey because we all feel our emotions the same way.

This makes us separate and united all at the same time. However, it is our separateness, which makes each of us as unique as the snowflake. This is exactly what I teach in my practice. It is not difficult to sit with people in pain if you have had pain and you are okay with your pain. It provides the deepest experience of understanding. The triggers never have to be the same. If you have felt an emotion and you are in acceptance of it, you will be able to accept people in their feelings as well.

**Are you a good listener?*

**Were you listened to as a child?*

**How do you see your relationships improving when you become an active listener?*

Extra Credit Advantage:

Healing reading for home-work

A Child Called it and The Lost Boy (David Pelzer): Wow, these books were life changing for me. I did not experience near the abuse that David did, but his survival was something that resonated with me, as well as his gut feelings that things were very wrong in his home. In the second book (*The Lost Boy*), he meets a social worker who does for him much of what my Human Angel did for me. It is a powerful description of how someone genuinely listening to you can absolutely revive your hope in life and people.

Toward a Psychology of Being (Abraham Maslow): Maslow is one of my favorite psychologists EVER! This book is written educationally but it is readable by those who are not well versed in psychological language. Brilliant, it gives purpose to life and a process to life. It shows that one of our very core basic needs is the need to belong. It is normal, natural, and 100% necessary to have a sense of belonging.

Differentiating Opportunity:

Just suppose every emotional experience you have with another person is designed to bring you into better knowing who you are. From this woman, I learned what it felt like to be genuinely taken care of and nurtured. The experience taught me what I needed. Knowing what I need helps me to be clear about who I am, as I share myself with another. Just suppose you could learn to meet your own needs. She taught me what I needed and that taught me how to meet some of my own needs. *When you are taken care of properly, you naturally learn to take proper care of yourself.* This is a gift. As you differentiate, you will stretch your skill set to learn on many levels how to provide for yourself. As you look at what you did not get in childhood, you will see what was missing and know the direction you need to take to fill in the empty spaces.

The benefit of learning to take care of yourself is it makes you so much more capable of being in healthy relationships. Listening is a key way to take care of another. If you haven't yet learned to take care of yourself, you will not learn to be a good listener. You will be so focused on your own needs and the need for it to be all about you, there will be no room to really listen to the other. Listening is not only healing to the person being listened to, but it is a maturing experience for the listener. It requires patience, an open mind, and the ability to humbly step aside and to let it be about someone else. Really listening to another person feels incredible. It is a liberating experience to create such a safe place for someone else. This is why relationships are important.

Some of the grandest individualizing opportunities you will have will come through the other. You can feel in your gut when someone sees the real you underneath all the drama. It is a moment of awakening when someone can see you and identify. It means you are real and valid. Understanding yourself is the most important understanding you can have, and this is why differentiating is so important. Sometimes talking with or sharing your deepest feelings with another can help you carve out your unique Self. When you find understanding in another, you exist psychologically. You can also use your emotional pain to develop more empathy. Empathy is a sign of psychological health and maturity. All of your emotions, whether positive or negative, say something unique about the way you take in the world. You can use these experiences positively to identify with another.

Through your emotions, you are experiencing and expressing your unique interpretation of the world. I heard a saying once that goes, "a wise man has many delegates." I take that to mean, you cannot do all of this life on your own. The limits to what you can handle in life help define you as a unique human being. Your healthy sense of limits is there to remind you that you need others. No human being can make it alone. Look at your limits as differentiating opportunities to let you know what you can handle and what you cannot. This helps to develop a sense of who you are and who you are not. This is why we differentiate.

Back in the boat,
still freezing cold,
frostbite nipping
at the tips of my toes.

But,
this memory did
offer me
a little taste
of warm empathy.

So grateful
that someone
gave me a moment
and nurtured me.

Sitting in silence at this scene
I am overwhelmed
with the emotion in brings.

Still aware of the cold,
This memory gave
the me then
some hope.

I feel movement as the
boat travels on.
I can see my breath
in the cold air.
My ears are freezing,
not covered by my hair.

My lips are blue,
my hands and feet numb,
taking in the memories of
me when I was so young.

I begin to sense
many years of stress.
I feel the uncertainty
start tearing at my heartstrings.
In one moment of sensing these things,
I am raw inside with the feeling of anxiety.

The me back then during these years
was so......

The way rivers work, there are smooth sections, rough sections, and all types of different movements in between those two poles. This is the exact same movement life takes us on emotionally. As you travel and re-visit defining moments, you are in the direct process of really getting to know yourself, the first step into Self-love. As you get back into guided transformational work, you are learning to sit with the uncomfortable. Life is so painfully uncomfortable at times and so incredibly Unstable.

Unstable lands are prone to disaster, earthquakes, tsunamis, hurricanes etc. As you arrive here in the land of the Unstable please step gingerly and be aware of your surroundings. When you do not feel a sense of stability, you feel a loss of security. This is something you will experience at all ages, throughout life, most painfully as a child. Feeling Unstable is a universal feeling and there is no land immune to its dangers. As the next section of travel unfolds, enter into your inner world and contact the fear of instability. Allow the poetry to help you see your own early stories of this feeling.

Unstable

Life so unstable,
I was not able
to cope with
what was normal.

Between all the parents,
and all the school change,
I lost myself
to an inner rage.

The latest step-dad,
I could not stand.
I knew he was not
a good man.

My previous step-dad
I loved so much.
He disappeared,
no explanation for us.

He ran off and married
my live-in babysitter.
He left behind
me and my brother.

He never even gave us
the blink of an eye.
He left without even
saying goodbye.

Why were we so easy to
push to the side?
This, so hard to understand
from a child's eyes.

So confused,
I loved him so much:
yet another fracture
in my already waning trust.

In school, I tried to fit in,
my weaknesses so visible,
the bullies clued in.

Not focused at school.
Not getting good grades.
I almost failed
5th, 8th and 10th grades.

So scared of my peers,
I lived in fear.
Each week unclear
if it was my week
to be treated as inferior.

Each week, it was horrible.
The not knowing

created severe
anticipation horror

My mind would fill
with endless pictures
of what my fate might be.
The bullies had
total control over me.

One day, I went to my locker,
and there it was.
An "I hate you" note had appeared.
It had the signatures
of ten of my peers.
Between home and school,
nothing was stable.

Me?
I became a depressed
empty vessel.

With life,
I was not compatible.
I became antisocial.
I experienced people
as mostly evil.
All of them were unpredictable.

This world,
so confusing to me.
I learned not to attach
for my own safety.

At home, I felt drained.
My parents, reacting to my grades:
"What the hell is
wrong with her brain?"

I was so angry.
Couldn't they see
that it was them
that created
this me?

Maybe I was wrong.
Maybe it was me.
Maybe I just wasn't smart.
After all, my brother was
outdoing them all.

He was the bright, shining star.
Everyone knew he
would go so very far.

The presence of me
caused chaos and frustration.
Why wasn't I doing better?
My failure defaced them.

Little did they know…

I began to hate them.

As you traveled by, you saw that not only is the landscape Unstable, but so are the waters surrounding this place. There is nothing stable in the water or on land, and so balance is not available. People, who could have stabilized your world, are unstable themselves. You lose faith in them and begin to fill with negative emotion. It is the negative emotion that creates the disasters and the unpredictable nature of this landscape and its waters. It is a dark place and the eye-sight not clear. As the boat pulls to shore, you will have to discover how to navigate this land, the culture and its people. You will need a survival pack to take with you in case a disaster happens. Exit gently. You are here to learn about instability and its impact on the state and culture of your inner world. There is much intelligence to gather from a visit here. Allow yourself to look through these distorted views.

Eye-Sight

Unstable home environments and children are a dangerous mix. If there is instability in the home, there is usually instability socially. I cannot emphasize enough how important it is for children to have love. Not superficial love, I mean *real* love. Love that is deep focused on the child and attuned to the child's needs. Each child is divinely unique and will require a totally different set of parenting skills from parents.

I was a *very* sensitive child. My step-dad was a stability for me. I loved him. When he left so abruptly, I went into a deeper state of sadness and confusion. My vulnerability leaked out of me in every way possible. I had no idea how to protect myself. My vulnerability could be felt in my energy. Thus, I became an easy target for bullies; I did not develop mechanisms for sticking up for myself. I had only developed mechanisms for pleasing other people. Pathetic, I had not had enough nurturing to develop the confidence I needed to cope in peer relationships.

Pleasing became my way of staying safe and invisible. I tried to fit in, but I suffered. I did not have consistent access to self-worth. I had no control over my emotional world. This made life-navigation very difficult. My eye-sight was that I was consistently at the mercy of the other, whether peers or parents. I got so afraid to go to school that I felt physically sick. I constantly had a nervous and upset stomach. The emotional pain was so intense that it crippled my nerves.

I frantically pleased all the wrong people, shrank myself to make others comfortable, and stuffed all my feelings. I was afraid of my own shadow. I was a disappointment because I did not get the good grades expected of me. I could not function in school. History class, in particular, was not as powerful as my sick nervous stomach.

As children, we are often robbed of our rights to anger/frustration because it is considered bad behavior. How come my parents could be angry, but I could not be angry? How come my parents thought I should respect them when respect was never afforded to me? Nothing felt fair. At home and at school, I was in environments where rules only went one way.

I could feel my frustration building into the beginnings of *real* anger. I was confused. I felt I lived in a house of mirrors, where everything was distorted but I was made to feel it was me that was seeing incorrectly. I could not find my way through this confusion, school was not interesting or helpful in any applicable way to my life, and I got stuck, a lost child.

In-Sight: Self-confidence is nurtured through mutually beneficial relationships.

Reflections:

Unstable is not deep enough a word to use for this time in my life. My too sensitive nature was a curse. I was raw on every level and intuiting my environment so clearly. I remember my live-in babysitter sitting in between my step-dad's legs and I remember knowing inside this was not right. I loved this step-dad. I loved him so much that I had asked my real dad if he would be mad if I loved my step-dad more than him. The loss of this man was profound. I later learned he married this babysitter, and I felt betrayed by both.

I did not like the new soon-to-be step-dad from the very first moment of being in his energy. I was living with my Dad and I was begging my mom to come home. She was trying to reassure me by essentially dismissing the seriousness of my pleading. The new soon to be step-dad rolled his eyes in annoyance at my desperation for her. My feelings had the potential to stand in the way of their need to be together. My needs were in constant conflict with the needs my parents had for their own lives. Because I was younger and more vulnerable, my needs came second. I did not have the power of choice. I was to accept and go along. Because my mother was happy, I am certain she thought it would also eventually make me happy.

Once my mom moved back, I was relieved to be in my little girl house again, but I hated her. This was the first moment I felt such pure hatred or rage. My inner life was disturbed. My sport, figure skating, gave me some reprieve, but that eventually faded because I became too visible. Nasty people, who were poisoned with jealousy, abused me. The more I tried to please them, the meaner they became. I eventually began to take my anger out on my sport and was told I could no longer participate in it. No one considered asking me about my feelings.

At home, I tried to communicate the level of my fear and pain, but my feelings were dismissed and in some form or another, I got the message I was too sensitive. My peers made my life a living hell. This was a deeply lonely and scary experience. Both my age and older, they had the power to make me feel utterly worthless on top of the worthlessness I already brought to the table. I was ignored, left out, alienated, and given dirty looks. Notes were written about me in front of me. I was physically threatened by the older girls. Things were written all over the bathroom walls about me and my sport. My coaches did nothing, my parents did nothing. The adults in my life *did nothing.*

I quit my sport and lived a life of feeling sick to my stomach. My only form of success was gone. I had sleep problems and was failing my classes at school. All the adults in my life knew what was going on, but somehow they also saw me as the cause. My reputation was changing from being too sensitive to being the *bad kid*. The bad kid role still follows me today. I spent a lot of time alone during this period of my life. On my own, I could find a calm, cool energy within me. Being alone became my heaven. Socially, I had no confidence. I was a pleaser. I was hyper vigilant, always cautious. Survival felt like all I could do each day.

My false-self was growing. If you repress your emotions, you keep them in. You hide them by ingesting them. When you internalize them, you become them. This is literally like poisoning the Self. As you hide and you try to become what you think others want, you experience compression. If you compress yourself, you shrink. You become a smaller version of who you are really meant to be. As you become smaller and smaller, you take more abuse. As you take more abuse, your anger grows. Anger will eventually turn to rage.

One of the more challenging things you will learn is to stand up for yourself. When you stand up for yourself, you respect yourself. When no one has stood up for you, it is difficult to stand up for yourself. When you lose self-respect, you literally lose belief in yourself. This is the most profound damage. The reason you don't stand up for yourself most often is the fear of the other's reaction. I lived in this type of fear for a very long time and still, at times struggle with this today. I used non-attachment to take care of myself, rather than confrontation. I did not know how to get my truth to my mouth in a way that was effective with peers or parents. With peers, I pleased; with parents, I raged. There was no balance.

Because my emotional state was an unwanted part of my family system, I had to internalize. My emotions had become my identity. I was now a sad person, an angry person, an out of control person, and an afraid person. I did not feel like a *good* person. It became difficult for me to get close to anyone. The more I felt myself to be less than others, the more I saw my choices as limited. The more I saw my life as unstable, the more I experienced myself to be unstable. I was not safe anywhere especially within myself. I was alienated from within and without.

I lived the eye-sight of lack. I felt flawed, and this distorted my view that all others were not flawed. I saw other people possess the qualities I wanted, and it made me angry and envious. How come they could have those qualities, but I could not?

We all have these types of issues in one way or another. We have all had peer abuse, we have all had some form of abandonment, not fitting in, and not feeling important. Conflict is scary, and most of us avoid it. When we do, we get further away from ourselves. If you are pleasing others to stay safe, how safe are you really? You are only safe for the moment that you avoid conflict. If you are raging at others, how safe are you? After rage there is usually regret, shame, and self-hatred. Pleasing and raging are not effective ways to tell our truth. In both instances, the truth gets lost.

All truth resides in the emotions. The emotions give you instant

20/20 vision. The truth is always simple, if you can express it without defenses. You learn to defend from your outer world conditioners, the adults in your lives. The stronger the conditioning, the further away from your natural emotions you get. How can you recognize your natural emotion? It is the first feeling that comes up. Someone or something either makes you feel good or bad. It is that simple. The first feeling is your personal truth.

Life Class Lesson:

In this section you are going analyze and wonder about the greatest human emotional affliction of not feeling good enough. As you have been analyzing your negative beliefs, you have seen your beliefs were formed in childhood. This conditioning formed your thoughts, feelings, perceptions, behaviors, and beliefs. If you desire to undo this faulty conditioning and change the experience of your life, you have to uncover how exactly your parents behavior impacted you.

Before starting this lesson, take a moment to visualize your childhood. In this visualization, you will see yourself not feeling good enough as a result of parental criticism. When you see them being critical, frustrated, annoyed, you are also able to see how their reactions to you made you feel small, ashamed, embarrassed, and deeply hurt. You determined you must not be good enough, or your parents never would have reacted in those ways.

As you step back from this visualization and look at what mostly stands out about the vision, it is your parent's behavior, not yours. What does that tell you? Maybe it means the parenting was the issue. You are so deeply open and vulnerable as a child that when you are punished for doing something or being a certain way, you feel not good enough, especially if the parents didn't follow up induced shame with love and explanation. Shame/criticism should always be followed up with reassurance, love, and explanation.

It is worth looking at not feeling good enough since each of us suffer from it. The more you feel this way, the less efficiently you will live your life. Let us move into learning to live as efficiently as possible so as to make life a bit easier. Asking questions helps you zero in on the emotions. The emotions give you direct access into the center of your pain of not feeling good enough.

**What and who has made you feel the feeling of worthlessness?*

**What did you believe about those people, and why did you believe them?*

**What decisions or lack of decisions have you made because you held this belief about yourself?*

**What fears did you develop to stay connected to people who did not value you?*

**Make a list of what you were told about your value?* Example:

- You are in the way.
- You are a burden to my freedom.
- You are a pain in the ass.
- You are too emotional.
- You are weak.
- You are a nuisance.
- You are not a priority.
- You are too sensitive.

I look at this list, and it is no wonder I had low self-esteem and could not thrive.

How can you transform that list?* Example: This list is a goldmine. To have it written and solidified now gives me the opportunity to take my life in the exact opposite direction of those negative beliefs. Just because my parents treated me this way does not mean it is true. I will now transform that list: *You are in the way* transforms into ***I am on this planet to make my own way.* *You are a burden to my freedom* becomes ***I am here to be independent and self-sufficient.*** *You are a pain in the ass* transforms into ***I am okay with me regardless whether others are or not. I do not have to have relationships with***

people who feel this way about me. They do not resonate for me. *You are too emotionally weak* beomes **I am emotionally in touch with my feelings and recognize who I can trust with my feelings.** *You are a nuisance* becomes **I am divinely important and here on this planet to have an impacting purpose.** *You are not a priority* becomes **I am now my priority and I love me.** *You are too sensitive* can transform into **I am beautifully intuitive and correct about my emotional world.**

**How were you negatively conditioned by your parents?*

How were you positively conditioned by them? Example: I was mostly conditioned positively by my Mother because she was always around. I have always loved her touch and her smell. My Dad was gone for a lot of my defining moments of growth. My Mom modeled for me to take care of myself physically. She fed us healthy food, kept a clean and organized house, and was always exercising. She taught me to dress nicely and to care about how I present myself to world. She also taught me to be on time to all appointments and to be respectful of any environment I am in.

The most valuable thing I got from her is being organized and hard working. My mom's number one stable love in her life was always her job. She was her best when at work, and I am now largely the same way. I love my job; I am not afraid of hard work, commitment and dedication; and I am grateful I had a mother who worked hard to model this for me. Because of this I have a full, dynamic, and interesting life. Also, my mom and I may have our challenges emotionally but she is always there regardless of the difficulties we have had, and I am grateful for this in a very deep way. She and I are incredibly different emotionally and on this level, I need to let her be who she is. I have to make sure I set my boundaries to be able to be who I am. I need a certain amount of freedom from her and I need to give her the same from me. I love all that she has taught me and modeled for me because the benefits have been incredible.

**Do you run from conflict? If so, why?*

**When you please another are you abandoning yourself?*

**If so, what part of you are you abandoning?*

**If you could say anything to someone you have pleased, what would you want them to know about the effect they have had on you?*

**If you could give advice to your pleasing Self, what advice would you give?*

Extra Credit Advantage:

Healing reading for home-work

The Power of Positive Thinking (Norman Vincent Peale): I read this over and over. I could not get enough of this book because it reassured me somehow that not only am I completely good enough but that I am 100% good enough and that belief had to start within me. At first, my belief was in the book and not in me, but with enough reading I started to adopt it as my belief. This may be why I read it over and over because at first the good enough belief only lived in the words on the page and not in my heart. With each re-read and actively practicing what I was reading, I eventually was able to believe that I am good enough.

*A Guide to Confident Living (*Norman Vincent Peale): In this book, I learned that confidence is actually an energy that we put off to others. This book helped me to generate and practice living the energy of the newly confident person I was becoming. This book put me in touch with my inner power that before this time was essentially unknown to me because I never learned of my power. I only experienced my deficits. Both of these books gave me practical advice that I was able to apply. They helped me to have faith. Thank you Norman!

Healing Your Emotional Self: A Powerful Program to Help You Raise Your Self-Esteem, Quiet Your Inner Critic, and Overcome Your Shame (Beverly Engel): This book helped me understand my childhood and the impacts the abandonments had upon me. I was not just abandoned by my parents but also by step parents and other significant adults. All of this made me feel unlovable at my core. This covers all of childhood and the impacts adults have on us and is a book that brought me into a deeper sense of self-awareness and self-acceptance.

Differentiating Opportunity:

Just suppose you have unlimited resources to change your mind about yourself. Suppose you learn to love yourself, to find yourself interesting and unique, and to accept who you are, sensitivities and all. If you are sad, suppose you can nurture and understand your own sadness. Suppose you can be the source of what you need from the other.

Differentiating is about transforming your limiting beliefs. When you are able to eliminate limiting beliefs, new possibilities open up, and you discover that there is a lot more to life than you had ever imagined. There is a lot more to you as an individual then you ever imagined. Your beliefs determine your reality, and changing them can have powerful results. When limiting beliefs are eliminated, you become limitless. New possibilities open up, and you quickly discover new thoughts, new behaviors, new feelings, and new realities in which you can thrive, prosper, and feel joyous. Just suppose....

You do not need to remain the product of your past, you can stay in the process of taking responsibility for yourself and making your life and your experiences individual. How is your anger yours and not caused by the other? If it is your feeling, it is your responsibility to take care of it. This does not mean that others didn't cause it. I am saying it is your responsibility to take care of it, to resolve it. Step back and see what it was in you that responded with anger. Were you defending your self-worth? If so, define what you were defending. This will allow you to see who you are.

When you can resolve your emotional issues within yourself, you have an opportunity to individualize. Ask your anger what its purpose is and learn how important it can be for you, as a unique individual. Find books written on the subject and learn about anger. To *feel* worthless is not to *be* worthless. What is the great learning experience you can get from feeling worthless? Feeling worthless is feeling worth less than you deserve. Having the emotional experience of worthlessness gives you perspective on how well you are accomplishing your life classes. Once you know worthless, you can begin your search to create, discover, and find your worth.

When *Not Good Enough* has become a belief – in the form of a thought attached to a feeling – it has become a core wound. To transform this belief, make the decision right this second to believe you are good enough. You are good enough in every way. Focus on the positive in your life, and redefine your ideas of perfect. Perfectionism is about control. Control puts you at odds with life. Those who get the most of out of their lives have the following qualities: they are first and foremost flexible; they are courageous, willing to make mistakes; and they are open and humble.

Gazing at this scene,
I wanted to unleash
on everyone who had
hurt me.

Instead, I reclaimed
the me that was there.
I know in her life
she did her unleashing.
For that later in life,
did her apologizing.

From this memory,
I relived that stress.
The ache in my belly,
I was always a mess.

Believe it or not,
I felt slightly warm.
The adrenalin within
kicked in,
as I revisited
the me that was then.

I became aware of my surroundings.
The water from the
icy ceiling was dripping.
The boat again began moving.

Up ahead another memory.

I see her; she is
thirteen-years-old.
She is coming home
to a scene that is...

In-sights all along the way are your new-direction Omens. This is the wonderful thing about traveling. As you travel and you learn new things, you head in new directions that would never have been possible had you not visited the exact places that you did. This is the gift of self-examination. As you enter the boat to continue, put your analytical mind away and allow your emotional Self to get back into the space of relating. You are soon to arrive in the land of the Unbelievable. When something Unbelievable happens to you emotionally, you are consumed with shock.

Unbelievable

I came to the door.
I had lugged my bags
up two floors.

I had been away
on a field trip
for the 8th grade.

At that time,
I was living with my Dad
because my grades were bad.
I got sent to him to stay.

I approached the door
and turned the knob.
It was locked.
I wondered what was wrong.

Impatiently, I knocked.
I looked. My Dad's car
was in the parking lot.
Didn't he know
I was coming home today?

Of course, he would know.
He would have missed
Me, while I was away.

After some time,
he answered the door.
He was wearing a suit and tie.
He looked at me with
astonishment and surprise.

He forgot I was coming
home that day.
He pulled me inside
and told me to get
quickly changed.

He was in the middle
of getting married.

As I entered,
there were several
strange people
staring at me.
I was tired and dirty
from the last eight hours
of traveling.

I went to my room,
sat on my bed,
and tried to catch up
with the thoughts in my head.

What the hell
was going on?
How do you forget
your child's coming home?

I had no idea
he was even thinking
of wedding,
but at that moment,
he was making the commitment
in our living room.
Was he crazy?

Unbelievable.
As I changed,
I began to cry.
I was full of frustration,
and now I had to lie.

I went out to join
the ceremony,
wearing a fake smile.

I watched them get married.
They acted so happy.
Me, I just thought
the whole thing was crappy.

His intention had been to
marry her behind our backs.
He said he wanted to
surprise us after the fact.
So seethingly angry,
I wanted to attack.

I hated her,
and I hated him.
I cannot believe
he just got hitched
in the living room.
I don't get it.

Don't adults
ever think about
the opinions
of their children?
It would have been
nice to know
this wedding was
going to happen.

You can see from the boat that this culture is full of the element of shock, coupled with disappointment and amazement at the ludicrousness of what the inhabitants of this culture will do. This is the land of the self-centered. It is the place where people do not care how their decisions impact those around them. There is not a lot of love here. This is a place consumed with wanting. The people here want what they want when they want it, and they don't care much how anyone else feels about it. The place of the Unbelievable creates separation and division among its people. Gently step out here and make the most of this opportunity to learn from those who want without regard for the benefit of the other. What you will learn is that the people of the Unbelievable feel justified in their actions, and this always makes another feel wrong. Let us look through this distorted perception.

Eye-Sight

Shock is unbalancing. When you get caught in the unexpected, your central nervous systems take over, and you are awash in primitive chemicals and automatic responses. In *Unbelievable* I realized my parents never considered my opinions or feelings. Children and teens have opinions. They have valid opinions and are essential members of any family. When children/teens share opinions and their opinions are considered by the parents, the young person derives a sense of value from being heard and respected. The four most important words to ask any child are: *What are you feeling?*

Feeling as if you have no voice invokes a toxic belief system that is shame-based. You begin to *believe* you do not matter in the world. To cope, you develop a false-self. You act one way to the outside world, but have low self-worth on the inside. When this type of behavior becomes normal, you lose touch with your essence.

The development of a false-self leads to the beginnings of poor life-approach habits. You may begin to approach life with an "I do not care attitude" because you have learned you are not cared for. The only way you can learn to care about life and others is if you are cared for. But you learn not to share your feelings and opinions and adapt to the belief systems around you. Once you learn not to share, you lose yourself. How can anyone know you or care for you if you stop sharing or if what you do share is a false-self?

To some extent, each of us has developed a false-self. You were given the eye-sight that your inner world did not matter. You cannot be authentic if you are consistently living from the place of pleasing others. To embrace the real self means you have to take personal ownership of the behaviors which cause you to be false and begin to express the real-self with confidence and exuberance. This means undoing all the old programming. How do you do this? You differentiate.

In-Sight: If I am a false-self, then I am not my Self. I become false to fit in.

Reflections:

On this day when I came home, I was mostly dumbfounded my Dad didn't expect me home from my week long field trip. How would a parent not keep track of something like this? I was clear, on a deeply confirming level, that I was not a child but rather a decoration in the life of my parents.

The next shocking thing was my Dad was getting married to a woman I had met only once. It was humiliating. When I met her in my Dad's living room, I did not like her. My intuition said she would see my brother and me as interference. Obviously, her presence would impact me in a profound way. This woman was self-centered, had no clue about teenagers, and lasted only a couple of years.

Mostly, what I thought and felt did not matter to the adults in my life. I had already shut my voice down. The voice is the vehicle for being heard. The throat is the mechanism for sharing who you are with the world. No other species has language like human beings do. Language is how you connect with others. It is how you express your individuality. Because of language, humans have the capacity to bond in the deepest way. The voice is often used for warfare as well. The power of words can destroy, or they can validate.

When you are not allowed your voice, you are not allowed an opinion, a place in the world, your self-expression, or your truth. When you do have a voice, you are given your value. That does not mean what you have to say will be well received. I have learned those who are the most resistant are those who are the most afraid to look at themselves. If someone is defensive or self-protective they are not open to new information. They have a need to see you and themselves in a fixed way. At fourteen, I was seen in a fixed way and was beginning to see others in fixed ways.

The throat gives you a voice; it can also be a vehicle for repression. Interestingly, for many, many years, I would be plagued with sore throats, strep throat and upper respiratory issues. When you are not invited for your self-expression or it is rejected, you can begin to engage in self-doubt. There is no worse feeling than self-doubt. My parents and many people in my life, behaved as if what they were doing was totally normal and what I was feeling about it was what was abnormal. Because they were my parents, I figured they must be right, and I must be either wrong or too sensitive. When this happens, you get even further away from the *knowing* you have inside. You become conditioned to avoid the truth and confrontation. Everything about you becomes fabricated out of the basic need to survive. The false-self grows. You become a gifted actor or actress, acting happy about people and situations which you are truly not happy about. You lose the ability to say no.

Life Class Lesson:

You are now going to open your mind to how you have become who other people need and want you to be. You essentially become a false-self by accident. You begin shaving off essential aspects of who you are to fit into who you are not. The desire to fit in is natural. When you receive a message that something about you is undesirable, you shave that part away to be what others want. This places you in the unnatural state of being who you are not. Over time, you can lose track of who you really are and end up in an identity crisis.

Why are opinions/choices important? All individual members in a family create the whole. In other words, the whole is greater than the sum of its parts. Each member in the family is deeply impacted by every other person in the family. Any change or action in a family impacts the stability of the whole and creates imbalance. My parents operated from an "I" mentality, not a "we" mentality. This "I" mentality was something I had to go along with in order to remain a part of the system. Each family member having his/her own agenda created so much of the internal chaos I would feel. Nothing was stable, and nothing remained the same. This was not just about the environment. The love was not stable.

There are different types of family systems. Some are "we" based and completely enmeshed, some are "I" based, and each person has their own agenda. Whatever system you grew up in is your mustard seed for transformation. You began the false-self in childhood. Let's look.

**How are you a false-self?*

**Do you find yourself repressing your truths so as to not make waves?*

**How do you feel after?*

**How do you feel long-term?*

**Do your feelings matter to you?* Example: I have had to learn how to make my feelings matter to me. Because I did not experience how they mattered to other people, especially my parents, I learned to make my feelings not matter to me as well. As long as others were happy, then I *should* be happy. However, as time passed, my feelings just got louder. I would do anything and everything to act and feel like I just didn't care. This was my defense mechanism. Communicating my feelings did no good and made no difference so I began to repress them.

However, because life is about open-ended growth, and I am designed to be sensitive, I was never able to fully repress my feelings. I had little choice but to feel them. Once I began writing in a journal around the age twelve, I was able to share my feelings. I did not share them with other people but I always felt better after I wrote them down. I didn't trust I could share them with others without getting some form of rejection, and so I kept them to my Self. But at least, I kept them. I acted like I didn't care out in the world, but I had a place to put my truth at night when I wrote my thoughts and feelings out. It would be easier if we could genuinely not care but that is counter to how we are designed. We are designed to be emotional creatures. I learned over time that my feelings were the most important sources of information about me. My feelings served as the answers to all my questions. Now, my feelings matter to me and to everyone who loves me and vice versa.

**Do they matter to others?*

**Who can you share with?*

**Can you describe your false self?* Example: I know I am in my false self when I am: Acting happy when I am clearly not happy. Attending social outings I really do not feel like attending. Keeping my emotions in to not to have to deal with confrontation. Making others more important and wishing I wouldn't do that but doing it anyway. Always being the flexible person in my relationships and bending around everyone else's lack of flexibility. Keeping my opinions to myself and putting on a face of agreement to others when I really do not agree.

The False self hides who you really are. Who I am would get so hidden that sometimes I would not be sure who I really was because I was too busy being what I thought others wanted me to be. This is how the false-self can gain a long term identity. Enough hiding and shape-changing and that is who you are. Your identity is "I am who others want me to be." This happens all the time, and the long term prognosis of this is not good. Adults, who suffer this, have chronic feelings of emptiness and an unstable sense of self or identity. They tend to have tumultuous relationship patterns and can often get lost in addictions etc. I am grateful that I have a strong enough *me* inside to realize when I was and was not being my real self.

**If so write it down and get a good look at this part of you because it needs healing.*

Extra Credit Advantage:

*Healing reading for home-*work.

Healing the Shame that Binds you (John Bradshaw): This book taught me that whatever shame was inflicted upon me as a child had a way of traveling with me into my adulthood. At its core, my induced shame destroyed my sense of value. Shame drives us from our deepest feelings about ourselves. This book helped educate me on shame and the feeling of being flawed and defective. This education alone was enough for me to better understand how I became the me I had become. It was enlightening. I read this book until I got what I needed out of it and then stopped.

Differentiating Opportunity:

Just suppose you being yourself drew you to the exact right people with whom you could authentically fit. The gift of knowing what not fitting feels like is it makes you desire to find where you do fit. Fitting is as internal as it is external, meaning you must have acceptance of who you are. When you like yourself and feel comfortable in your skin, then you fit. As you put that energy into the world, you will find others with whom you fit as well. This is the value in Differentiating: as you become your authentic Self you will draw a whole new group of people to you. Like attracts like. If you like yourself you will find the people who will like you as well. These people will be the *right* people, the people with whom you feel safe to be yourself.

When you are stuck with people you do not fit with, it becomes easier to shrink than to fight. You become a go-with-the-flow person. While it is necessary to be flexible in life, never going with your *own* flow is Self-abandonment. Suppose you were able to use all this information to start your journey into Self-acceptance, and you could have the courage to express and hold onto the values and opinions that are unique to you. No doubt it takes courage to separate from the group that you have always been with, but *our most successful people have courage, they are willing to abandon what doesn't and who doesn't work in their lives in search for who and what does.* This may mean you go at life alone for a time but again, whatever you release in life has to be replaced by something else. Opinions and having a say take courage. Suppose you have the courage to start putting your thoughts out into the world...

Reflecting back, my opinions did not matter to my parents, but they did matter to me. I kept my uniqueness stuffed deep inside. Although it was unexpressed, I held tight to it internally. My opinions make me unique. Your opinions make you unique. Opinions are not about being more *right* than the other; opinions are our internal world *shared* with the other. They make up my perception of the world and my perception of the emotional environment I was and am currently in. How I take in the world is what makes me different than the people who raised me. If you believe in something strongly, your perception is correct for you. I encourage you to hold onto it and let it elevate you to your next level of learning.

While we all tend to keep our opinions to ourselves, sharing opinions is a clear and direct way to show our boundaries or our separateness from the other. This is a statement of who you are. I encourage you to share your thoughts and to be open to them being accepted or not. It isn't about that. It's about the statement of who you are that matters. Opinions have a bad reputation in many circumstances because to be opinionated means to be closed or not open to new information. I am not speaking of opinions in that way. I am speaking of opinions as your unique perceptions. Once shared, they can be altered, stay the same, be validated or invalidated. For instance, I now believe my parents were not trying to make me unimportant. They were simply focused on their own wants without insight into how this would impact their children. This understanding feels good even though it doesn't change my experience.

Sitting in the boat
gazing at this memory,
I am in shock at its meaning
for the me that was then.
To her parents,
she felt she meant nothing.

I feel her sadness
as she changes her clothes.
She came home to a scene
that was unbelievable.

It was at this moment
she was reminded again,
in the minds of her parents
her opinion was irrelevant.

Anger pushing
through my body,
I wanted out of this boat.
I wanted to jump into
that scene and hurt somebody.

The me then was too weak.
She had no voice to speak.
She put on a happy face.
Inside, she felt angry.

In the boat.
the cold is stinging me.
I barely have any feeling
aside from the anger
rushing through my body.

I sit and embrace
the me that was then.
I felt so sad for her.
Her opinion didn't matter.

*Oh my God,
up ahead so much fog.
The adrenalin had worn off.
The brief warmth
was gone.*

*My whole body damp.
I felt so frozen.
Up ahead I was approaching
a me that was broken.*

*It was so foggy;
I could barely see.
The boat pressed on.
It had a memory to bring me.*

*The fog spoke to me
metaphorically
of what life is like
when living with deep…*

Up ahead is the land of Insecurity. This is a most interesting place. Inhabitants talk too much or totally isolate themselves or a little of both. As you approach this place, you can see there is much wisdom to this culture if you learn how to nurture your inner soil, the fertile ground you have within. All insecurity comes from within. Let yourself have a soft landing into this next scene. It is nice to be able to approach life gently, especially when you are traveling. The more gentle you are with your emotions, the better you will be able to understand and love them. Love and understanding nurture the soil. Insecurity tends to bring on some tumultuous travels, but since you have feelings of insecurity, you can have comfort in knowing you are not alone because you can relate to every person in existence. As you learn to give love to the Self within, you will see that your insecurities are your great guides. The best way to get to know who you are is to look at what makes you insecure. So push play and allow the story to unfold into the scene of Insecurity.

Insecurity

Insecurity,
alive within me.
No more innocent purity.
I was angry.

My trust had been shattered.
It had been squashed,
beaten and battered.

So early in life
I had no security.
I lived in a state
of pure uncertainty.

There is no light.
I have no more fight.
I am exhausted by life.
Please God,
won't you take me tonight?

My insecurity
gnaws at my insides
with relentless fury.
Everything that was painful
I had to bury.

The consistent ache inside,
From it I could never hide.

My insides,
always aching and churning.
This emotional bleeding
was a sickening feeling.

I was always wound,
so tightly bound
by my insecurity.

Fear, the only feeling in my life.
I lost my sight
on the meaning of my plight.

The words from my mouth
became so unkind.
As the words escaped,
I always seemed to be
several steps behind.

My anger, the vessel
for the hurt inside.
It defended me
and guarded my
vulnerability.

I began to feel inherently mean.
But, my anger protected me.
I was just defending
what was sacred to me...
My sanity.

It seemed to come out
mostly at school and home,
on those adults
responsible for putting me
into that zone.

Feeling misunderstood,
I didn't want to me be mean.
I just felt I was always
having to defend me.

I turned my anger inward
when I stopped eating.
By turning it on myself,
my emotions were finally shelved.

No longer outwardly angry.
Maybe now
I would be accepted
by my family.

It is typical to feel a little motion sickness as you pass through the fog and the lack of clarity surrounding the landscape of Insecurity. The waters are deep and foreboding, the population isolated and starving for a sense of inner peace, and yet, these people seem not be able to find it. It is a sad and desperate place. The desire of the people here is to find acceptance. As you exit the boat and walk the shores of Insecurity, you can obtain great knowledge. There are treasures hidden all over the landscape. It is time to explore and find the treasures. Insecurities are somewhat similar to Omens. You will learn that they are here to signify what you have to change. Walk gingerly, gently and with awareness of your Insecurities. Here that you can begin to heal them.

Eye-Sight

Insecurity is a permeating darkness which comes from a deep seeded shame-based belief which says you are not good enough, lovable enough, successful enough or important enough. Shame based beliefs are developed in childhood. My eye-sight was that I was not good enough. I was not good at life. Life didn't like me. These beliefs grow throughout life. The brain works like a filing system. My abandonment file was full. Current abandonment brought up the entire file and I re-spiraled into the familiar feelings of old abandonment. In this way abandonment accumulated. These files are *core wounds*. As you grow, they grow to encompass past, present and even future fears of abandonment.

Abandonment is recycled mostly through the relationships we choose. In *Insecurity,* I express how this feeling raged inside of my emotional system. I was a melting pot of chaos with the outside world being the dictator of my emotional rollercoaster. As my insecurity grew, so did my anger. As my anger grew so did my lack of control over my life. I was not only feeling angry, I had developed an anger problem. It was the only thing that made me feel powerful, at least in the heat of the moment. After the heat of the moment I was back to shame and regret. Although the rage *released* emotion in the moment, it did not *transform* the emotion. My shame-based beliefs were constantly being reinforced. Once you dip into living in shame, life becomes cold and dark. Your entire frequency communicates this darkness.

When you are depressed, your brain chemistry is sending out neuropeptide chemicals which suppress every cell in your body. When you are depressed, your whole body, mind, and spirit are depressed. The electrical charge dispersed in your aura is dark. You are experienced as lazy, sluggish, and non-productive to those around you. Living at a low frequency causes you to attract more and more low frequency life experiences. When you live the idea of lack, you become lack, and you attract more lack to yourself. In other words if you stay focused on your suffering, you will get more and more suffering. You continue in the pattern of reinforcing old shame-based core wounds. This is a hard trap to escape. Your beliefs determine what types and levels of life experiences you attract.

Insecurity is alive in every person. It is part of the human experience. I believe that a certain amount of insecurity is healthy as it keeps you from narcissism, but deep insecurity can keep you from growing. You cannot pass life classes without a healthy dose of insecurity and humility. The mission is to understand the insecurity so it can be examined and released to mend your broken pieces.

In-Sight: Each insecurity has an evolving purpose. They are not meant to go away; they are meant to lead our way to healing.

Reflections:

I was a sad and angry person by this point in my life. I had heard so many negative messages to myself about myself that I was lost in those perceptions. I had gone through so much change due to my parents shifting partners and shifting life decisions that I had very little consistency. I did not have choices as a child. A life without choice is a life without a voice. I could not test out inner security when I was not allowed my opinion. When you are allowed, at least your opinion, and it is taken seriously, you learn to take care of the feeling-self within. Confidence is developed this way. My parents did not consider what their life choices and what their life behaviors would do to me as a person. I was not closely bonded to either parent. My attempts to talk and say what I was feeling were not heard. My parents did not want to hear that anything they were doing in their lives was messing up my life, even though signs of my failure were popping up everywhere. Driving my anger was the feeling of hurt. *I believe that had love been consistent and had I had a deep connection with even one parent, I would have better come through my changing circumstances.*

Grief/sadness is the emotion that naturally arises when you lose something you are not ready to let go of. It could be a pacifier for a baby, a friend that moves away, a lost stuffed animal, a broken relationship, loss of health, loss of a job, loss of money, the death of a loved one, loss of someone's approval and/or recognition, loss of a friend, etc. I was losing homes, schools, sports, consistency, parents, step-parents, animals, etc. If, as children, you were allowed to experience and express your sadness, you would have learned your sadness was normal and okay. You would have developed no fear or shame around your feeling of sadness. When children are validated in their sadness, heard, loved and understood, they become so comfortable with this emotion they learn to move through it quickly and efficiently as adults. They see it as something that is to be expelled, expressed, and let go. They understand that all is well even when they are feeling sad. Sadness does not create instability.

However, most of you as children were told not to cry. You got the following messages "To cry over that is silly," "That is nothing to be sad about," "Be quiet can't you see that other people can hear you?" "Don't make a scene." You have gotten the message throughout your life that your sadness needs to be silenced. This is because your sadness causes your parents to feel responsible for causing it. Thus, most sadness goes invalidated by those closest to us. My sadness and failure were too strong of a mirror for my parents to look in. They were the least likely to take responsibility for my emotions because it was too easy to make me the bad kid.

If you pull the word insecurity apart and it reads in-security you see that security has to come from within. Inside, you either feel good or you feel bad, it is that simple. If you do not have security within, you will naturally turn to anything in the outside world to help you to feel good. Some turn to substances, some turn to anger and power to feel good, some turn to sex, and some turn to food. I turned my sadness into anger (power). With anger, I felt a rush of adrenalin that made me feel powerful. I can see that I gave up. I got to a place where it became easier for me to be what others thought of me than to try to deal with my emotions and their truths. The adrenalin made me feel good. After the moment passed, I felt shame and that was my insecurity.

Life Class Lesson:

In this lesson, you are going to look at the seeds of insecurity. Insecurity is the root cause of many other problems. Its foundation lies in a lack of Self-belief or Self-confidence. When you feel insecure, you develop fears of not fitting in, rejection, abandonment, and disapproval from others. Due to these fears, you can end up isolating yourself. Insecurities are the abusive voices that exist within you. You may have learned you are not good enough from the outside, but once you internalize that, you begin to tell yourself you are not good enough. Once that process starts from within, we become self-abusive.

This is what keeps you locked into your old conditioning. Your insecurities allow the past to rule and run your current belief system. As this happens, you become stuck with your inner critic, and life becomes difficult and unhappy. You will get stuck in the trap of comparison which will prove to you that you are not enough.

It is challenging to undo negative messages, but you must see your insecurities as great teachers. I suggest you look them right in the face and see what you can do to dismantle their power. Once you are clear on where they originated, it is easier to see how you came to believe falsely about yourself. It is important to contemplate the reasons behind your insecurities for the purpose of taking steps to transform. The next step is to share them. Sharing your insecurities decreases their intensity. As you continue to reflect upon them and their origins, you will find your way to solutions.

**When you were young how was your self-esteem?*

**Who helped you to develop it?*

**What can you do to undo negative messages?*

**What parts of your Self became these messages?* Example: I was taught I was substandard, and so I lived substandard. I gave up on school. I did not find it interesting. I could hardly concentrate because I was so full of self-doubt. I was not praised for good grades nor directly encouraged to work for them unless they were bad. I had a hard time feeling good about who I was. I wasn't emotionally parented to have positive beliefs about myself. I wasn't a superstar performer like my brother. Nothing I did made them look good, so I did not receive what I needed emotionally.

All children need to be treated as superstars regardless of their talents. All children have the same needs. We need to feel full emotionally. We need to be full of positive praise, and we need to see love and excitement in the eyes of our parents. I am a parent now, and I can discipline my daughter and still show her love and compassion. She is a star just for being on this planet. We all are.

**What is the shame that holds you back?* Example: Not feeling good enough holds us all back. It has certainly held me back. It is hard and scary to motivate when we are feeling not good enough. It drives our insecurities and places our fears at the wheel driving our journey. We become timid, afraid, do less than we believe we can, and somewhere in our guts, we know we can do better but cannot figure out how. The *how* comes in choosing to heal and in choosing to develop our own new beliefs about ourselves. The how comes in *doing*. That is what we are doing in this read. I am simply teaching the formula I have learned, lived and now teach to my patients.

*****If you look back on your life and see the changing circumstances as unchanged but you see that you had parents who validated you and emotionally affirmed you throughout, do you think you would have come through your changing circumstances differently?* Example: It is my belief that had I had even one parent in total commitment to me and nurturing my feelings, I could have come through much healthier. It is not a matter of how many people are available in chaos but the quality of love given. It makes me sad my parents were too self-consumed to make that commitment to me emotionally. However, from this lack in my childhood, I am now able to love my daughter with quality love through all the changes she has gone through, is going through, and will go through in the future.

**How were you loved by your parents, and from this, how did you learn to love yourself?*

**Make a list of all your positive qualities and focus only on those. See the change. (Don't hold back on this one because it's good to toot your own horn.)*

Extra Credit Advantage:

Healing reading for home-work.

Jonathan Livingston Seagull (Richard Bach): In this book, I was given tools on how to imagine myself to be all that I could or wanted to be. This is about breaking all perceived limits. I was learning to change my ideas of my Self and my life from negative to positive. I hated feeling so insecure. It was aggravating to say the least because I could not live efficiently. I did not want to turn out to be substandard or average. When we image something bigger and better, we are seeing it in a new form. That new form feels good and we become drawn to it. I began to image myself as a new and improved me, the me I knew was lurking somewhere within.

The Way of the Peaceful Warrior (Dan Millman): I could relate to the character who was plagued with his own insecurities and limiting beliefs. This book was a life changer, and one, I read more than once. I truly studied this book and felt inspired to see everything in my life as opportunity. It is all about breaking free of perceived or believed limitations.

The Four Agreements (Don Miguel Ruiz): This book is one I still reference. I think I could read this book at every new life stage and get something new or deeper out of it. For me, it is the guide to focusing on my Self and not giving my power to others. I see it as the Four Responsibilities I have to my Self. If I can keep those responsibilities, then I will not be as impacted by the uncertainty of people and anything in the outer world. It is the quickest way to get me back in touch with my purpose when I have been seduced away from my Self.

•

Differentiating Opportunity:

Imagine all the possibilities that will open up as you cleanse your insecurities. Insecurities are your emotional baggage. Suppose your insecurities can be thought about differently, and you can see them as the places in your Self which need work and transformation to get you to the life experience you desire to have. If you got rid of this inner critic, how much more at peace would you feel? All it takes to get rid of this inner critic is to override its voice with the opposite positive thought. What if you do this over and over again and are able to reduce these voices to a small hush, easy to quiet with a simple shift in thinking? How much better you would feel in your world! Suppose you can see others as having unique gifts of their own without their gifts making you feel as if you fall short somehow. Suppose when you feel inferior, you look to the positive things about you that others do not possess, and you feel proud. Suppose each insecurity is actually a treasure leading toward more fulfillment, rather than something that robs you of fulfillment.

Differentiating is about changing and transforming. It is about changing the ways you think, feel, and behave to get to your natural, individual expression. Thinking positive is just one effective way to alter your insecure feelings. Thoughts that are positive in nature have an uplifting power and can help you conquer false beliefs. Another tool for differentiation is to avoid the trap of comparing yourself to others. When you compare yourself to others, you set up an unnecessary sense of competition which results in you feeling insecure.

Insecurity was my identity for such a long time. It was what I was experiencing and expressing myself to be. It caused me to feel different than others. My insecurity was my responsibility, and it took me a long time to stop blaming others for it. I had to make people accountable for their contribution to it, but at the end of the day my insecurity was mine uniquely, and I had to take care of it.

My parents' insecurity did not *make* me insecure; it *taught* me to be insecure. It was as much of a learned state as it was an induced state. I had many of the same insecurities as both parents, but they expressed theirs in their unique ways, and I lived mine in my unique ways. The point is to take responsibility and make a choice not to suffer over your own suffering. My insecurities have offered me more gifts than not. I find them fascinating topics of study. I feel them, I research them, I read about them, I write about them, and then, I change them by doing new and uncomfortable, but more productive, things. This is my uniqueness-building opportunity.

The fog has cleared.
As this memory appears,
I feel so sad
for the me that was there.

I lived in a cold fog
of insecurity.
This made my life blurry.

My knees are shaking,
all my muscles are aching.
My clothes are damp,
my chest feels clamped.
The cold is overwhelming.

I can feel the
hypothermia setting in.
I have black frostbite spots
on my skin.

I am so cold, I want to cry,
but I reclaim the me
that was suffering
from such deep insecurity.

The journey must continue on.

The boat again begins moving.
It is now cutting through ice.
It is chipping and cracking
underneath the boat at its sides.
The boat is struggling to get
to the other side...

Another memory,
this one is angry.

It is directed toward?

The adrenalin within is in high flow. I encourage you to hold on tight. As you arrive in the land of Authority, there is some anarchy. The culture of Authority, in general, means a lack of freedom which is why many of you rebel as children and young adults. As you examine what it is like here, trek carefully. Deep within you have the urge to be yourself, and when you are experiencing natural or unnatural, logical or irrational constraints on your self-expression, you get adrenalized and ready to fight for your independence. The rapids will be intense and the ground unstable in this place, so a life-jacket and some padding may be necessary. Anger is a necessary and evolving emotion as it serves to help you fight for yourself. I encourage you to feel your anger from being told to be less of who you are. Allow that feeling to carry you through this next scene you will have it to take out and examine when we get out of the boat.

Authority

Authority,
neglectful of me,
mean, abandoning, rejecting.

I scream.
My soul knows
the disgust I see.
No one listens to little old me.

"Oh don't mind her, she's crazy."

I drift into a
sea of depression.
My sadness has
no place for confession.
Authority,
full of lies and deceit.
Who cares about the children?
I was preferably hidden.

My parents,
so self absorbed.
The next man or woman,
Me: pushed aside,
them: welcomed aboard.

Them: the priority.
The children never having
parental victory.

I yell, I scream,
please listen to me!

"Oh don't mind her, she's crazy."

The anger,
the rage,
I just want to be saved.

Wishing they would die,
so new parents
would love me
and keep me alive.

I know more about them,
than they wish to see.
I am the child;
they fantasize
that I know nothing.

Too much chaos on each side.
My parents, both, married
multiple times.

They are crazy.
It is not me.
I want to tell them
so they will see.

My words go unheard
as I yell and scream.
I am punished for
embarrassing them and
creating a scene.

It is easier for them
if I am crazy.
That way
they escape responsibility.

Parents, teachers, coaches –
all the same to me –
usually not on my team.

You see…they already knew about me
from my reputation.
They heard I was crazy.

I am stuck.
I suffocate.
I am the scapegoat.
My words not allowed
to go past my throat.

"Shut up child, don't rock this boat."

No one to help me.
God, please let my
car drive off this road.
Please take me;
I cannot carry this load.

Never thought to be credible,
I became a rebel.
I became what they needed me to be.
It was easier for them
if I were crazy.

Freedom from responsibility,
my parents' life theme.
Why do people such as these have children?
So self absorbed,
they just emotionally neglect them?

This was my experience of authority.
So bound by their projections,
I lived a life of
emotional repression.

Authority,
squelched my identity.
I wasn't liked
for me being me.

Me, so sad,
I stopped eating.
As the pounds came off
I got lost.
It was so gratifying
to be my own boss.

I loved being sneaky
instead of overtly angry.
I was winning
because they chose not see me.
In fact, they rewarded me.

"My what's different, you look so pretty."

It became a game of deceit.
Me against authority.
My outward rage deceased.
I finally fit into Disney.
All it took
was being pretty.
Thirty pounds later,
the game went on.
Authority?

Living in their natural state of oblivion,
they never asked any questions
as to why did I
live in isolation.

I didn't care.
I had control.
My own world,
so much more predictable.

With the rage gone,
I became invisible.
The thinner I was,
the less vulnerable.

The less of me to see,
the perfect escape

for someone like me.
I was finally done being
pacified as crazy.

I could disappear.
With food I had no fear.
I was now
my own authority.

They taught me
how to treat me.

I modeled them unconsciously.
I became my own worst enemy.
For such a long time,
I was empty.

As you passed by this war torn land, you witnessed the violence of rage, and you watched truth go into battle with denial. It is sad that often denial and distortion win. The truth had to surrender as the distortion was too powerful a force for this war. As you see, those who surrender here often turn their rage in on themselves as they learn to live among the lies.

So, as you exit the boat and stop the story to discover what is here, let yourself see how hard the truth tried for victory. You can see how many people, not only believe the distortion, but how they live it as if it is truth. Several outsiders, on the side of truth, are being forced to live among those in denial. These outsiders are loners. There will be much to learn as you look through the rose colored eye-sight of those who see through the lenses of distortion and denial. It is important to learn of these people and of their weapons. It is easy to get lost here, so be careful and pay close attention.

Eye-Sight

Challenging authority is a natural part of growing up. In *Authority* I express the rage alive inside of me. I was raw, exposed, and unprotected. The eye-sight I was given was that I was the *bad kid*. I experienced anger like a mounting pressure, a fuel. Anything that touched my emotional self the wrong way, I attacked with my rage. At some point, I began to feel an entitlement to my anger. The emotion was not allowed for much of my life, and I was ready not only to own it, but to dominate with it. I was still submissive with peers but I was angry with the adults in my life. I did not feel any of them deserved my respect. Respect to me seemed like it should be a two way street. I had never felt respected, thus, I did not know how to respect adults. *Children do not do what their parents say; they do what their parents do.*

I had a lot of truths I could not keep in anymore. My truth's need to come out was stronger than my will power to keep it in. If I felt misunderstood, I raged. If I felt not heard, I raged. If I felt disrespected, I raged. Once, I raged, my message was out, but it was poorly received due to its delivery. My bad kid reputation stuck. I *was* bad at that time. Unfortunately, this perception of me became fixed. The bad-kid program still gets recycled each time I do not do as others in my family wish. It does not matter how far beyond my childhood I am. Old belief systems can still dominate in family systems. *When one person changes but the family system remains the same, old views still reflect the old programming.*

I had gotten to the point of such deep rejection because of my anger that I became ashamed of being bad. I had gotten out of control and could not figure out how to stop myself. It was then I started to feel fat. I pushed all my anger into my body. I was fat with anger and shame. I used food to stop this. I wanted to please so badly that I displaced all of my anger onto food and developed an eating disorder. I wanted to not only to be good, I wanted to be *perfect*. I wanted desperately to feel some sense of control, authority, and predictability in my life. Reading labels and planning my food schedule for each day became my obsession. I did not allow myself to think of anything other than food. This rigid will power and thinking pattern transported me into a new universe away from all my pain. Food control, exercise, looking in the mirror and hiding my body became my life.

The less of what my mother fed me I ate, the more power I felt I had over my relationship with her. I felt as if I took all her nurturing capabilities away from her. She would pack me a lunch for school, and I would throw it away. It made me feel like I had control over her and all others in my life. The fact that I was strong enough not to eat made me feel stronger than everyone around me. I felt stronger than all my peers. At lunch, I saw people around me eating and thought to myself how weak they were. In hindsight, I am grateful for the false sense of power I got out of not eating. I developed a strong identity through this experience. I am afraid to think of what I may have done had I not found a sense of power somewhere. I did not have an *eating disorder* I had an *emotional disorder.*

Anger is a natural core emotion, and every person will experience anger and rage in their lifetime. My messages of truth often got lost because of my rage. This is what rage does. If you express the truth without self-control, it gets lost. With my anger, I was trying to preserve my self-worth. Unfortunately, the inappropriate expression of anger, always led me back to shame. Anger is about power, and power turned inward onto the self can manifest as unhealthy ways to maintain a sense of control. In my case, I used food.

In-Sight: We develop disorders out of our emotions. At the core of any disorder is the need for control.

Reflections:

I was angry and misunderstood. I was not parented with any boundaries so I did not know how to keep or to respect the boundaries of others. I knew the truth of my family, but when I tried to communicate it, it not only fell on deaf ears, it systematically got turned back around on me. If only I were a good, quiet kid, then the family would *look* good, and it would all be good. I was on a merry-go-round. The more, I fought for myself, the more it was turned around on me. The more it was turned around on me, the angrier I got.

Anger that is repressed turns to rage. Rage is violent and the end result of rage is shame. Shame is fixed and unmoving. Shame creates more rage, and rage creates more shame. It is a vicious cycle, all resulting in self-hatred and the hatred of others. Rage is the body's way of getting someone to take you seriously. Yet, the louder and more belligerent you get, the less people listen. Also with rage, you tend to be ten steps behind your thoughts and actions, and you are only batting average on the truth. You are just spitting out venom. Why? In an effort to preserve your self-worth.

The issue lies in the fact that most of you are saying yes, when you need to be saying no. You feel guilty if you say no when you are being coerced in some way to say yes, and so, you go against your instincts. People-pleasing creates an anger sickness inside of you.

Every time you say yes when you should be saying no or say no and it is not respected, you add resentment into your emotional self. You feel weak because you said yes when you should have said no or bad that you weren't strong enough to make your no respected. You collect your angry feelings, hoping that next time you can do better, but when the next time comes, you still are not doing what you need to do. The result is more anger.

Imagine if as children when you said "no thank you," you were heard, listened to, validated, and received some acknowledgement of the feeling you were having. You may not have always gotten your way, but you would have been given the gift of understanding that your no-thank-yous were important. When children are made to feel unimportant, they are made to feel defective, as if something is horribly wrong with them. My rage was the only way I could have any power. The purpose behind my rage was to gain access to feeling some sense of control over my life, some sense of dominance. When I felt the power of my rage, I felt less defective because I felt strong. My rage was stronger than my authority figures, and it helped me to not care. When I felt this power over the authority in my life, I felt less small and less vulnerable.

Rage can also be turned on the Self. Some people cut

themselves, burn themselves, and have chronic intimacy problems, substance abuse issues, or chronic infidelity. Others develop eating disorders. My rage turned inward had an interesting impact on my life. I focused on what I hated about my body instead of what I hated about my family. I raged that I had a paunch and used food restriction to make it disappear. I lived in a guilt-world around food. Bad foods could make me feel guilty. My parents could make me feel guilty. But I had control over my food guilt and no control over induced parental guilt. If I ate good foods, I would feel free of all guilt and be rewarded with a feeling of success. By controlling my food and becoming perfect, I ended up having complete control over my parents. Thin equaled *good* to them too. My rage was all displaced and food became my obsession. Getting thinner and thinner made me feel like a better person.

Life Class Lesson:

In this lesson, you are going to observe the emotions of anger and rage. As you discover their origins, you have the opportunity to gain understanding into their purpose. They are messages from within used to get you to define the boundaries in your life. Anger is a natural emotion, and in its natural state, it is simple, non-violent, and expressing a dislike. It is your ability to say "no thank you." Anger that is repressed turns to rage.

Rage by definition is abusive. It is much stronger than anger, and with rage, your primitive brain chemistry prepares you for war. You rage when you feel your limits are not being respected, heard, or validated. When you rebel against anything, anger and rage tend to lead the way. Rebellion is driven by the need to have a sense of independence from a system that does not fit. I feel the drive to be independent is more praiseworthy than the desire for dependence in that this drive is the beginning of wanting to be loved for your unique Self.

Rage may not be the most effective way for you to express your need for independence, but if you have been conditioned to feel defective you often rage in an effort to preserve what little self-worth you have left. If you have little self-worth, you are probably angry within at the feeling of being flawed, therefore, when someone in the outside world adds to this perception, it can evoke rage. Let's examine the natural emotion of anger and its fixed counterpart, rage.

**Where in your body do you feel your anger?*

**How does your anger express itself?*

**Are you silent or loud when angry; are you silent or loud when you rage?* Example: When I am angry, I tend to be silent. I am feeling a no-thank-you but not expressing it. I shut down when I get to my limits, maybe out of the fear of conflict. It didn't feel good to have a no-thank-you come up because I was feeling an uncomfortable emotion. I could feel my being contract almost like I was wounded and wanted to be left alone. If my no-thank-you was not well received, I pulled in even more and started to wind up to an explosion. When I raged, I was extremely loud, adrenalized and forcing my way into being heard. I believe the original pain underneath the anger was hurt. (We get hurt when we do not feel heard or validated.) The only ownership my mother took was to take a victim role and say something like, "I can't say anything right." This would then evoke more rage. The only ownership my Dad would take would be a verbal attack or abandonment.

Anger serves to protect you by letting you know that you do not like what is happening or how you feel. We can show our anger with a low serious tone, as we say no.

I have learned to find the gifts and deficits of each parent. What I have had to accept in my relationship with my mom is that she is emotionally unaware. For me to go to her expecting awareness is now *my* mistake. My mom is generous, and that is how she shows her love. She is a blast and extremely active, and that is where I let my love for her reside. I have had to let go of being emotionally close with her because I am not emotionally safe, and that is okay. I have to accept and love her for who she is. My relationship with her taught me about anger and rage and how to deal with them. It is important to know how all the emotions feel. Every emotion needs to be experienced. This way, you are having the full experience of your humanity. When you experience unwanted emotions you have the opportunity to learn about yourself and others, and this leads to better relationships.

With my Dad, I have had to accept his deep insecurity and rigidity to be on his own program in life. He is not confrontable. If he is confronted, he abandons, attacks, or does both simultaneously. I stay out of all areas of relationship with him that deal with confrontation. I keep my talks with him more intellectual and spiritual in nature because he can provide refreshing ways of looking at things. Confronting my Dad puts him into a tailspin of abandonment, blame, and a lack of kindness. I think this must be his way to defend his own core wounds. I respect those wounds in him enough that when I am unhappy with him personally, I just change the way I interact with him.

**Do you feel powerful or powerless when angry; what about when you rage?*

**How do you feel after you are angry?*

**How do people respond to your anger? How do they respond to your rage?*

**How do you respond internally when you are angry?*

**Does your rage lower your self-esteem? Why?* Example: Rage lowers my self-esteem when I do not express it appropriately. Typically when we are angry, we lose our center, and we react in emotionally out-of-control ways. We start lashing out and pointing the finger. When we rage, we are completely disconnected from the thinking parts of our brains. We are not in touch whatsoever with reality, with truth, or with solving any problems. I learned rage from my Dad. I saw him rage all throughout my childhood physically and verbally. The truth and the desire to heal may be buried under the rage but once we rage, there is no solution. Rage is always followed by shame. Shame is about who we are, whereas guilt is easier as it is related to what we have done. *It is much easier to fix what we have done than it is to change who we are.*

Anger does not lower self-esteem. Anger does not have to be out of control. Anger is simply a response to something where we know it is a no for us, and so we must set an appropriate boundary. Anger can be stated as a dislike, whereas rage is about power and domination. They are very different. We will all experience them. Rage tends to come when we have been pushed far beyond what we can handle emotionally. Rage comes when our dislike was not heeded. I have had enough experience with both to know that rage does not serve me and anger can act as the leader of my dislikes, driving me to communicate and make decisions which are best for me.

**Can you see when you are angry you are trying to say "no thank you?"*

**What other ways can you learn to say "no thank you?"*

**Can you see anger is coming from the more vulnerable emotion of hurt?*

Extra Credit Advantage:

Healing reading for home-work

The Anger Trap (Dr. Les Carter): This for me is the best book ever written on anger. This book does not look at the surface of anger, but it looks at the core of anger and the positive intention anger has, which is self-preservation. It also points out people pleasing or submission as other forms of dysfunction. This was a deep read and it took me a long time. It not only helped me to understand my own anger but also it helped me to understand why later in life I attracted angry people.

Reviving Ophelia (Mary Pipher, Ph.D.): I read this book when I was very young. At the start of my eating disorder, this book was recommended to me. It was deeply impactful. I felt understood, which is hard for any adolescent. It goes into why so many teenage girls are afflicted with eating disorders, depression, and other harmful ailments. Not all parts of the book related to me but enough of it did so I was able to use it to have a deeper understanding of myself.

Ask Elizabeth (Elizabeth Berkeley): I read this book as an adult. I purchased it as a psychologist but it evoked in me that girl that I was as a teenager. It touched on those feelings, those experiences, and those insecurities, some of which are still alive in the woman I am today. It is equally as healing today, as it would have been had I read it as a teenager. Brilliant book.

I Know Why the Caged Bird Sings (Maya Angelou): Through Maya's story, I was able to get in touch with my own feelings of neglect and simply wanting the unconditional love of my parents. I feel a lot of my anger, angst, and eating disorder was driven by the simple feeling of sadness. I felt inferior, and I was able to resonate with the inferior feelings shared in this brilliant book. I also identified with the shifting of homes, parents, and new parental partners as attachment/abandonment pains. This helped me see the feelings I felt in regard to my circumstances were normal. I love seeing myself through another person's story.

Differentiating Opportunity:

Suppose you could gain access to controlling your rage through a better use of your anger. This would all come down to communicating your limits, not expecting them to be met, but using the art of communication to know that you at least put your limits out there. You can follow your limits in any form you choose. As you differentiate, you are finding the gifts in all you have been through. At this time in my life, my anger made me feel powerful in the moment. It was not a long term power, but nonetheless, it was a feeling of power which felt significantly better than powerlessness.

It also felt good to vent the things I so diligently kept in, which taught me I needed to communicate my feelings regardless of how others responded to them. When you are angry you have the higher learning opportunity to handle yourself in new, more effective ways. Anger and rage are driven by fear: the fear of not getting what you want, the fear of not being heard, and the fear of not being respected. If you can dismantle fear and say no when necessary, you will be heard. If you can see your anger and rage as the driving fuels to be independent and you can become independent and free to express who you are, how different your life would be!

At its core, anger is a natural emotion. It is one each person feels. If you are angry, state it simply, "I am really angry." Then, express your no thank you. If you are unsure of what made you mad, ask yourself forward-moving questions such as, "At what point did my gut tell me I was mad?" "What made me uncomfortable?" "Who made me uncomfortable?' "What part of this made me feel disrespected?" "What do I need to say no to?" Answer your own questions, and you take responsibility for your anger response. Once you find your answers internally, state your boundary or limit in a few words. If you feel afraid your boundary will make someone mad and you don't state it in this instance, you will only bring on more anger. If you are saying yes when you want to say no, you are being deceptive. Believe it or not, people would really rather hear your truth. In telling your truth, you will find more respect for yourself and you will generate more respect from the other, all the while eliminating the repression and storage of anger that will turn to rage.

What makes you unique is how you take in the world. My parents may have made me upset and angry, but, again, it is still my anger. If it is my anger, then I have to be responsible for it. I have the right to say no thank you to *anything* that does not fit for me. It is another statement that differentiates me from the other. When I was younger, I was saying yes so often when I wanted to say no that I eventually lost control of my emotions. So that I do not do that anymore, I take a deep look at what I feel inside before I say yes or no to anything. I find what I uniquely want or need for myself and that becomes the new statement of who I am. This liberates me from the old story, the bad kid.

With this out,
I needed a rest.
With this last memory,
I lost my breath.

I sat in the boat,
stiffness setting in.
My body was so freezing,
I could barely
comprehend.

Up ahead, a little light shone.
Was I out of the land
of the me that was alone?

I trusted my fate
and reclaimed the me
that I just saw in
that terrible memory.

The boat traveling
at a gentle pace.
I embraced
all that I had faced.

Moving on
to the memories ahead,
I could finally sense
I had some…

The greatest thing about rebellion is that you can get so angry that you end up needing Help. We all need Help. Needing or asking for help can be difficult. However, as you prepare to land in the world of Help you will see the culture of this place is about togetherness. It is about teamwork, listening, empathy, and guidance. No one is alone here. The inhabitants come together as a tribe, each one helping the other. It is an accepted given here that all need help. There is nothing wrong with anyone, who has gotten off course.

You are not meant to do this life experience alone. You are driven to relate to each other and to help each other.

Relationships are instrumental as guides to keep you focused on your possibilities as people. As you observe this next scene, be open to the idea of getting help, of being humble enough to admit you want or need help and let that shame dissipate. This is Self-love. You help those whom you love, so why on earth would you not do the same for yourself? One of the bravest and most noble acts of Self love is asking for and getting Help. It is now okay to release the pause button.

Help

I need help
can't you see?
I am not like
the other people
around me.

My heart,
always aching.
My meaning in life
is quickly fading,
and I am only fifteen.

Both parents,
unavailable.
My mom at work,
she spent all her time there.

My Dad,
he wasn't speaking
to us,
and, from his last words,
didn't really care.

Alone,
I wasn't functioning healthfully.
I made my mom cry weekly.
Then, I would feel guilty.
That is when I met her...
her name was Laynie.

I asked my mom
to take me to therapy.

With Laynie,
I felt safe.
She was nurturing
for which I had such
a deep yearning.

She was interested
in me.
She cared
about my feelings.
She wanted
to know me.
That in itself
was so healing.

She asked
many questions,
and listened intently.
Never once
did she judge me
as crazy.

She saw my parents
for what they were,
a complete and total disaster.
She confirmed the truth
I had known
inside me forever.

She did not see me
as the cause of
all the family drama.
My behavior,
just a symptom
of all the trauma.

She knew
I used my anger
to protect me.

For once,
someone believed me.

I was so used to being
seen as bad.
Her belief in me,
hard for me to conceive.

Could I be
the potential
she saw in me?

For her,
I would do anything
from writing out my feelings,
to reading books.

With her,
I was able
to take a closer look.

She suggested I read
Jonathan Livingston Seagull.
From this book,
I saw in me
the possibility
of unlimited potential.

Maybe…
it wasn't all that
important to try
and fit in.

Laynie taught me
there was good within.
All I had to do
was learn
to tap in.

For three years,
she was with me.
She helped me organize
all I felt I had to hide.

It was her higher belief in me
and her stability.
Finally,
an adult who
inspired me.

I wanted to be
what she saw in me.
That higher belief...
to me was still
a mystery.

To do this,
I would have to
battle with my
internal negativity.

You have stopped here in the land of Help. It is such a beautiful culture of people. The people here have empathy. Help is always available and it is a culture of community. There are no loners here like there were in the land of Authority. It is known by these people that we all feel emotions the same way, and so we essentially all speak the same emotional language. These people help each other reach their dreams, live their dreams, and become their dreams. They are about mentoring, hearing, feeling, communicating, relating and achieving. They are a very work oriented people and wanting the best for someone else is their mission statement. Let us leave the boat to spend some time among the people who live here. They will help us to see the world through new eye-sight.

Eye-Sight

Needing help and knowing you need help come hand in hand with releasing control. I had the mature realization that whatever it was I was doing to survive was not working. Inside my heart, I was aching. I was mostly lonely. I felt fundamentally different than my peers. I could look at them and see genuine happiness expressed through their actions. But I felt heavy and without light. I was a sad, chaotic person.

I asked my mom to take me to therapy. Therapy was the most adult choice I could have made. I needed help, and the adults around me could hardly help themselves. With my therapist, I felt nurtured, heard, loved and understood. I was finally around someone who saw a glimmer of positive in me, who validated and normalized my anger. It was a defining time. *Sometimes, all it takes is one person to believe in you for you to start that belief in your Self.* I was inspired to live up to that higher thought. Laynie forever changed my life. My eye-sight was beginning its change as I saw my Self through Laynie.

Loneliness, not fitting in, and the trap of comparison occur throughout life. With loneliness, you use methods of avoidance, blame, or defensiveness to rid yourself of this feeling. I learned humility and getting help are the best ways to get to the other side of a negative self-perception. To go at life fighting it with your ego will create more and more pain. Humility, on the other hand, creates an open mind. *A mind that is open is a mind that can change*. This is power. To have an open mind means to adopt a life-approach of flexibility and awareness. If you do not possess the flexibility that daily life requires, you will fight life instead of live life.

I look at life as a series of classes. Each class has a final exam. Humility and/or letting go are almost always required to pass. I got sick of trying to pretend to the world that I was not falling apart. The fact was I was a total mess. I was just struggling to keep myself somewhat assembled. Therapy helped me to gather my emotional pieces and begin to make sense of all of it.

In-Sight: It's okay to need help.

Reflections:

From birth to age twelve, you are living and taking in your conditioning like a sponge. You are more passive in believing and assimilating the messages you are getting from your closest relationships. You suffer from what has been *done to you*. But once you hit the teenage years, you start to look toward a perception of *what you are going to do about it*. I did not like who I was or what I was doing. As much as I was blaming my parents for all they caused, I was becoming acutely aware I was the only one who could change anything. I genuinely wanted to be a better person.

I felt as if I were a total failure as evidenced by my grades, my anger, my eating disorder, my poor social relationships, and my low self-esteem. I felt isolated and alone. Not an unnatural feeling for teenagers, of course, but my loneliness had a pathological twist to it. I felt *chronically* empty because I did not have any substantial relationships to help me to see myself as a valuable person with an important existence in life. I had no sense of belonging. My sense of shame had become poisonous. I lived out the idea that I was substandard. If I continued to live this reality, I would become severely character disordered. At a fork in the road, I had to make the decision to change.

I was desperate to establish my own unique Self apart from my parents. My first step into this kind of control came through controlling my food. I had a focus and a discipline to follow, and this fundamentally changed my life. At the same time, I started therapy and had adult guidance and adult love that felt real to me. It was the most remarkable time. Looking back, I am so happy, I had this experience. Controlling my food taught me to be in control of myself. Laynie taught me that I could be anything and everything I could ever dream of.

Committing yourself to a new reality requires willingness to undergo continuous self-examination. I feared seeing myself as the false-self I had become. I did not like me. That is the prison that shame creates. It is the painful knowing of the failure of the Self by the Self. It is isolating in the complete sense because not only do others not approve of you but you are also exposed to your poor character. There is nothing more isolating than feeling totally disconnected from within. I did not want to live this way.

Here I came to therapy with very little insight. I was living my conditioned eye-sight. I had no real compass to get me to the places I wanted to go or into the emotions I wanted to feel. I was in contempt of my Self. There was no way to my Self that I could find on my own. Therapy helped me to access my inner world. It helped me to access the good in me. I had to learn to connect with my inner world, and to develop an awareness and communication with my emotions.

In therapy, I got the mirroring of my emotions which I desperately needed and was able to see them as not repulsive, but as me simply responding to life. When I was mirrored, I was able to exist in my natural emotional state. I was heard, which helped increase my awareness. My therapist was not defensive and so, could actually listen to me. When I was able to fully express myself I learned my rage did not surface. When I felt sad, I could be sad. When I felt angry, I could be angry. When I felt jealous, I could be jealous. When I felt love, love was reflected back to me. When I felt fear, I was allowed to be fearful. This is what therapy offered me. *I was given permission to feel.*

Children cannot know who they are without the mirroring from those around them. Knowing who you are requires the mirroring of significant others whose eyes see you pretty much as you see yourself. This is what I ended up getting out of my therapy. Without someone to reflect your emotions, you really have no clear way to knowing who you are. What I needed more than anything was someone to really *see* me and structure me.

Meeting Laynie, I felt so vulnerable, small, exposed, and infantile. As the relationship developed, I began to see myself as a *person*. I was someone who had needs and feelings of her own. I pulled away from peers at school. I spent my time reading the books Laynie suggested. I started writing my feelings in a journal, and I began to change my mind about myself. As she validated each and every feeling, I began to see myself differently. When I say validate, she did not agree with all of my perceptions, but she could see them from my point of view. She would suggest alternate points of view without demolishing the one I had. She made me think, and my defenses began to drop.

She modeled what I had been missing my whole life: an adult. Unlike my parents, she was calm, composed, discerning, interested, curious, probing, disciplined, effective, introspective, and a good listener. I had not been around anyone with these qualities. I felt safe with her. She organized my internal world and provided me structure. Through Laynie I began to practice different behaviors, to live different thought patterns and to think new ways. It was slow and arduous. It took many years with her, but my changes did begin to happen. She was my safe-base.

Life Class Lesson:

In this class, you are going to explore the concept of mirroring. Mirroring first occurs between an infant and the primary caregiver. It is the very root of communication. Mirroring is the interaction in which one person mimics the other. For example, if a baby smiles the caregiver smiles back. The baby gets to see its reflection in the face of the caregiver. This makes the baby experience its effect on the world and its own existence. As an adult when you are talking with someone and they begin to feel sad, your face – if you are attuned – will reflect back to them the feeling of sadness. This is beyond communication; this is the depth of relating.

Mirroring either exists in your relationships or it does not. If it did not exist between parent and child, the child will struggle with communication, shyness, feeling socially awkward, or not knowing how the natural flow of a conversation should proceed. Through mirroring, you learn how to listen and you learn to notice when what you are communicating has been received and when it has not. Exploring mirroring will aid you in understanding the frustration you encounter in communication within your relationships. You will learn that maybe due to your lack of mirroring, you have not developed good listening skills. Or, you may find you end up in relationships with people who do not listen to or mirror you.

Therapy, with the right therapist for you, is a perfect place to start. Therapy is essentially all about mirroring. It is the back and forth conversation where another person who is objective and secure gets to walk a mile in your shoes and reflect the emotional experience back to you, while also helping you to find solutions. You are often not objective about yourself and neither are those closest to you, so it can be eye opening to see someone who has no attachment but rather has clarity. Their clarity helps you to find our own clarity. Just like lost people get us lost, clear people help us get clear.

**What kind of mirroring did you receive from your parents?*

**What did you learn about yourself?*

**If you are emotionally unorganized would you be willing to start therapy knowing this is a place where you can get that mirroring?*

**How does being emotionally unorganized impact your life and your relationships?* Example: It has impacted them negatively because I always felt frantic and insecure, and I felt as though I was always making mistakes, not getting my needs met. I also felt incapable of meeting the needs of the other person. It is a crazy-making feeling to be disorganized within your own emotional world. This is why many of us are reactive rather than responsive. When we are consumed with reactive relationships, there is no way to find intimacy, harmony or connection. It is beyond frustrating not to be able to control your own emotions, your immature responses, or tendency to sadness. When we are emotionally unorganized, we operate at a level about ten IQ points lower than usual when we try and enter a conversation.

**When you look at yourself, what parts of yourself would like to change?*

** What resources can you find to creatively start that change today?*

**Are you willing to jump on the path of continual self-examination?* Example: Yes, continual self-examination is the only way to live an efficient, productive, and functional life. Life is always going to change. It is always going to be an up and down life experience. There is always going to be something in life that will force us back onto the path of self-examination. Some of us have a perception that if we do enough self-examination, at some point in life we will be unaffected by life's uncertainties and hardships. This is an illusion, since we cannot stop life's process and we would have to be in continual self-examination to be in a powerful enough relationship with ourselves to withstand change as life rips and tears at us.

As I continue developing my relationship with my Self, life simply becomes more understandable. Further, each change I experience catapults me into developing new skills. Each new skill can be utilized to survive and understand any current stressor. Life is not meant to be comfortable, and I no longer have that expectation. Life is comfortable at times and uncomfortable at other times. It is what it is. I do believe, however, I can go as deep as I choose to go within the relationship I have *with* life. This is the gift of being in a commitment to my Self. I can make life whatever I choose to make it – my choice.

**Have you ever been emotionally out of control? If so, why?*

**What can you do to get your emotions back in control?*

**What have you done in the past?*

**What has worked and what hasn't?*

**What are you still struggling with?*

**Is it similar to the emotions your parents raised you with?* Example: What I still struggle with is anxiety or the fear of the unknown. Yes, this is the exact emotional environment I was raised in. I was raised in the emotion of anxiety. I saw it, modeled it, was conditioned by it, and lived it. Anxiety was all I knew. So now, it takes quite a bit of rehearsing new thoughts over and over until I calm down and get back to the task at hand. Rehearsal and practice are the necessary ingredients for permanent change. It is amazing how much we are willing to do for others, but very few of us are willing to put the same time and effort into our own lives, into ourselves.

All healthy relationships are born out of the healthy relationship we have with ourselves. If our outside world relationships are not healthy, the place to start any type of change is within ourselves. What I now tell myself when I am anxious or frantic is to scale back and focus on what I can control. What I will always have control over is me. I cannot control what is outside of me, and when I scale back and get into myself, I realize that I am happy. There are many things I can focus on that I have some control over and all I have to do is focus on those things. The rest will fall into place. This is what helps me to let go. I scale back and focus on me and what I can do at the moment.

Have you ever thought about getting help from a professional?

What do you think the value of talking to someone could have on you?

Extra Credit Advantage:

Healing reading for home-work

The Joy of Therapy (Jeff Blume): This book explains in simple detail the process of therapy. It is described as a journey, and this book makes therapy appealing. Therapy is a process, not an event, and it is a place to grow and be mirrored by someone else. The book talks about therapy as the model for a healthy relationship. As a therapist I peek into this book every now and again and gather inspiration. It also reminds me of the beautiful relationship I had with Laynie. It was a relationship I was able to be myself in and still be loved, my first experience of unconditional love.

Mirroring People: The New Science of How We Connect with Others (Marco Iacoboni): This is a book I have not yet read but am very interested in reading. Understanding the science of mirroring is instrumental in improving all of your relationships. I learned about mirroring from less inspiring psychological theories as I was being trained. But I love anything communicated through neuroscience. I find it more believable and applicable. I am opening the pages now...

Differentiating Opportunity:

You should have gotten beautiful mirroring as a child. You deserved to have that mirroring. The first way you take in the world is through the caregivers and the emotional environment you live in. If you did not have mirroring, you were not given the opportunity to see yourself. There are many ways to get that mirroring now and have what I call *corrective experiences.* The first real mirror I had was Laynie. She saw things in me I did not and could not see in my Self. She affirmed my emotions and reflected them back to me.

Anyone who can focus on the possible positive outcomes of their pain is bound to succeed. Suppose you learn to be a mirror for yourself. One great way to become a mirror or an objective for yourself is through writing. Writing things down gives you a viewpoint from a distance. It helps you organize your emotions so you can find solutions. It is a powerful tool of transformation. Writing things down solidifies things in your mind and helps you to get clear. You will leave your writing feeling better and with a better sense of direction.

Journaling became and remains my greatest mirror. Some higher self is contacted in writing, and I have learned all my answers are within me. This is differentiated. I count on my internal world for my unique answers to life.

Reading is another way to receive mirroring. Reading helps you to see yourself. It helps you to look at yourself when no one else is watching. When you can see aspects of whom you are or what you are going through in a book, you are being mirrored. You can find understanding and a sense of belonging when you read. Reading is a vehicle through which you can make sense of your confusion.

If you engage in reading and writing, you will better see yourself, your life and your relationships. If you engage in some kind of self-reflective mirroring each day, you will also be a better mirror for others. You will be able to offer a depth of understanding and empathy from doing your own internal work. If you truly understand and believe in the validity of what you feel, you can act as a mirror of understanding within the relationship you have with yourself.

As I sit in the boat
and watch the me then,
that memory,
a little slice of heaven.

I am amazed
that this me then
knew she
needed help.

Laynie...
was a God-send.

At this moment,
I realize I am not as cold.
I saw the me then
have some hope.

I can feel the boat
move underneath me.
I need this memory
to sustain me
on the rest of my journey.

As I look down,
I have more sight
due to the light
I can see
the ice chunks floating by.

I can hear the
the water dripping
from up so high.

My clothes still damp,
and ears still cold,
but right now,
the cold is
much more endurable.

Up ahead,
another memory.
That is when I met...

When you get help you grow, and as you evolve, you will attract special people into your life for longer periods. Your next destination is the place of Belonging. The culture of belonging is about fitting. You learn more who you are when you have the experience of belonging. When you land, you will journey through the feeling that when you have a sense of belonging, it increases your sense of Self love. If others can genuinely love you, then you must be lovable. It is an eye-opening experience to feel someone else's love for you. You may not initially know how to take it in, but you know it feels good and it raises your thoughts of yourself. You must be lovable. It is as if a light has been suddenly turned on. As you experience that you are lovable, you will have new thoughts about yourself, which are more positive and loving. As you enter this plane, allow yourself to feel the acceptance of love and to look into your own history and see and be grateful for those who have shown you your lovability.

He and She

He,
so calm, so collected.

Me,
at that time,
so disconnected.

This adult,
so foreign to me.
I lived in a world
of reactivity.

Could someone like him
love someone like me?
I am sure he could
sense my insecurity.

Overwhelmed with the
presence of him,
his stature
so tall and thin.

What he represented to me
I only had in fantasy.
I guarded my heart from him.
He intimidated me.

He
did not fit in
to what I knew
about authority.
He was a mystery.

My heart
so guarded and protected.
I had no trust,
my inner world,
confused and fragmented.

Around him,
I felt exposed.
I felt naked
but, for whatever reason,
I connected.

The first adult male
to contain me.
My heart unprotected
with him,
never rejected.

I think he loved me.

On long drives,
he shared his soul with me.
One time as he shared,
he cried.
Holding his hand,
I witnessed his vulnerability
so alive.

He trusted me.
I felt such a tender pride.
He chose me
to confide.

He was sent to me
to keep my heart
alive.

Before him, my heart
had died
many times.

Her,
so strong, so sure,
a stable base.
Around her,
I felt secure.

She sacrificed everything
down to her sanity,
all for the love
of her family.

A purity in
woman and mother.
This role
never used as a cover.

It was her authenticity,
her commitment
to her family.
This, so alien to me,
I admired her capacity.

Her love for her children,
so visibly deep.
My yearning for this
made me silently weep.

As life began to change,
she made a promise to me.
He and She....
would never stop loving me.

I was set free.

Gazing into the land of the special, you can see this is a warm place. It is calm, gentle, and based in the pure acceptance of others. The people of this culture can see a diamond in the rough and give it love. With a little love, the chosen person begins to shine. It is here where lost people feel found. There is no more significant way to feel like you exist than when someone chooses to love you. As you enter their land and tie the boat to the shoreline, you will explore what it feels like to belong, to be loved for exactly who you are, flaws and all. You can see the people, who live here, change the lives of those who visit. When you are chosen, it says you exist, it says you are important. These messages uplift your thinking, and you begin to see yourself through renewed eye-sight. Let us visit now and discover their secrets. Let them take you to a higher belief in yourself. These are the teachers of love.

Eye-Sight

Life brought me stability when I met He and She, the parents of my brother's high school girlfriend. Our families bonded through their relationship. He and She showed me what *family* was in the traditional sense. I essentially became a member of this family for several years, and it was a pivotal turning point. Through this family, I learned much about love, togetherness, respect, discipline, and true acceptance of others. I was shocked they accepted me, because they knew I was a bad kid. It was healing for me to be accepted and loved by such good people.

I had a sense of family for the first time in my life and half felt like I belonged. The other half of me belonged to my biological family which I felt connected to, but not a part of. Being an outcast had been a wound for many years. The outcast eye-sight started to shift as I became involved with this family.

It was the consistency He and She offered which helped me discipline myself and focus on getting myself together in the now. With them, I was not an outcast. He, especially, found me interesting, smart, insightful, and of great value. My therapist genuinely loved me, but I saw her by appointment. He and

She *chose* me. Before them, I had never been chosen, I had been rejected. They helped shift my perception of myself to the next higher level.

Love changes life. Each new perception we gain into ourselves gives us a whole new way of experiencing our lives. It seems to happen in layers. He and She were an important layer.

In-Sight: I am lovable enough to be chosen.

Reflections:

Reflecting back, I have such happiness these people were a part of my path. I had never felt anyone really understood me until Laynie, and now, from this family, I learned *identification with something larger than yourself is one of the most basic human needs*. We all have the need to identify, because it provides us a sense of belonging. When you belong to something, it gives you the sense that you are safe and protected from the larger world. I never felt this type of safety in my own family. When I became close to this family, I began to feel like a real person.

They provided me a sense of structure where I had limits and responsibilities. A bond was formed because there was mutuality between us. They loved me, and I loved them back.

They treated me with respect, and I respected them in return. I had the experience of fitting in to an intimacy that I had never experienced before. I had not been in a family environment which had a natural back and forth pattern of sharing, reflecting, mirroring and affirming. Everything I was learning in therapy, I got to practice and experience with this family.

I had too much freedom in my biological family and having this, was a recipe for destruction. I was drinking alcohol, smoking cigarettes by the eighth and ninth grade. Once I stopped eating, I used food to create a rigid structure that I think saved me from getting too far off into the world of alcohol and drugs. Once I stopped eating, I became pathologically structured. After meeting He and She, I began eating again, and they provided me structure.

The power of mirroring, structure and identification assisted me in creating a newer and more powerful version of myself.

Life Class Lesson:

You are now going study and understand the basic need all human beings have to belong. People have a strong and primitive need to belong and to be accepted by a larger social group (family, religion, friends etc). People need to love and be loved. You are a social creature at your core, and you essentially learn the most in life from the relationships you have, good and bad. You have a genuine need to belong to a group so you can experience loving others and feeling loved in return. If you do not have this sense of belonging you cannot establish self-esteem.

You have a basic need for frequent, non-conflictual interactions within an ongoing interpersonal bond. These bonds provide you the opportunity to give and receive mirroring. You learn you exist, and you learn to mirror another's existence/ importance to them. Non-conflictual bonds are key because you learn softness, nurturance, relating, and empathizing. When bonds are highly conflictual, you are receiving large doses of criticism which contribute to your lack of worth beliefs. You will stay attached to these bonds if it is all you have. Traumatic bonding is bonding out of the simple need not to be alone.

Humans are driven to attach. There is nothing wrong or needy about the desire to attach, love, and be loved. A lack of attachment is linked with many adverse long-term problems such as ill health, loneliness, and lack of well-being. This is how powerful the need to belong is to each human being. It is the fundamental drive of human motivation. When you belong, you have people in your life you can count on, who can help you solve your problems and in times of crisis. Belonging gives a person a sense of emotional safety.

**What are your experiences about belonging?*

**Do you feel you belong?*

**If so, with whom do you belong?*

**How did you know you belonged, and what did you feel a larger part of?*

**If you feel you do not belong, why?*

**With who have you always wanted to belong?*

**What happened to make you feel you do not belong?* Example: My parents' frustration with me when I could not go with their dysfunctional flow, made me feel that I did not belong. Their frustration made me feel like I was flawed and defective. There is no more isolating or lonely feeling than the feeling of you do not fit. We all want to fit, and we especially have the desire to fit into our families and to bond with those who brought us into the world. When this bond is not formed, we can feel like a miss-fit. Missing the mark can be a lifelong feeling if we do not heal and find those with whom we do fit.

The greatest feeling to come from healing your Self is that as you heal, you can find *ways* and *certain places* within your family that you can fit. For example, my family is very athletic and outdoorsy and so am I. In these activities, I can fit. The only and the most important place I did not and do not fit is in the emotional environment of my family. Having this consciousness allows me not to go there for emotional support, and yet, I can still enjoy my family in other ways.

**What are your feelings about belonging?*

**When someone identifies with you, how does this make you feel?*

**How does it impact your identity?*

**If you still feel you do not belong, what would you have to work on to allow yourself that opportunity?*

**If you did not feel you belonged to your biological family, what have you learned about belonging since then?*

**Have you found a place or people or belief to belong to?*

Extra Credit Advantage:

Healing reading for home-work

Little Women (Louisa May Alcott): This book was transformational for me even though it is a book for young women. It is about having the sense of belonging to a larger structure, a sisterhood. Of course, I identified with Jo, who was the rebel. Her character made me feel normal. Self Help books are not the only way to healing. Stories evoke the human relational experience and can teach us so much about what we want, our pain, and how to handle it. They provide an escape into another world. This is also why movies are therapy. Sometimes, it is healing to escape into another person's pain.

The Secret Life of Bees (Sue Monk Kidd): As I got to the end of this book, I was grieving at the sheer idea the book was over. I so identified with the elements of abuse, abandonment, and finally fitting into an entirely new and unexpected group of people. It was emotional, enchanting, and inspiring in terms of having a sense of belonging. Belonging is a basic and very important human need. He and She were my unexpected family of belonging.

Differentiating Opportunity:

Suppose you found a new group with whom you feel belonging. Imagine what that would feel like to you. Imagine the opportunities afforded you from finding the correct group for yourself. Sometimes, you are forced to be in groups that are not correct for you and instead of venturing out to find your own group, you shrink yourself to fit into the places you are forced. These are your traumatic bonding groups. Suppose you were here on this planet to be free and loved only. Suppose you have the power to make any and all decisions around who is good for you to bond with and who is not. Suppose you can find the courage to leave those unhealthy bonds, how free would you feel? Just suppose in doing this, you find a group that offers you genuine acceptance, how comfortable would you feel?

Sometimes I believe we struggle to fit with people, who are not correct for us. We are constantly conforming and shrinking to fit where we think we are supposed to or should fit. This does not allow us to be differentiated. Suppose the correct group of people is just waiting for you to heal so you can find them. Trust me, as you differentiate, the right group of people will show up. Whatever you release in your life must be replaced by something else.

Just because you may not feel you belong in your family of origin does not mean there is nowhere you will or can belong. *You do not have to be defined by the family you grew up in.* You have the opportunity to define yourself. I have learned that once we take the first step in self-definition and get away from old projections, we begin to attract those people to whom we can belong.

So, your first step is to start to define yourself differently from what you were taught. Make a list of who you would like to be and live that list as if it were real. It will become real. Belonging is a creative venture. If you find you do not belong in your current marriage or at your current place of work or with your current belief system, *there are no rules requiring you to stay somewhere you do not belong*. The world of your feelings will tell you clearly where you belong and where you do not. Changing often creates chaos and consequences you seek to avoid and yet, there is no freedom if you stay. It takes more effort to tread water than to swim. Differentiate and find your way to the places and people to whom you feel you belong. Be yourself. Embrace change as it is the path to you becoming a bigger and grander form of who you already are.

He and She
so necessary for me.
I am filled with
such gratitude
at the magnitude
of this memory.

My angels
sent them to love me.

In the boat,
I am unaware
of anything
but the content
of this memory
that was then.

As I sit and reminisce,
I feel a happy sadness
push itself
into my chest.
I try and resist, but
my tears begin to flow.
I am so eternally grateful.

I feel the boat
moving ahead;
inside, I feel
nothing but dread.

I want to stay
at this place
in my head.

I want to stay
where it is warm
and away from
where I am
half alive,
but mostly dead.

The boat does not care.
It moves on.
I take in the me,
who was loved by he and she.

I will need this memory
to carry me,
as I embark
on the rest of this journey.

Up ahead I see a me
that is...

Before you make the next landing, take a moment and look at the treasures you have collected along the way. Feel a sense of gratitude, and take just a minute to breathe. You have an understanding and knowing of yourself which has brought you in-sight or sight within. You have seen as you have been traveling that the rivers are sure to be rough on and off throughout any journey, and your in-sights will serve to show you the way.

At the next destination, the feeling of being totally Lost is played out. The culture of being lost expresses itself with fear. This is another dark place, and the inhabitants walk nervously around constantly changing their direction until they finally sit and rest. There is not one person on this planet, who has not experienced this feeling. Feeling lost is often attached to the emotions of helplessness and fear. To feel helpless is to be embraced by the total vulnerability of having no clear direction. There is value in being lost because being lost does one thing: It creates space in time. When you are lost, you have no direction, and so you are placed in a position to wait for clarity. As you disembark here, bring your own emotions of that feeling of being lost along with you so you can get the most out of the experience.

Lost

Inside me,
I had no perspective.
Each day was a struggle
to keep my emotions
collected.

Away from home
too soon after my healing.
I went to college,
not mature enough
in my coping.
The scariest part
was every now and again
I lost control of my emotions.
I cried for no reason;
there would be no
thoughts in my head.

I would just get overtaken
with feelings of dread.

I could feel the pain inside,
but I felt unsure as to
what brought it into sight.
It was like something
snuck up on me
and gave me a bite.

It took away my laughter.
Sometimes, I would cry for hours,
so unclear of what happened
to make me cry
without satisfaction.

I was so afraid
of overwhelming
those who loved me,
I would try not to cry
if they were around me.

My self doubt
was so immense
I felt continually
paralyzed by
unexplainable stress.

I wanted to go back home
where I was just beginning
to figure me out.

Here, I was lost,
I had no footing.
I was away from
all of the things
I had to help me.

Needless to say,
I made my friends
and got good grades.
But, I was haunted
by the feelings
that lived in my internal grave.

These feelings had
a bad habit
of whispering my name,
triggering feelings
of very old pain.

Being alone
was the only place
I did not have to be fake
to make those who loved me
think I was okay.

Struggling in identity,
I came from
such a fragmented family.
I wanted to search for
the good within me.
I knew it was there,
but I didn't know where.

All I could contact was
nervous anxiety.
I could not figure out
how to love me
consistently.

I spent many years living this way.
Just surviving day to day.
I lived nearly
unconsciously.

Inside, I was aware
that although
I was searching,
at this time in my life
I was...
lost and still guessing.

I am certain you can empathize with this culture. The weather of this land is inconsistent and the wind blows in no one direction. Its people pace back and forth muttering to themselves and always seem to be looking for which way to go next. The emotional climate showers storms of anxiety and time seems to move so slowly here. As you stop here and explore, you will find a hidden group of people sitting and feeling okay in the slowness of the time. These people have somehow figured out how to be okay with being lost. They take this space in time and learn about themselves and in doing this, they eventually find their direction.

This land is not meant to be a place of permanency, but rather it is a transitionary place only to be inhabited in times of confusion. Yet, you do have choice. Some will stay here, as they cannot seem to make the move to decondition their old programs, and they will live here, continuing to feel lost. However, you are a traveler, and you can learn from those who know how to use this space: feeling lost as their way to be found. You can model them and change your eye-sight.

Eye-Sight

The feeling of being lost may be one of the most unsettling experiences you have. It is a time of confusion. You may experience this many times throughout a lifetime. When I left for college, I was not emotionally ready or mature enough. I felt abandonment. I had just connected with a group of people at home. Now, they were gone. Life had an insensitive way of nonchalantly moving on regardless of my readiness. Every day became a struggle between me and my sadness. My sadness won the battle on most days for a couple of years. If psych meds were as popular then as they are now, I am certain someone would have medicated me. I faced my sadness raw and in its full form.

Crying did not give me a sense of relief, release, or satisfaction. I was full of self-doubt. I felt alone and isolated. I had friends, but I did not let anyone in. I was ashamed of my sadness. I did not see my peers having it the way I did, so I continued living in this core wound with the eye-sight that I was just not like other people.

Luckily, I only knew one way, and that was forward. I moved forward each day feeling like I had cinder blocks attached to my feet. I did not know who I was without my outer stabilities. I did not know where I was going or what I was aiming for. I was just moving forward, going through the motions day by day. But, I did not stop, did not give up.

What I would later learn was *I had to be lost to be found.* Action is the only way through sometimes. *Feeling* lost does not mean *being* lost; there is still the one step at a time progress you can make each day. I did not allow myself to get stuck, because that would mean to stop. Stopping felt more unsafe then moving. I knew if I stopped I would die, at least emotionally. I was well enough at this point to know I needed to keep moving. I may not have had a good internal compass, but I did know forward. There was something ahead of me I was drawn to. My depression has always been an agitated depression. I was too nervous to sit in it.

In-Sight: I am at my best when in action. Always look forward.

Reflections:

I had to keep moving to ensure I would survive. What was buried at my core was not something other people my age seemed to be going through or dealing with. They may well have had similar issues, but I didn't see them and felt too ashamed to share my pain with others. I was a lost person. I felt shy, afraid, ashamed, and preferred to be alone rather than with people. I was the only one of my friends, who chose to live alone rather than live with a group of girls in the college owned apartments. I did not fit in and did not want anyone to see the world of sadness I was living in. Because I felt so different, I felt lonely and empty. In journal entries from this time, I write about being in fear each day and not understanding the sadness dominating my world. The sadness was scary because once it started I could not turn it off. I wanted it to go away.

In my journal, I let the emotions come. I let myself grieve. I can see now that as I was maturing, my ability to look back on my life and consolidate memories and emotions was developing. I was beginning to see clearly all I had been through, all I was not allowed to feel inside my family, and all that I had to bury. My going to college and away from He and She and Laynie put me on my own. This alone time must have created the space for these emotions to come up as strongly as they did. They needed out.

My friends did not know me. I put on a fake face to socialize. I was not capable of intimacy. I was dealing with the inner confusion about who I was and which of my friends were true friends. Any attempt to explain my feelings to family was dismissed as "it is just a phase," or "I don't know what to tell you, maybe you need therapy." My family, I had to learn, was not a place I would ever be able to go with my feelings. I left every conversation feeling frustrated, belittled and angry. In each attempt to get affirmation, I was left with more destruction, and I was never able to heal.

Most of the time, I looked forward to coming home to my solitary environment and my journal. It was the only place and way for me to be authentic. My nurturing was self-nurturing. The solitude had many gifts. It was conducive to the development of my spirituality and my ability to count on my Self. It forced me to get to know all of my vulnerable parts, and when I would write in my journal, what I call 'my higher self' would talk to my vulnerable self, and I would find my way through the confusion and sadness. Due to this, my low self-esteem did not shut down my efforts at achievement. I had few friendships but the ones I had kept me social. I used my time to get good grades, exercise, and simply maintain one step at a time.

In hindsight, I can see all the grieving was because I was losing the life I had always known. I was in the process of getting rid of my false-self in an effort to find who I was at my core. All the tears I was crying were cleansing the old eye-sights. I was in the gray, in process – neither here nor there. This is a scary place to be. I just kept hanging in there believing someday, some way, it would get better.

Life Class Lesson:

In this class, you are going answer questions about the feeling of being lost in life. When you feel lost, you feel disconnected from your current life's purpose, current relationships, and from any sort of clear direction. It can be a time of isolation, invisibility, and depression. Life is a journey after all, and throughout this story, you have been floating on the river of emotion. During any journey, you will feel alone and lost at times. Life feels uncertain, as if danger is lurking behind every corner. You can feel full of anxiety about not knowing if you will ever find your way. But as the beautiful Mother Theresa eloquently said "This too shall pass."

It will pass. When you find yourself in this uncertain space, remember this phase is not forever. There will be a light at the end of the tunnel. Any time you are lost, the experience you are having has purpose. These times are meant to take you to places and people meant for your next level of learning, living and loving. Further, each time you lose your way, it offers the opportunity to slow down and examine what you are doing, where you would like to go. You find ways to get yourself moving forward.

When you have been lost, you have the opportunity to re-evaluate your life, the people in it, the relationships you have chosen, your purpose and direction and you can find a new compass. When you are lost, it is like life is offering you a space in time to reflect, gather, be creative, and examine. When you are lost, time literally feels like it slows down. This is the exact opposite thing you want to feel when you are lost. I am sure you would prefer these painful times pass as quickly as possible, which is normal. However, you are not offered these spaces all the time, and I say you can take advantage of them to be creative and develop an awareness of how you feel. There is value in uncertainty. It tests your fortitude, your faith, and your endurance to keep on keeping on under difficult circumstances. These strengths are gifts necessary for you to be successful long-term.

As you are feeling lost, time is on your side. Time is always traveling forward and solutions that already exist are just waiting for you to bump into them. This is why it is vital when you are lost to keep putting one foot in front of the other. As I look back on this time in my life, I can see that just one step forward each day was all I needed to make this phase pass.

**Were you ever a lost person?*

**If so, describe the phase and its gifts. If you cannot see the gifts, describe its pain.*

**Have you ever had a time in life where you were so alone that all you had was yourself?*

**What did that feel like?*

**How did you come through it?*

**Were you able to turn to yourself?*

**Could you find yourself?* Example: There is a certain silence in being alone and feeling lost in life. Thankfully, there are gifts to silence. Silence more than anything creates space. When we create space, we have the opportunity to be creative. This space allows for the *new* to come into form. Without space, the *new* cannot enter. It cannot squeeze itself through. When I was running around focusing on the old, I could not be creative. I just kept juggling the old eye-sights, making a mess of things. The silence of nothingness can feel louder than all the mental chaos we are used to, and this can be a very scary and isolating experience. However, I ended up finding my Self through my alone time. This silence in my life allowed me the space to re-establish trust in my Self. Any and all healthy relationships must be based in trust. This time created the space for me to listen to my own inner dialogue, emotions, and perceptions.

I found myself through reading, writing, and sharing my feelings. In this way, my silence wasn't empty, it was just inward. Everything I did took me deeper into my Self. I was learning and discovering the ways in which my inner voice communicated with me, and I was beginning to uncover my own answers to my life questions. I was starting to become my own leader. It was a one day at a time process, but it worked. I forced myself to focus on the task directly in front of me, and these tasks carried me into each next moment.

Life moved slowly during this time, as if I were in emotional slow motion. It was a certain kind of rest I think I needed. I have learned since this time that life does not offer these little rests very often. I feel I was learning to be in the present moment as I was undoing my past, looking at an uncertain future. I had to purge the old before I could enter the new and that took a lot of tears, introspection, a one step at a time approach and courage. I was learning about my higher Self, the one that would write through me and guide me. There was no need to go anywhere except within. I just had to let things be and accept that I was neither there (past) nor there (future), I was here.

I had to get in touch with what was *real*. True healing can only happen from the place of reality. It cannot happen in distortion. I was coming to reality. Maybe this is why so many of us are afraid of silence because we are afraid of the *real* and more comfortable in our distortions of what we tell ourselves is real. In my silence, I had to listen. I had to listen to my inner world.

Extra Credit Advantage:

Healing reading for home-work

There is a Hole in My Sidewalk (Portia Nelson): This book is all about being lost in one's identity, purpose, and relationships. It's brilliantly funny, relatable and it made me feel normal. This is a read I will touch upon throughout my life just for the joy of Nelson's intelligence and authentic humor, and her inner process. It's an every person's read.

Stand Like Mountain Flow Like Water (Brian Luke Seaward Ph.D.): The title alone captivated me. It made me feel calm within the unpredictable movement. I devoured this book. It is all about getting in touch with your own inner resources.

Reality Therapy (William Glasser): This book is all about learning to fulfill your own needs and become responsible. There is nothing safer and sometimes more painful than reality, but reality is the only place we can truly heal from. This is a read I can revisit often, at any stage in my life, and it will help me.

Differentiating Opportunity:

Suppose each time you fell, you got back up again and were stronger than you ever imagined. What if you learned from falling that you had an inner strength and wisdom never known to you before? Just suppose your hard times of feeling lost and uncertain are your guides to differentiating. When you differentiate, you have to dig deep within to find what you need to get back up and take one more step forward. Each step forward is one more step into your differentiated real self.

Being lost makes being found that much deeper and meaningful. If you are lost, the only person you can depend upon is yourself, and this is the beginning of learning to depend upon your abilities to carry you through. It is a time of significant creativity when it comes to doing new things to survive. Being lost can be a time full of possibility and discovery.

I was in the process of differentiating from what I knew during this time. I did not have a parent who was capable of being there for me emotionally. Because of this, I did not feel I had the right to depend upon anyone. Although not completely clear on how to be there for myself, I was at least in the process of learning. This one step was making me distinctly different from my family of origin. I was learning to do something in my life that was never taught to me, something they never learned to do for themselves.

Sitting in the boat,
the me now has a
small glimmer of hope.
I see that the me then
was seriously grieving.

She was finding a place
of her new beginning.
One step forward
was all she could do.
Sometimes, it is the only way through.

She was taking notice
of the ghosts in her
internal grave.
They were yearning for a voice.
Crying was the sound of their noise

From this perspective,
I see that the me then
was being unexpectedly
frostbitten from deep within,
letting go of what was then.

Our worlds are getting closer
as I sit in this boat.
The me here and the me there
are in some very distant way
coming together.

Although cold beyond what
I can physically hold,
I clutch tightly to my tissue
for my sniffly nose.

Aching from the cold,
I have a sense
that something up ahead
will very interestingly
unfold.

These two worlds
at some distant time
will collide, but not until
life stabs in her sides
a few more times.

Up ahead, I can feel it coming:
A memory, accompanied by
some horrible feelings.

The cold becomes unbearable.
There is not an ounce of light.
I hear an icicle drop
from up so high.
Landing close to the boat,
I fear I will die.

The water splashing,
the boat rocking,
I hold on tight.
As I look up, I see her,
She is unveiling the …

If you are really living, you will experience all the human emotions. I encourage you to feel all of them in their wholeness because there is so much to learn from each emotional understanding you have. The next destination has much to do with betrayal. Why is it good to experience betrayal? It is good to know what a lack of trust and a lack of respect feel like. If you know you do not like these feelings, then you can choose to love your Self better. When you get betrayed by someone you had faith in, a whole host of emotions appear for you to travel with. These emotions are designed for decision making.

This is a land where you can never tell what is real and what is not real. It is a house of mirrors. Here, people tell you what you want to hear, whether it is true or not. This place is emotionally provocative. While you are here, you will have to listen to your intuition rather than what people tell you. As you learn to listen to your intuition, you develop a deeper love and trust for yourself. Push play once again and bring your own experiences of betrayal so as to put you at an advantage in knowing yourself and your feelings even better. Observe the emotions and damage that can be created through betrayal. Remember anyone who betrays another first, betrays themselves.

Bad Man

For fifteen years,
he was in my life.
I knew from the first moment
when I was nine,
this man was full of lies.

His energy
was that of a salesman.
This man was selling lies,
and my mother
bought them.

After some time
of him still being around,
he had outlasted
the previous two rounds,
I tried to connect
since I figured
he was permanent.
But, in each attempt
I never experienced him
as authentic.

My mom and brother
were fooled.
Me, I was confused
as to why
they couldn't see
what I could.

I began to question
if it were just me,
that he was what
they thought him to be.

I saw him
as a chameleon.
He was just using them
for his ego satisfaction.

As the years went by,
more problems seem
to arise.
I noticed him commenting on
the sexual beauty
of much younger women,
the age of me and my friends.

This gave me the creeps.
Around him I could not be;
he did not act appropriately.

I found him to be
disgusting and embarrassing.
I felt sad for my mom.
This man was humiliating.

So it did not surprise me
on that day,
when I caught him
going astray.

It was on that night
walking my dog,
I saw him drive past.
She was hiding behind
some hanging clothes.

At first, I was shocked
at the mere reality.
Then, I was angry.
The fifteen years of him
were nothing but a travesty.

He was just a weak man,
being led around my his
male anatomy.

I confronted him
the very next day.
I exposed his pathetic ways.

Ironic, it was me.
The only one who knew
his true identity.

In his office,
he was mine.
He got a piece of my mind.

This man, the victim.
I stabbed him with
what I had always been
told by my intuition.

To me,
he could say nothing.

I had caught him.

As you arrive in the land of Betrayal, you will see the impact dishonesty has on a group of people. As you exit the boat, notice the sign posts, which all read "beware." At first, it is hard to believe you need to be careful here. The people, who live here, seem so charming and trustworthy at first. They seem to have only genuine intentions for you. But in this land, many people pretend to be someone they are not. In your gut, you feel that something isn't quite right but you cannot tell what that is. Explore and discover how tricky dishonesty can be and how it can completely mislead you away from what you know in your instincts. Be careful here because at the other end of dishonesty is destruction.

Eye-Sight

Children are purely intuitive, instinctual beings. They can often sense when someone or something is not right around them. I was a deeply intuitive child, and I knew the energy of my new step-dad was not right from the moment we met. I never allowed myself to attach to him beyond a superficial, cordial level. He felt creepy to me.

In *Bad Man*, I caught this person having an affair on my mom. I was full of anger at the betrayal and manipulation but was also filled with satisfaction because I was correct about him. This was empowering. I confronted this man by myself. One of the many benefits of being the bad kid was that I was brave enough to do what no one else could. It was especially liberating for me to expose one of my parents to be bad. In a way, I got to set myself free with each truth I discovered, uncovered, and brought into the open.

Your intuition is experienced as a feeling or an inner knowing which resides inside your body. In-sight. It is not a mental process. This is an emotional/instinctual process. The emotions are felt within the body. As an adult, you often ignore these bodily sensations and justify and rationalize away your gut feelings. You internally accuse yourself of being insecure or paranoid. This is the eye-sight I lived with. I believe with enough time, however, intuitions do always manifest as truths. You need to be less critical of and more in tune with intuitive responses, because they are usually correct.

I was conditioned through the eye-sight of I was wrong and my feelings were wrong. Because of this I would push away all in-sights and treat them the way my family treated my feelings as wrong. I essentially lost my compass due to this conditioning. If you can act on your intuitions more in the moment and allow your feelings to be your guides, you can save yourself a lot of emotional trauma. This was a moment where what I *knew* internally actually manifested.

In-Sight: My answers live in my body.

Reflections:

My life was consumed with crazy-makers, people who presented themselves one way but were not that person at all. I have always been able to *feel* people. I have always been able to know when people are bad. I couldn't see how other people could not see what I could and this frustrated me, often leading to anger outbursts.

My first meeting with this man put me on high alert somewhere deep inside. He oozed con artist, but everyone else in my family bought into the charade. After a while, I began to question myself, thinking it must be me. I must be too sensitive and was not really giving this person a chance. But the feeling deep inside me never went away. I never looked at him as my Dad, nor did I see him as someone who had anything of value to give. He was empty. But my mother and brother loved and adored him.

Once again, I was on the outside looking in not understanding the dynamics of my family. This was a guy, who was using my mom and my brother's regard to meet whatever needs he had in the moment. When my mom could no longer meet his needs, his twenty-six-year-old secretary seemed to meet them just fine. These types of people are creatures of the dark and are the most dangerous if you fully trust in them. He had no qualms using my mother and brother. He took their effort, their money, their love, their attention, their admiration, their bodies and their souls to meet his own insatiable needs.

This man was able to turn himself into whatever people wanted to see which allowed him to lure people in. I believe he even fooled himself into believing he was the person he portrayed himself to be. Ironically, this man was born on April fool's day. Whenever I was around him, I felt uneasy. He was constantly commenting on the sexual beauty of girls my age and demonstrating immature boundaries. His maturity had never progressed past his college days. This man had totally failed to grow up emotionally, financially, sexually, and physically. He was one thing and one thing only: a manipulator.

Redemption is a powerful experience. When I confronted him that day, I had absolutely no fear. I felt vindicated to everyone who ever doubted my ability to see through this person. One of my gut perceptions was finally having its day. It made me feel whole. It was a beautiful confrontation. I looked him in the eye, set the right boundaries, and blasted him with the truth. It was a wonderful feeling to watch him wiggle, try and justify, show that he had no insight and finally, get caught. I saw a little boy in front of me. All the fake-self that he showed was gone in that moment in time. I saw him shrink. I did not see him have any shame, but I saw him feel small. He justified and rationalized what he was up to and tried to convince me that he still wanted a relationship with my brother and me. I laughed at him.

He was an emotional leach and I had known it from the start. I was rewarded that day in a deeply personal way. I finally had an inner truth to show all those people who doubted me. For once, I felt like I proved myself and my truth to be true. It was a great moment. *All of our answers truly lie within.* This was a powerful victory for me, one that was worth winning, not because it got the bad man, but because it confirmed to me that I was in touch with the truth from the very beginning and that *I could trust myself.*

Life Class Lesson:

You are going to uncover the beauty of intuition. Intuition is basic for survival. It offers us the ability to deeply know something without the process of analytical reasoning. This bridges the gap between the conscious mind and the unconscious mind. Only 20% of your brain is used for conscious rational thought, the other 80% is dedicated to the unconscious thought process. The unconscious mind is emotional rather than intellectual, and it is where you get all your gut feelings. In this part of the brain, the mind searches through the past, present, and future and connects with your sixth sense in a nonlinear fashion.

You are sent hunches about people, events, and circumstances, about whether they are going to be positive or negative experiences in your life. Intuitions are not often incorrect. However, you may doubt these gut feelings or not like their messages, and choose not to listen. You are especially prone to doubting internal messages when you cannot see anyone else experiencing the same feelings. Everyone in my family liked the bad man, and this put me in conflict with my gut feelings.

I learn over and over that my first response is often the closest to the truth. Because of these types of situations (bad man), you can be uncomfortable with the idea of using your intuitions, let alone, believing in them as guidance tools. You get into self-doubt and may even be embarrassed to say you follow your hunches. You can also mistrust them if they are unfavorable to your desires. When you do this, you diminish your capacity to use this amazing internal guidance system to your benefit. You may feel that if you follow your hunches, something disastrous will happen. But when you follow them, what you actually see is your life gets better.

Have you ever known a truth inside yourself that no one else agreed with?

How were you able to hold on to your truth, or did you doubt yourself and let it go to stay with the 'in crowd?'

If the truth finally came out, what did it teach you about yourself and your ability to trust your gut?

Have your gut instincts ever placed you in the position of the outsider? Example: My whole experience in childhood placed me in the outsider position. I was a miss-fit. I was rejected any time I made an attempt to tell my truth from within. But my intuition about the bad man came true. What I had always known inside of me manifested as a reality. I was a miss-fit only because I wanted to talk about the reality of my dysfunctional family. Our gut reactions bravely connect us with truth. Sometimes the truth sets us apart. Most people live in distortion, and truth can make us the miss-fit. But maybe, truth pushes us out of mediocrity, and distortion keeps us average. Truth will always bring things into the light.

How did you handle that?

What did you feel about yourself?

What are the gifts of being an outsider?

Extra Credit Advantage:

Healing reading for home-work

The Runes (Ralph H Blum): These are magical little rocks that come in a bag accompanied by a book. You pull a rock and look it up in the book, and receive a message for you to interpret. This is such a great way to practice coming from your intuition. I use these Runes regularly in my life for inspiration, guidance, lessons, and new directions. They have inspired me, and they are timeless. I always use them when I am in pain. They fill me with hope and guidance and something to focus on, which is forward moving. The messages, which I interpret, help me gain access into my inner world.

Don't Take it Personally, the Art of Dealing with Rejection (Elayne Savage): In this book, I learned that rejection is simply a part of life, an absolutely necessary part of life. Being rejected is one way to clear away someone or something that doesn't resonate with *us*, and we can simply say "next." Rejection can hurt, and it can inspire. I prefer to transform rejection hurt into inspiration motivation. The more we get rejected, the more we can use that energy to hold tighter to our dreams. The only NO that will ever make a difference in our lives is the limits we set upon ourselves. *Rejection is not personal; it is transformational.* The point is to be guided by our own intuitions and dreams. Rejection can lead us there. Rejection is how we develop strength and fortitude.

Differentiation Opportunity:

If you followed your intuitions as they arose, how different would your life be? Your intuitions provide you the signals, which guide you to survive. These hunches assign direction to decision making and help you develop a more trusting relationship with yourself and others. Intuition is like a muscle: the more you practice using it, the stronger it will get. Suppose you allowed this mechanism to guide your life to all the correct places and people that are waiting to take you to the next level of living. If you allowed your intuition to aid you in getting all the toxic people in your life out of your life, imagine how much more efficiently your life would flow.

As you see that following your hunches works, you will begin to believe in yourself, developing faith and trust within. You can let them push you gently towards taking necessary risks and into trying new things. In my case, I was able to confront someone in my life who was poisonous and get him out of my life.

As you learn to follow your intuitions, you will fundamentally change the way you make decisions. Suppose you stop making decisions with the mind and start making decisions by following a feeling, trusting the emotion to be the vehicle you are riding to find the correct decision. As you follow your emotions for a while and let things unfold, you arrive at the right decision. *This way you are not making decisions, you are arriving at decisions*. In this way the correct decisions end up being made.

Your gut reactions are your uniqueness compasses. But is common to suppress what your guts tell you for risk of being an outsider or for lack of trust or for other reasons. How do you know if you are dealing with intuition or fear? Intuitions stay constant and unchanging, while your fears are in constant change. Sometimes a fear can go away with a good night's sleep. Fears are transient and loud. Intuitions are more quiet but consistent. You may feel them like a little alarm going off. You notice the alarm, but often do nothing about it, except doubt yourself out of listening.

Learning to follow your intuition can sometimes feel like you are living on the edge. Another way to look at this is that you are learning to live without the false sense of security you get from trying to control everything that happens to you. Gradually, you will become less and less afraid of uncertainty.

Here are some simple ways to help you to use your differentiating gut responses: First, when you are writing your thoughts and feelings down in your journal, keep the left brain (rational) engaged and distracted so that your more right brained activities of emotions, creativity and sensitivity can reveal themselves. Even if you think you have nothing to say as you begin writing, write down all feelings that come to your mind. This helps the non-conscious part of your brain open up. When you are writing, you will be looking for emotional responses not intellectual responses.

As you are writing, turn off your inner critic. Oftentimes, when it comes to your intuitions, you rationalize away those voices which are there to guide you. This time as you write (after all no one is watching), allow your inner dialogue to happen without judgment or ridicule. It is only you and your journal, so you are safe. Write in a solitary place where you can just let your emotions flow. This is imperative to finding and retaining the building blocks of intuition.

There are other solitary activities that bring up my intuitions. When I run, I find that my mind is full with my deeper thoughts and feelings. Sometimes, I bring a small pad and paper to jot them down. Reading is another way that my left brain gets distracted and my intuitions pop up. All of these are great ways to bring about this inner process. It is key to differentiating. As you are in touch with your inner world, you become your Self.

In the boat,
I sat and stared.
At this scene,
I looked long and hard.
In some ways liberated,
in other ways,
torn apart.

I felt so angry.

Consumed with hate,
this step-dad
from day one
was a fake.

Aware of the cold,
it unmercifully nips
at my body.

My tears are flowing;
the cold is enticing.
It is starting to take over
the emotional world within me.

So incredibly cold,
I wrap my arms
around my middle.
I sit and stare
at this scene.

So much anger inside me
I could not get a handle.

The boat slowly presses on.
I knew what was to come.
I had a job to do,
a job no one would
want to have to pursue.

The weight of the job,
feeling so heavy.
I felt the horror

of what was coming.
It was my job to deliver
to my family the.......

The land of Betrayal is next door to the territory of Secrets. Secrets are hidden and often poisonous, and you experience their poison once they release. Secrets seem to have an actual need to release. You have to be careful while you are here, because Secrets operate much like volcanoes. You have kept secrets, and you have probably exposed them. Pain is always the result and on the other side of this pain, is often the feeling of relief. As we begin this part of your transformation, allow your Self to contemplate through my story how secrets have negatively impacted you and your life. Secrets and love often cannot co-exist. As you are learning to love yourself it is important to be mindful of this.

Secret

I had caught him,
him....my victim.
I had seen through
his shenanigans.

Now, I knew
I was carrying a bomb.
One that would create
mass devastation.

My mom and brother,
who loved him,
would now become
his victims.

How could I tell them?

Me, I was paralyzed
with sickness.
I did not want to face this.

Driving home with my secret,
my insides brewing
with anticipation.
My life was going
to change again.
I had no idea
what was about to happen.

I knew this secret
was going to rip and tear
in ways that would
be cutting and bare.

This pain for me,
the loss of family,
was all too familiar.

It made me yearn and miss
the fantasy of
my own daddy,
who still was not
speaking to me.

On the way home,
I drove nearly
unconsciously.

My mind was flooded
with all the possibilities
of what was coming.

The secret I knew
was now so heavy.

How was I going to handle
what was about to happen?
I began to wish
I had never caught him.

It was a night
I will never forget.
So much pain
and so much resent.

My brother... so devastated
he went to vomit.
His psyche could not contain it.
It was too much.
He did not want to
believe it.

My brother, shattered.
He wanted a dad
to feel like he mattered.
He had lost so many
already in his life,
this one drove in
like a knife.
My mom lost control.
Her depression stole her soul.
She could not sleep,
or stop crying.

She really tried with this man
to get it right,
now...she was
no longer a wife.

Inside me, I was fractured,
not sure why he mattered.
I was numb and internally cluttered.

I felt dark inside.
There was no voice.
I was empty and hollow,
and somewhat paranoid.

Astonished at this scene,
I began to worry.
My life felt like a
stand up comedy.

Like everyone else,
I wanted the fantasy.
For me and my family,
that was never a reality.

This secret caused
unimaginable damage.
With a core felt loneliness,
I silently questioned

Is this what love is?

Observing the land of Secrets as you glide in, you can see the potholes of annihilation left where secrets have exploded. You must be very careful where you step as you exit. Secrets are hidden like land mines and once stepped upon, they explode. What you will learn here is that Secrets, like truth, have the need to surface. They can be hidden for long periods of time, but eventually they will erupt. It is the truth's way of bursting forth. Unfortunately, explosions and extinction often follow. You can see people here are all bandaged and broken, and yet there is a certain breeze of relief blowing through the lands of the Secret. A pressure is released upon their eruption. Secrets keep your eye-sight distorted. Learn how you can undo this as you explore this land.

Eye-Sight

Secrets are painful. *Secret* exposes what it was like to stumble upon a major betrayal. My satisfaction in catching my step dad having his affair was short lived. I now had information I knew would destroy my family. My initial excitement and personal validation were quickly washed into the emptiness, devastation, and destruction this information would have on the rest of my family.

As I dropped the bomb, I watched my sense of family fracture all over again. Whether I liked my step father or not, he did provide structure to our family and he was a part of my life. He also had four kids of his own that were a part of this situation. For fifteen years, we were a family and had both positive and negative experiences with each other. Not everyone got along, and not everyone was happy about the union of our parents, but we were all a part of this mess, like it or not. Now, I felt like a terrorist. I remember thinking if this was what love was, I wanted nothing to do with it. This was my eye-sight: *love always ends in pain*. As Eminem raps "love spelled backward is evol."

The family experience ranges from hope to pain to hope again, and kindness to meanness to kindness again. Family disasters cause you to question love, to question people, and to question relationships. Out of these questions and experiences, you begin to mold and define yourself. You define what you want love to look and feel like. Sometimes it makes you want to stay away from love all together. On this day, I hated my intuition.

In-Sight: The truth can hurt.

Reflections:

Vindication was soon replaced by destruction. I learned the impact parental infidelity has on children regardless of their age. Whatever their age, children – whose parents have been unfaithful – often react with intense feelings of rage, anxiety, anger, shame, sadness, and confusion. I went through all of these feelings. I had rage about everything. I was mad that everyone was so upset. I was sad everyone was upset, and I was enraged because my mom reached out to my biological father at this time for comfort. This was a man, who wasn't even speaking to me and had chosen to be out of my life for years.

Reflecting back on my growing up years, I never saw a faithful marriage. Further, in every marriage/relationship one of my parents was always regretful over a previous relationship that had failed. I grew up listening to a parent constantly talk about wishing they would have stayed with a high school sweetheart or another past relationship.

Neither parent fully committed to the relationship they were in. Both parents complained about their partners. Obviously, neither parent ever reached a level of wholeness where they were happy enough with themselves that they could see the gifts of their partners rather than their deficits. Conversely, neither parent was whole enough to know who would be a good partner for them and who would not. I would see in my future life, I would not have a good compass for choosing partners either.

Each child reacts to infidelity uniquely, but it is common for children to experience a roller coaster of different feelings. I experienced loss of trust and was, again, given the message I had no right to depend upon anyone. I found it extremely difficult to trust that someone I loved would be honest with me or fully committed to me emotionally. I was always fearful of abandonment or of being rejected. I learned not to put my faith in love. My eye-sight was that love was a joke. I also lived with the eye-sight that love was disposable. Along with a loss of trust in people and in the concept of love, I felt ashamed of my family. I was ashamed of my family before this affair, but it took my shame even lower. I was embarrassed to be associated with this mess.

Confusion was a part of this emotional roller coaster. I drew the conclusion that marriage was a total sham and love an illusion. I couldn't develop any reality around love because I was surrounded by people who were too lost to get it right. It is not that my parents were bad people; they just did not know themselves well enough to find a quality person. I never saw my parents learn or grow from their mistakes. I just watched them live the same mistakes over and over again with different people. All of this dysfunction impacted me and the future choices in love I would make.

Being exposed to all the infidelity, as well as all the men and women in between my parents' marriages, provoked intense insecurity within me. I had a need to resolve a lot of unfinished business from my childhood as I traveled through my adult years, often making many of the mistakes I saw my parents make. The difference between me and my parents is that I chose to learn from each mistake. I had the insight to examine why I made the mistake. This understanding turned each mistake into a corrective experience.

Life Class Lesson:

Secrets are most destructive when they are present in the family system. Families are designed to be support systems. Our identities and abilities to form close relationships all begin in the family. In the family, you should be able to depend upon others with a level of trust and communication. If family members keep secretes from each other, the emotional fallout can last a life time. Secrets build wedges between those who know and those who do not. Infidelity in the family can divide family members permanently. Secrets break all bonds of trust and accountability and can freeze psychological development which is crucial for the growth of the self and identity. Secrets fill the bonds between family members with guilt and doubt. They create interpersonal paranoia.

This is a lesson about secrets and infidelity. Infidelity brings instability into a family system which is often unrecoverable. Those who experience infidelity as children are more likely to have affairs as adults. Parents, who choose infidelity, make this choice normal for their children. It is often not conscious. No one sets out to have an affair, or to become an alcoholic or to commit suicide but parents model these as viable options.

The larger lesson here is not infidelity, but dishonesty. Dishonesty, more than anything else, prevents you from becoming the type of person you desire to be. Dishonesty is at the root of many problems in life. If you are dishonest, you cannot ever fully know what it is like to be complete. If you are dishonest, you will be divided from within.

**Have you ever seen any form of infidelity acted out by either parent?*

**What did it make you feel about the concept of love, marriage, and commitment?* Example: I thought love was an absolute joke. Love was a joke that made me sad. It was not an emotion I felt or experienced to last the test of time, and I learned to pick people who were difficult to love. I picked people, who were impossible to please and who held out the commitment carrot for me to chase as long as I made my world about them. My parents essentially did the same thing. This was a pattern I was all too used to. My parents need to be the center of attention created in me a person who picked people who had that same need, and I was too conditioned to see it. It was the only pattern I knew and whether I liked it or not, recognized it or not I found myself constantly in the midst of this pattern, feeling all the same ways I felt as a child: unfulfilled, exhausted, bored, uninspired, guilty, and confused. I wasn't feeling a whole lot of love. Rather I was living the type of love taught to me.

**What did it make you feel about the concept of trust?*

**Have you ever made relationship mistakes similar to those your parents made? If so, how did you handle them differently?* Example: In all honesty, yes I have made similar mistakes in spite of myself and my commitment not to make those mistakes. This shows how powerful unconscious emotional programming really is; it is cellular. I believe that whatever was unresolved or painful for us as children, we will often repeat in some form in our adulthood to heal the original pain. The mistakes I have made may just be a whole other book, but I can say that I analyzed heavily why I made the mistakes, where I learned them, and why I couldn't see it as it was happening. I was actually able to heal a core wound caused by my childhood through my own experiences in adulthood.

My mistakes humanized my parents and showed me where my parents stopped short in their own healing. I was able to repair my inner world with self-awareness. The more aware you are of an unconscious pattern, the more on top of re-training that pattern you will be. This is how you learn. I am not regretful about the mistakes I have made. I see them as completely necessary corrective experiences. I have become wiser, better and happier for each and every pattern I have been able to transcend

**Where did you learn to put your trust?*

**If you felt no trust in others, how did this make you as a partner in your relationships?*

**How can you heal these wounds?*

**How did parental infidelity impact you directly?* Example: For one, I had a secret, and the secret put me in the place of having the information that could destroy a family. The pressure to carry this secret was immense. I felt afraid, I felt angry, and I felt somehow that I was responsible for having the secret in the first place. I was in complete conflict regarding my step-dad and his relationships with my brother and mother who so believed in him. The entire time he was simply an imposter.

After I delivered the news and everything blew up, my brother and I had to take on the role of parent to our mother, who was devastated. She became the hurt child and we, the parents. She counted on me to make sure her emotions were taken care of. On vacation when I was getting male attention, it made her angry, so *her* issues had to be *my* issues. There really was no separation, no family structure, and now, I was the caretaker. I had to be therapist, nurturer, and best friend – all the roles, she never played for me during the normal developmental experiences in my life.

Infidelity splits people into good and bad. I could see my step siblings and my brother struggling to equate the dad they thought he was with the unfaithful dad he had become. He had had an affair on his first wife as well. All children want to see their parents as honest, good, family-oriented and responsible. When a parent has an affair, that parent essentially becomes a stranger to the children. He looks like their dad and seems like their dad, but once the affair happens they do not know this dad. Everyone becomes foreign to everyone else.

The kids end up with a love/hate connection to the parent who strayed. The original bond of trust is forever severed. Children also see the betrayed parent with new eyes. Whose side do we take? Can we be on the victim's side and still love the perpetrator? We need our parents to be solid. We need that from our parents because we depend upon them to be our leaders. When affairs happen, kids become leaders and comforters and their parents become children, liars, deceivers and followers. This impacts the identity of the children and creates confusion about their roles. Once the affair is over, the parents want to resume being parents and it all becomes convoluted.

Can you love yourself even if you make some of the same mistakes your parents made that damaged you?

If you make similar mistakes, how can you take responsibility for them?

Each mistake is a life class designed to bring you into a deeper sense of wholeness. Can you find your wholeness through your mistakes?

Can you see how to make your mistakes benefit you?

Extra Credit Advantage:

Healing reading for home-work

Parents Who Cheat: How Children and Adults Are Affected When Their Parents Are Unfaithful (Ana Nogales): This was a great read for me. I read it years after the event but I could see how the affair impacted me. I can see how all the smaller levels of infidelity also impacted me. This is one of the only books I have come across addressing how infidelity impacts children. It is an amazing book, and I learned so much about myself from this read!

Differentiating Opportunity:

Suppose you became a person, who was free of secrets. To be this means to face the fears of telling your truth and consequences your truth may cause. If you avoid sharing your truths, you cannot differentiate. If you are afraid to be truthful, you are in essence acting out of the false-self, not the authentic self. Making mistakes is the way to differentiating. *After all, your mistakes are your self-created learning experiences.*

Mistakes you learned to make as a child give more meaning

and understanding to your childhood and offer you a more clear direction for your future relationship choices. Suppose you used your mistakes so you could perfect and make adjustments to who you are. For example, I learned to pick poor partners but the relationship endings in my life also taught me to leave relationships that did not work for me. I see the leaving I did as a gift I could have only gotten from how I was raised.

Sometimes differentiating means repeating what was modeled until you have so much pain that you choose to learn from the mistakes, undo the patterns, and create a different outcome for yourself than you saw in your parents. Patterns are hard wired into your brain and are repeated on an unconscious level. Whatever was unresolved is carried in your subconscious. Your subconscious is often the driver of the mistake car. You drive the car, and you crash into the *wrong* person for you to have the *right* corrective learning experience. When you make mistakes similar to your parents' it humanizes them. You see you did not mean to harm anyone with your mistakes so you can then assume your parents also were not out to intentionally harm you with their mistakes. The gift of differentiating is to go beyond what you repeat, to look and see that yes you repeated a pattern, but that now it is *your* pattern. *If it is your pattern then you can take responsibility for it and change.*

Grief work is an essential aspect to differentiating because you have to be responsible for all you do in life. You have to see you are human, that your parents are human and grieve through your losses, your shameful feelings, and your public humiliations. I believe you are here to evolve. That is your only purpose. If you evolve, you differentiate. If you do not evolve, you stagnate and continue hurting yourself and others. Do your inventory, the shame and all. Grieve, grow, own your stuff, and you will transcend old programming. Sometimes you have to really dig to find yourself, but with enough digging the individualized you will begin to surface.

As you differentiate, you are searching for a sense of integrity. Integrity means to feel whole, complete, or undivided. If you find yourself the victim of someone's lies or a perpetrator of your own dishonesty, you divide yourself from within and create division in your relationship world. You fall short of your full potential, and you cannot differentiate. Learning to be honest, you increase your potential for personal fulfillment. Suppose you could see deceit as a roadblock to long term growth. Imagine taking your grief at being at the hands of dishonesty and turning it into your passion for honesty.

For example, let's say you fall in love with someone while married to someone else. You tell your spouse that you believe you may have feelings for someone else before your feelings progress, and you start therapy with your spouse. However, the marriage is not salvageable, and it ends. Because you were honest right away, you have your integrity regardless of whatever story your spouse tells the world. If you can operate this way, you will be healthier regarding any and all mistakes you make in life. Imagine how freeing this would be and how it would lead to self-acceptance.

In the boat,
my head was reeling.
The me then
was as cold
as this icy scenery.

The two worlds
were unfortunately meeting.
Both were consumed
with darkness and sad feelings.

I feel nauseas
as I relive these memories.
The boat is rocking;
my head is spinning.

So cold and damp,
my muscles aching,
they begin to cramp.

I cannot move.
This me then
was completely consumed.
At twenty-four, my life was cruel.

That girl then,
her hope was fading,
life not making
much of an impression.
She had lost sight
of her previous notions,
of her inner light.
She was now so dark inside.

The boat shows
no signs of continuing on.
Paralyzed with fear,
I do not want
to stay here.

I have to reclaim
the me that was there.

I have to save her,
life has to get better.

The icy cold air
swirls and flares.
Chilled to my bones,
I do not care.
I have to get the me then
out of there.

As I embrace her,
the water begins to get rough.
I hold tight to her,
she cannot give up.
She has to do her best to
embark on the......

Departing the land of the Secret, you are now aware that real meaning in life comes from the truth. You can see that when you continue running the same pattern and are getting the same results, you have to start to do things differently. So, here you are, passing through the land of Finding Meaning. When you can find the meaning behind what you have suffered, your life begins to make sense. The inhabitants here do not feel punished by life. They accept things as they are and do not need for things to change. It is the land of depth and understanding.

Finding meaning in your life can only come from a sense of love for the Self. To find your meaning you have to venture into new behaviors, new thoughts and new experiences to enrich your life with fresh meaning. Meaning comes from within, from your own emotions, from your own answers. As you observe your own ineffective patterns in love, I encourage you to search within for your answers to your questions. Step back into the river of transformation and observe through my story, how to go inside yourself to find your questions and your answers.

Search for Meaning

Searching for meaning,
I was so empty.
For so long,
I sought outside of me.

My vessel for meaning
became men and being pretty.
Attracting men
was never a problem.
There always seemed to be
one waiting for me.

I used men for security.
Unfortunately, I attracted
men, who had nothing
to give to me,
and in reality
I had nothing to give of me.

So many men,
all with different faces,
but inside, they were
all very similar.
The majority of them
were empty containers.

I showed up, and the
only thing I had to offer
was codependency.
I wanted them to
fill me emotionally.

After breakups,
I would experience
unbelievable pain.
Many of the men
thought it was because of them.
But, they took way too much credit.
My pain really was
only mine to mend.

My pain reflective
of my inner grave
that was there before
any of them came.

The ghosts in this place
wanted resurrection,
so any moment of sadness,
they allowed themselves out.
They needed attention.

With relationships
unbeknownst to me,
I modeled my parents.
You, see…I learned from them.
To be alone, I learned,
was some kind of sin.

I tried to search for God
in my moments of pain,
but he seemed so distant
and so far away.
He felt impossible to obtain.

The depression and emptiness
left me so vulnerable.
I realized I had to be careful.
If I continue to attract
where I am at….
I am in trouble.

I knew it was time to examine
and to commit to things
that made me happy.
I had to find me.

I had to find what would
keep my heart alive.
It certainly wasn't men.
It certainly wasn't being pretty.
At some point, I realized
happiness did not
live outside of me.

To my parents,
this was a lost discovery.

The culture you are passing by is one of the most significant places in the emotional world to travel to, and you should travel here often. This is the place of alchemy or learning to take a common experience and turn it into something of great value. The people here do not have maps, and they are no longer looking outside themselves for their direction or answers.

The natives of this culture engage in a deeper, inward process to discover their answers. They are a beautiful people, and they have a certain glow to them. If you cannot find the meaning in your suffering, you will have despair. If you have despair, you will stay in the land of the Lost with unclear eye-sight. It is important to take the lessons of the natives in the Land of Meaning, and to learn from them how to search the inner world. As you exit the boat, you will learn to see things spiritually, to see life and events as not haphazard, and to see that each life class you take helps you find the deeper meaning in the circumstances you have suffered. You will learn to alleviate the eye-sight of seeing life through the lens of despair. This is a land where patience and acceptance are taught because with patience and acceptance you are able to see the bigger picture.

Eye-Sight

Life brings you emptiness, so you work to find wholeness. Life is full of dualities. What you do want is the opposite of what you don't want. The place of the *don't want* is powerful. Once you fully embrace, feel, and experience what you don't want, you have direction. You cannot know full unless you know empty. You are essentially lonely because there is only one of you. You have to travel your emotional world independently, regardless of outside support. Your emotional world is your responsibility.

I was constantly searching the outside world for my meaning

through what I looked like, boyfriends, friends, grades, jobs etc. I specifically used relationships to make my life feel meaningful. I only felt the love of myself through someone else's love for me. This pattern was established very early on in my life. If someone else loved me, it helped me to feel lovable. If they went away, my lovability went with them. I felt unlovable.

It was treacherous for me when people left. Even when I was the one to leave, I would *still* feel abandoned. This was what was modeled for me. Meaning came through being validated by a relationship. Rejection and abandonment became my way of life. I attached through traumatic bonding – bonding out of not wanting to be alone. At some point, I realized what I was doing was only leading to deeper and deeper levels of emptiness, but I didn't know a different way.

I believe we all, to some degree or another, do not like or want to be alone, so we search for that internal contentment in another person. I have learned real power is inside me. It is not *out there* somewhere. It is inside *me*. It is constant work to stay connected to my internal power. It is easy to lose and difficult to maintain. Codependency is ugly, it is needy, and it is desperate. It is not a place where happiness can develop. Happiness and neediness cannot co-exist. My eye-sight was I had to clutch onto life and people or else I would be alone. To bring about change, I had to look inside my own personal life for meaning which meant focusing on what I could control and do-by-not-doing all the things I felt desperate about. Learning to let go was madness. I felt fears that were larger than my knowledge to cope with them.

In-Sight: It is hard to let go.

Reflections:

Desperate for love was what was modeled. I became desperate in spite of myself. I can see I was so starving for love and attention that I was looking to relationships to give me what I needed to learn to give to myself. I was a walking vulnerability looking always to the outside world to feed me and make me feel better. If I got into a relationship, I made my whole life about the man I was in the relationship with, hoping it would be reciprocated. Needless to say, I have been with a lot of takers and men who did not value me. My vulnerabilities were always exposed.

I was easy to take from because I did not let anyone give to me. I felt more control if I was the giver. I did learn takers don't give so we were a perfect dysfunctional mess. I think I wanted to make myself irreplaceable. I saw the giving of myself and the endless meeting of the other's needs as my way to be that. If I received anything, I felt like I immediately had to give back to make things equal. This is what happens when you feel deeply unworthy inside. It is also what happens when you are conditioned as a child to believe that your parents' happiness is your responsibility. My parents made me feel disposable. Both with them and in my romantic relationships, I was attempting to replace *disposable* with being *irreplaceable*.

Neither of my parents ever modeled independence, aloneness, or being comfortable within themselves. If my mom was single, she was miserable and either pining for a past relationship or desperately trying to find another one to get into. This is what I learned from her. It was gross, sad, and pathetic. I actually thought I could change the people I was with and help them to be better lovers of me. The sad part was I had no idea how to be a good lover of me. That had never been modeled for me. This core wound was one that took much pain and many years to resolve.

This part of my life was all about codependency. I needed a relationship to feel whole. I picked all the wrong relationships and was continually left feeling empty. If a break up occurred, it took me months to get over it. I went through months of tears, of working through feeling rejected and worthless, and sadness. My abandonment issues were so intense that current abandonments would open that file in my brain and bring me back to every time I had been abandoned and confirm for me that I was worthless. If I was worthy, then people wouldn't be able to leave me so easily without remorse, missing me, or pain. Yet, they seemed to leave and not have one feeling about me. I recognize this to be a core wound.

It was natural for me to be the sweet girl, the accommodating person in a relationship, in the hopes that they would see me, change and be a better partner. This never happened. I was emotionally raped over and over, and sadly, it was self-induced. Ultimately I had nothing of value to give to a relationship because I didn't value myself. I became a shape changer, changing form to keep a relationship. My emotional reactions gave my partners attention, control, and the feeling of embellished importance. They made me feel small, pathetic, lost and ashamed.

This was a defining moment in my life where I began to have the insight that what I was doing wasn't working. I began to see that what I had learned about love was not love at all. It was bartering. It was desperate and afraid. I was taught that being alone meant you had no value, and I already felt I had no value. My parents' needs for relationships were in conflict with my needs for them to be my parents. I was not their priority and therefore, I was not my priority, and hence, I was not the priority for anyone who dated me. It was a sad, sad cycle

I needed to find myself. I needed to risk being alone to find out who I was and who I wasn't. I was learning over and over that my happiness was not manifesting from my relationships. This was the start of my first life turning point (there would be many up ahead). I was beginning to become aware from my experiences with relationships that what I was doing was not working. My awareness was showing that the problem was somewhere within me. Awareness was the start of my self-reflection.

In-Sight: I am the common denominator in all my relationship failures.

Life Class Lesson:

This lesson is going to help you analyze how you have become the common denominator in all your relationship failures. The typical pattern in relationships is one partner becomes focused on changing and molding the other. When we focus on changing our partners, the relationship is doomed to fail. Under the delusion I could somehow change them, I picked people who were emotionally unavailable. I preferred to focus on changing someone or 'helping them to grow' than to face being alone.

As you look at this lesson, you will learn you are responsible for your 50% of any relationship failure. Analyzing what your 50% contribution is will be your path to freedom. The more you understand who you are and what your 50% is, the more meaning you will find in the circumstances in your life. You will have the opportunity to adjust and change what is not working. Make your happiness your responsibility and learn to let others make their happiness their responsibility. This eliminates codependency. What you want is inter-dependency where two happy fulfilled people come together to share life.

Interdependency can only occur between two equally responsible people. If one person is responsible and the other is not, what you have is an adult/child relationship. This dynamic alone will create division and frustration in the relationship. If you have two irresponsible partners, you have a relationship that cannot function on any level. If you have two partners who are 'independently' living their lives, they are likely to drift apart. If you have two people who are responsible in their lives for themselves and for their own emotional world – who love, relate, and share with each other – you have a healthy interdependence where love can grow.

**Have you made the relationship in your life a priority over your own self-esteem and self-needs?*

**Have you looked to your relationship to be your need-meeter?* Example: 100% yes. I have made this mistake and I have also made the mistake of being the need-meeter of my partner. I gave to get in relationships. Happiness and love became a bartering system: "If I give to you, then you should give to me." This all came from a place of love and good intention, but it was filtered through need and expectation. I have read that neediness, expectation, and jealousy are the three relationship killers, and I was living that experience. I was operating from the idea that if I gave, then I could *expect* the other would *want* to give back. Unfortunately, the others I chose to be in relationship took in response to my giving, making me feel hurt and angry.

People often saw my giving as weakness. I was giving because I didn't feel I was deserving. This made me prey for the takers of the world, not only because I would give, but also because I would give-in. I wanted better, of course, but I wouldn't have known better if it hit me in the face.

**How have you sacrificed your own self-worth to keep a relationship?*

**Can you see this as self-abandonment?*

**Did you make all the effort in a relationship to have it fail anyway?*

**What did this make you feel about yourself and your partner?*

**What kind of awareness can you glean about yourself from looking at these types of patterns?*

**What about yourself would you like to change?*

Extra Credit Advantage:

Healing reading for home-work

Codependent No More (Melanie Beatie): This book taught me what codependency was and how every relationship I had ever witnessed or been in was codependent. When we're codependent, we are desperately trying to control others rather than take care of ourselves. Many affairs, addictions etc. are part of codependent relationships. Reading this book was a great start for me in educating myself in the unhealthy patterns I was raised in which had transferred into the unhealthy relationships/friendships I was engaging in. Once we know of a pattern, we have the information to transform the pattern.

Mastery of Love (Don Miguel Ruiz): This is one of the best books written on relationships. It all comes down to responsibility. I am only responsible for my 50% of the relationship. I am not responsible for doing my partner's 50%. It was such an awakening experience to learn that all I had to do was be responsible for my portion: I have to be responsible for my happiness and my partner responsible for theirs. I have to be responsible for my finances and my partner theirs. I have to be responsible to my feelings of love in the relationship and my partner has to be responsible for taking care of their love in the relationship. I have to be responsible to communicate my feelings and my partner theirs. I have to be responsible for my spiritual growth and my partner theirs. I had consistently chosen people who were incapable of being an equal partner and my mistake was doing their part hoping it would make the relationship work.

God Wears Lipstick (Karen Berg): This is another book I read more than once. I learned how to have compassion without being a pushover in the covers of these pages. I learned how to take responsibility for putting myself first without feeling guilt for not doing enough for the other. I learned how to love myself without becoming self-centered. *If we give to ourselves half the commitment we give to others, we would all have better relationships.* I learned it was my responsibility to change my life for the better even if the man in my life was not on the same page. Due to this commitment, I did not stay with unequal partners.

Why We Love: The Nature and Chemistry of Romantic Love (Helen Fisher): This book was such an insightful read. It was written by an anthropologist, who helped me realize how we can fall into the feeling of love so easily and have it fade so quickly. It made me think about love in a completely different way.

Differentiating Opportunity:

When relationships come to their end, you often feel lost, devastated, and alone, wondering if you will ever be in another relationship again. It is here you have the opportunity to differentiate. When you hurt after loss, you wonder if the deep rooted pain you have will ever go away. You are left to depend on yourself to get through the loss. This is your opportunity to dig deeper, to ask new and different questions, and to gain some in-sight about what life changes really represent. Loss offers the opportunity to dig for something deeper within you as you push for a better understanding. Life changes are difficult, but you can use these challenges to bring yourself into a deeper in-sight along your journey to wholeness.

Suppose you not only become aware of what you contribute to your relationship problems, but you also get clear and change those patterns. Think about what an incredible learning opportunity this would be and how wonderful it would be to have all the power within you to change who you are rather than wasting your precious time and effort attempting to change another person.

Awareness is the defining moment in being able to differentiate. You become aware of yourself and the patterns you learned from your parents. With this awareness, you can then be clear enough to change those patterns and do things differently. Awareness does not come all at once. Rather, it comes in pieces that are digestible. This way you can work on yourself one step at a time, one pattern at a time. Growth is the result. Psychological health is synonymous with maturity and mental illness is synonymous with immaturity. Immaturity creates repeated patterns with little in-sight. Maturity takes in-sight. With new in-sight you can navigate your world with better eye-sight.

In the boat,
I watch the me, then
wonder her emotional world
so lost and unguided.

As I sit and gaze
at this memory,
I feel an icy cold frost
bite at the very edges
of my psyche.

I sit and witness
the me that was then
give herself away
for the fantasy.
She wanted
to feel wanted
in such a deep way.

She wanted love.
She was searching
in all the wrong places
and from all the wrong people,
just as her parents
had modeled for her.

In the boat, I feel
somewhat helpless.
I am watching her try.
Her trying was authentic.

Her search for meaning
ended up to be fruitless
in the manner in which
she was trying to achieve it.

I feel for her.
My body begins to shiver.
I feel my tears like a river
leaving a path of wet coldness
down the landscape
of my face.
Life sometimes feels like a disgrace

The me then was coming
from such a good place.
It just did not manifest that way.

I had had
such terrible modeling.
For the me then....
I was in this boat grieving.

In the boat,
I sit and close my eyes,
and I embrace the me
that was then,
and thanking heaven...

There is a wealth
of hidden meaning
in this scene that
would someday help her
to make good decisions.

The boat begins to glide.
I wipe my tears
and hold my head high.
The memory ahead
I feel its essence
so alive.

Finally,
she knows
she has to...

What you often struggle with in life is finding solutions. As you more fully understand the meaning in your travels, you learn that your next destination is mandatory in being open to solutions. You are going to explore the land of Surrender. Surrendering is letting go and giving yourself to the truth of your current circumstances just as they are. Surrendering puts you into the truth and pulls you out of denial. To love yourself, you have to surrender to the changes you see you need to make in your life. Surrender seems to come when you have exhausted all of your faulty beliefs and behavioral patterns. If surrendering seems vague, then allow your open mind to glide over the emotions of the poem. If the mind is open, it is ready to take in new information. Surrender is not about giving up, it is about gaining presence of mind. When you have presence of mind and are aware of yourself, you open up to loving yourself in new ways, with new patterns and new thoughts. Let's travel through Surrender.

Surrender

It was time;
I had to change.
No more
creating my life
to be insane.

From my pain,
I no longer wanted
to abstain.
It was now or never;
I had to change.

I was so scared,
but now, I had to dare
to take on this venture.

I made a commitment.
I would be alone
for at least one year.
I would have
to be my own home,
no men or false security
to fill my bones.

I had never lived there…
inside me.
I was too busy
avoiding me.
I was empty.

I had to surrender,
if I wanted to get better.

I had to enter
the empty vessel.
I had to strengthen
my emotional muscles.

I cried the deepest tears.
Being alone was
my biggest fear.

Alone in my life
had always been
so unfair.

It triggered long ago
memories of
a little girl,
who after so much
abandonment
lost all hope and care.

My life needed to be clear.
I had to face what was there,
if I wanted my life to get better.

In being alone,
my vessel was hollow.
It was where my pain
dwelled and wallowed.

How could I love anyone
if I didn't love myself?
If I didn't love me,
how could anyone else?

In being alone,
I realized I did not love me,
at least not wholly.

At this time,
I had to surrender.
I had to try and learn
to get to know me.

I surrendered.
I let the pain come.
I did not hide or run.

My sadness came on
like a rushing waterfall.
At times, I felt
I would not survive;
I felt so small.

Where did all this
sadness come from?
All the pain
I did not fully understand.
It came from some strange,
cold, dark familiar land.

Some pains so deep,
it was not time to look.
I had to start little.
I got some help
from some amazing books.

In this surrender,
I was learning.
This life is
100% my responsibility.

That thought…
daunting.

It was up to me
to fill me.
I had to learn
to make myself happy.

In being alone,
I learned
I wasn't so fond
of my own my company.

I was taught to like others.
Liking myself,
I wasn't taught to bother.

On this venture,
brought on by my surrender.
A metaphor came to me:

I came into this life
with a pile of bricks.
It was my life's job
to take these bricks
and build myself
a crystal palace
for my soul to live.

Whatever it took
I had committed.
With each brick,
I would face
another problem.
To this process,
I had to surrender.
At this time,
I started to get better.

Surrender is the land of faith, receiving, and openness. As you view this from a distance, you can see that the people of this culture spin their wheels fighting for a solution until they come to realize what they have been doing is not productive. You will learn from the bravery of these people, because this is a culture that lives by the laws of humility. It is okay not to be perfect. It is okay to be doing things the wrong way. It is all a part of learning and growing.

As you get out of the boat and let the movie stop here for a while, you will have the gift of learning that surrender often means accepting things as they are without needing them to be different. It is here you learn to let go and work with what ***is****. You will learn here that you do not need to waste your energy "trying" and putting in all this extra effort, because in the land of Surrender,* *you stop and allow yourself to do by not doing. It is the path of least resistance and the place where needing to be in control does not exist. In this culture, the idea of control is considered an illusion and a sickness. When you surrender, you will learn that the space of the solution naturally opens up. Your eye-sight will be greatly expanded from your visit here. Come, and learn.*

Eye-Sight

To surrender is to cease behaviors and beliefs that are not working, to step into the new life class and learn new ways. My life was an emotional roller coaster. I had to learn to live *with* myself and figure out how to make my way into internal happiness without dependence on an external source. I knew I did not love myself, and I had no idea where to start. It seemed like such a strange concept. I needed inner stability – something permanent I could count on. The problem was this seemed conceptual. I did not know if inner power was just a fancy idea or if it really existed, if people could really obtain this. I was unsure of what kind of work I would need to do to produce that state of mind.

I had been living with the eye-sight that other people were my cure to loneliness. I looked to everyone outside of me to make me feel good. I made them responsible for my happiness, like my parents had made me responsible for their feelings. I had to jump into the void of aloneness and loneliness. It was the only way. I felt half-crazy taking this leap, but I had exhausted all other options. I had opened all other doors and tried every other way. I had gotten to a point where the only choice was to choose this. I had kicked down all other doors, scrambled to make each door be the door that would finally work.

It came to me that I should not kick the doors down because the key was in my pocket. The key was surrender. I had been so focused on the door; I did not even think about the key. The only way to happiness was to do the deeper, transformational work. I began to see that all experiences are designed to bring us into a closer relationship with the Self. As I let go and I stopped fighting and controlling all the pieces of me that were like confetti tossed haphazardly into the air, I found each piece would find the right place to land.

If I could surrender, it would all happen just as it should. Perfectly. The more I tried to control, the longer my pieces would stay up in the air, the longer it would take them to settle, and the more anxiety I would have. I had to stop. I had to surrender. I had to let the pieces of me fall. Once all of my shattered pieces were on the ground, I would be able to look at them. I would be able to see my Self. I would be able to be clear about what needed my attention. I would be able to put myself back together by simply letting go.

In-Sight: I am not by myself, I am with myself.

Reflections:

I had gotten to a place where I was either going to continue on my needy path, or I was going to change. In the outside world, I was like a funnel; the good passed through me, but never stuck. Nothing within me felt good enough to catch and keep what I got from the outside world. None of the choices I made in the outside world had any real value because none of it was permanent. *If I was not in a consistent relationship with myself, I would not find consistency outside of me.*

My aloneness was at first unbearable. I could not believe the levels of sadness I was feeling. I did not like myself. I did not like that I could not be happy on my own and by myself. I did not like my neediness. I did not like my insecurities. It was a painful time, as I adjusted to being alone with myself. I did notice, however, that in choosing to be alone, I started treating myself better. I ate healthier, I worked out more, I read a lot, and I wrote in my journal. I needed to keep myself busy so I would not drown in my sorrows. I began to give to myself what I had previously been giving to others. Out of nothing to do and no one to spend time with I focused on keeping myself occupied. The first part of my connection with *myself* had begun.

In looking at the pieces of me that had settled, I could see I had to shift my perception of the world. The world was a not a place to *get* things. I had to get my needs met from within, and then the world would open up to me. I had been living the expectation the world owed me something, and I was constantly let down. The world did not need to change. I needed to change. I was becoming more interested in what life would be like if I enjoyed it. I wanted to know what joy would feel like and how could I produce it. Joy, up to this point, had only come in moments, and I wanted to learn how to make joy a commitment. To do that, I would have to get to know myself well enough to figure out what made me happy. I did not even know myself well enough to know what made me happy.

I had begun to learn the lesson that nothing outside of me could save me from my pain or from my insecurities. In fact, I had evidence to the opposite. Everything I gained in the outside world left me abandoned and more empty than before. My task would be to find the path to my inner world. All the love I had been searching for was here within me. I could not demand love from others until I figured out how to give it to myself. I had to learn I *could* give it to myself. I was a loving person. I could see I gave all my love away with the expectation that in giving it I would get it in return. Upon reflection I could understand as long as I was desperate and chasing love I wasn't really giving love. As people, I believe it is in our very nature to love. If it is my very nature to love, then there should be no need to search for it and no need to work for it. I just had to *find* it. *Love would be the path to my Self*. I was now willing to learn to love myself.

I was aware I had many insecurities and idiosyncrasies. These would be my challenges to face on the path to the love of my Self. The beginning of loving my Self came down to surrendering to all of my bad habits and having to take a look at them. I was insecure about the way I looked, I did not think I was lovable, I was needy and I had no ability to deal with and face conflict. With all these bad habits, I had become someone who required too much work, too much attention, and too much praise. Why was it too much? Because I was so empty I could never get enough.

Life Class Lesson:

This lesson is a series of questions designed to get you in touch with the origins, avenues, and gifts of feeling insecure. Insecurity is marked by a general feeling of unease or nervousness where you feel a sense of vulnerability or instability which undermines your idea of yourself and your value. Insecurity is a natural part of the human condition, mostly derived from the trap of interpersonal comparison. Often as you compare yourself to others, you see yourself as lower or not good enough. You begin to doubt your abilities, your capabilities, and you lose belief in yourself to be everything you desire to be.

When you are letting your insecurities run your life, you become full with the frantic energy of needing to prove your worth to others. When you surrender, you let this go. Ultimately, you have a deep desire to have inner fulfillment and to know yourself. It is your higher purpose to be differentiated and true to yourself. When you surrender, you are giving up the struggle between yourself and your insecurities. Surrendering requires you to dip into self-acceptance. You have to accept what your insecurities are and then decide what you want to do with them. *Surrendering is not about giving up, it is about opening up.* When you open up, miracles come.

When you are a ball of insecurities, your choices in life are extremely limited. The process of surrendering quickly filters the true from the false, and it shows you where your choices are. As you relinquish control, your choices become plentiful. As you are able to take a realistic and deep look at your insecurities, you will begin forging a path to the life of fulfillment. When you can honestly accept and look at who you are, the choices of who you can become are unlimited. Surrendering is a deeply personal experience and it requires introspection, acceptance, love and letting go.

**What can you learn from surrendering?*

**What are you insecurities?*

**How do they impact you? How do they impact your*

relationships? Example: My insecurities weigh me down. They do not allow me to feel comfortable within my Self, my world or in any of my relationships. If I am not comfortable with me, how can anyone else really be comfortable with me? And the worst thing about insecurities is that being around other people often made me feel worse. Insecurities drive the idea of comparison. The idea of *more than and less than, better than and worse than.*

There was no way I could feel my magnificence when I was so focused on my lack. Because I was so focused on my lack, all I could see was everyone else's magnificence. It was such a terrible and defeating way to live. I saw the world in quotas. Some people had things I didn't, and because they had them, there was now none left over for me. Living this way internally is common to us all to some degree, and it affects us in our relationships to the same level and extent we live it internally. *Insecurities then serve as blocks to intimacy.* It is difficult to accept love from others when you cannot even muster that same love for yourself. If you heal your insecurities, you become more available for intimacy. When you are insecure, it is impossible for you to give your attention to something or someone else because you are consumed with feeling not good enough. There really isn't much room for anyone else.

**What have people told you about your insecurities?*

**Are they right?*

**What can you use from that feedback to grow?*

**What are the opportunities you have in becoming aware of your insecurities?* Example: When you can transcend negative self-talk, it can change your whole life. I had to recondition my mind to think differently. I had to flood my mind with positive thoughts constantly. I surrounded myself with positive books and affirmation cards. I repeated positive thoughts in my head and listened to positive thinking books on tape. I still practice much of this today at a different level and for different reasons; the method works.

As we change our thoughts to positive, bigger and better opportunities come our way. Negative energy isn't attractive to anyone. It is not attractive to those we have relationships with, it is not attractive to employers, and it is not attractive to potential opportunities. It is impossible to have a great life when we are living negative beliefs. Positive thoughts lead to positive feelings, and positive feelings lead to positive thoughts. I want all possible opportunity available to me. If I choose to want even more then I have to work on my thoughts, feelings, and beliefs to resonate with the larger opportunities I desire. Even with the simple repetitive rehearsal of positive feelings and thoughts, we can open up endless opportunities. It is truly transformational.

**Are you as annoyed with your negative thoughts and characteristics as others are?*

**What have you used from the outside world to fill you emotionally?*

**How long did it last?*

**What was the end result?*

**Most importantly, where did you learn all of the bad qualities about yourself?* Example: I learned them from my parents and their frustration with my inability to cope better with the constantly changing circumstances their decisions inflicted upon my life. I brought these internal instabilities as baggage into all other relationships and became even more insecure. I also learned some of my insecurities from the media and other powerful conditioners that are a constant in our society. This kind of conditioning is present everywhere we look. There are standards set up by family and society that are not attainable without an airbrush or constant negative feedback. To heal, we have to go within and decide that we have the power to determine our own worth, our own sense of beautiful, our own sense of our expression etc.

Extra Credit Advantage:

Healing reading for home-work

A Return to Love (Marianne Williamson): I do not affiliate with any religious or spiritual philosophy, but I can say that I am drawn to concepts that are more spiritual in nature. In this book, I was comforted in the knowledge that I can transcend my insecurities and I learned a lot in how to deal with challenges I was facing in my life. She talks about how our greatest fear is that we are essentially inadequate, and I was living this as my greatest fear. This book was incredibly life changing for me. I could pick it up at any point in my life and get an inspirational direction to follow.

Differentiating Opportunity:

Suppose you could directly eliminate your insecurities by asking and answering forward moving questions. What if you asked yourself things like: What is perfect about this insecurity? How can I use this insecurity to benefit me? What am I willing or no longer willing to do to heal this insecurity? Insecurity can be a precursor to growth.

Your insecurities are the things which keep you bound to your unhealthy parenting and childhood. The insecure voices in your head are the voices you internalized from childhood. The messages you received in childhood stay alive via your insecurities. Your insecurities are the voices in your head which tell you that you are not good enough, pretty enough, smart enough, tall enough, etc. When you are in the habit of scolding yourself or diminishing yourself, you are beating yourself up. You beat yourself up because that is how you learned to be in a relationship with yourself. It keeps your childhood abuse alive. The more you berate yourself, the more you deepen your insecurity. It adds more and more glue to your low self-esteem. It binds you to your current state of misery.

The way to differentiate is to be aware of the inner critics, undo their messages and open yourself up to becoming a new version of who you are without these voices. Or, you can get into a parenting relationship with these voices and discipline them when they are out of control. The habit of negative self-talk will require you to force your mind to think new thoughts about yourself.

You have a unique path to take and becoming aware of your insecurities is the way to get out from under an oppressive emotional world which does not serve your higher purpose. You can only be oppressed as a child. Once you are independent, you repress yourself with your insecurities. To become your own person, you have the task of calming these old voices, taking care of them, knowing them and choosing not to see them as the truth of who you are. *The truth of who you are lies in the freedom to choose whoever you want to be.* Those choices are limitless.

Here are a few steps to help along the path to surrendering and differentiating:

-Take each moment as it comes, and you will be at peace with who you have been in the past and with the unknown *you* to come in the future.

-See life as perfect in its design. Everything in your life was brought to you at the exact right time for the exact correct learning experience you needed to help you differentiate.

-Each time you feel an insecurity or a fear, reverse your thoughts to embrace something positive about the situation.

-There is always something positive and transformational inside each negative situation and/or insecurity. Look for it and identify it.

-Train your mind to think only in terms of positive outcomes and that when the world tells you something is impossible, don't believe it.

-Aim for the outcome you want and do not give fearful outcomes too much space in your head. --Have faith and hold your thoughts in the space of belief, positive intent, and feelings.

-Think of how unique, powerful and limitless your lives could be as you let go and transform your insecurities. Just suppose...

As I sit it the boat,
I am struck with
such pride.
I look at that girl,
and she wants
to be alive.

Our worlds are so close.
Soon, they will collide.

As I sit and gaze
at this amazing time
I feel graced…
This girl
definitely wants to create
her life's space...

As the boat glides on,
my eyes are having to adjust.
It isn't as dark as before.
This is the metaphor:

The me then
is touching upon
her light within.

I also notice I am not
nearly as cold.
My teeth are not chattering.
I seem to be out of the
the waters that were so
deep, dark, steep, and old.

I have reclaimed
many of the me's
that were maimed.

Now I sit and watch
this memory of the me
that was then
embark on becoming…

Her own woman.

We have been traveling along gathering your in-sights and becoming more aware of your faulty beliefs, and you have been transforming them simply by becoming aware of them. You are about to arrive in the land of Intelligence. You will see this culture is full of Books and wisdom. The inhabitants love to learn and live to learn. As you explore this land, you will observe the power of information and what that information can do to save your life. Books are direct guidance. They are compasses through the emotional and mental worlds. They help you understand your emotions and your faulty thoughts which trigger your emotional responses. Books are a necessary part of any journey. You have read books that you feel have been life changing. In this next poem you will observe how transformational books can be in your journey to love yourself.

Books

My guiding light
to rebuilding my life:
I turned to books,
where I learned
new skills to survive.

To get to know myself,
I had to ask,
"Who am I?"
and
"What do I want
out of my life?"

I want to be happy.
I want to be loved.
I want to be successful.
I want to feel fulfilled.
I want a man,
who is emotionally
available.
I want to love the part
of me that is
the most vulnerable.

I have to be alone
to meet this goal.
I have to go inside
to heal my soul.
I have to believe
that this healing
is possible.

I read books each night.
They put me back in touch
with my plight.
Their information
nurtured my vessel
and filled me with insight.

In the Meantime,
Yesterday I Cried,
A Woman's Worth,
Conversations with God,
Seat of the Soul,
Women Who Run with the Wolves,

among a dozen others,
each book taking
my healing
to another level.

My books were my dates.
With them, I journeyed
through my inner landscape.
I examined all the unhealthy ways
I had learned to relate.

Slowly but surely
I was changing my fate.
Inside me,
I stopped feeling lonely.
On my own and self created,
I began to feel
authentically happy.

The desperation was gone.
I was not searching
and hunting the outside world,
using whomever and whatever
came my way to make me
feel strong.

It took about three months
of tears and unbearable fear
to get to this place
of being able to simply
look into the mirror
and examine the person
that was there.

For the first time,
all of my good feelings
were generated from
within me.

There had been so much of me,
I hadn't the sight to see.
Some of the things were
so beautiful,
they astounded me.

I had never touched on
these parts of me.
I had gotten lost
in repeating the ways
in which my parents raised me.

I was stopping the dysfunction.
The first step I was taking
was to become aware
of the inner me
in the making.

My desire to love myself
coming into fruition.
I wanted to love me,
so I could be my very best person.

With my books,
I laid the cement.
I was in the midst of
constructing my foundation...

Brick by brick.

Books produce alchemy. They can help you metamorphose into the new you. Everyone here reads and writes in their journals. These people are full of excitement and motivation, and they often meet in groups in the evenings to discuss what they learned that day. They are dedicated life students and are always looking forward. They love and feel gratitude for the guidance offered in their education. They take no information for granted, and they study their materials. These people are hunters of information with the goal to understand who they are and how they can more happily and efficiently live their lives. They are wonderful, smart people. Go and keep their company for a while and see what you can learn from their efforts to educate themselves. There is a flag here that waves in the lightness of the wind which reads "Information is power." Let's step out and see why.

Eye-Sight

In my surrender, I researched and investigated my fractured emotional foundation. I figured out Self-love by recognizing I had no foundation. My eye-sight had been that I was never secure or safe. I had no foundation of belief, direction, or knowledge on how to deal with life by myself. In *Books,* I show that healing comes from information. Books became my companions, my best teachers and closest confidants. I spent much time analyzing all that was missing inside me. No matter the issue, I could always find the exact missing piece of information I needed in a book. Books became my evening dates and weekend conversation. The knowledge gained through them began to heal my soul. Books became my externalized parents. They supplied me with the good advice, direction, and understanding I could never find in my upbringing. I found that whenever I needed sound, logical, practical advice I could turn to a book and get what I needed.

Information is liberating. Information opens up new worlds. What I needed was to figure out how to build my foundation. From my research, I learned that starting over with self-love at an older age was going to be an adventure which would require training my mind to think different thoughts about myself. I would have to start by thinking things I did not necessarily believe about myself and rehearse these new thoughts to make them real. Just because others did not believe I was magnificent did not mean that was true. It was only true for them. Just because my family thought I was bad did not mean I was bad. They were responsible for their thoughts of me. I had to become responsible for deciding my own thoughts about myself. Changing fixed conditioned thoughts is repetitive, hard work. Most of us continue to want the quick fix or some external world solution. The quick fix is never the answer. Quick fix attempts at self-love recycle core wounds.

Authentic change only comes from hard work, commitment to healing, and willingness to be open and learn. The process of self-examination is the path I was taking. You will arrive at new-direction-moments throughout your life, so when things change, you have to be able to be flexible and change everything. Each life-class you take will require new skills from you to deepen and enrich your next level of development. As you develop, your new form begins to emerge, your frequency enhances and you have a more composed trust in life. Pain is simply a part of any transformation.

In-sight: Everything you need to learn is available as information.

Reflections:

The gift of having parents who could not nurture me emotionally is I had no other choice but to figure out how to resolve my own issues. Books provided me the exact parenting advice I needed. In my time alone, to avoid my loneliness, I went to Barnes and Noble with a journal and pen, walked through the self-help section and picked out books that spoke to me by title. I remember one book, *Foundation for Inner Peace*. I loved the title. Inner peace was certainly not something I possessed, but it sure sounded good. I found The *Power of Positive Thinking*. I wasn't great at positive thinking, so I knew I could learn from that. Once I had a couple books, I purchased them, found a cozy place in the book store, took out my journal and pen, and began my process.

My process went something like this: read a book, write the highlighted parts in my journal and process my feelings about what I underlined by writing them out. When I read these books, it helped me analyze my insecurities. I wrote about them and examined the impact they were having on my life. When I was flooded with insecurity, I had no inner happiness. If I wasn't internally happy, there was no path to fulfillment in anything in the outside world. I kept learning the same painful lessons over and over again.

I am lucky I have always been an avid reader and writer. It is the best therapy out there. If I have a problem, an insecurity, a dysfunctional behavioral, or a negative thought pattern I can find all the help I need in a book. However, the act of reading is only an intellectual process. I found the way to transform the information I was learning was to put it into writing and coach myself into a new way of thinking and behaving. When I wrote, the change would happen. I was in the process of creating myself into the image of the *me* I had always wanted to be. The blank journals were my canvas and my books were my paints. One without the other would not have worked. I needed both to create real and lasting change.

I began to live within the covers of these books, and they became more real to me than any other relationship I had in my life. My awareness guides, these books led me deep into my internal world. I documented my journey by writing every step of the way. In time, my inner world began to develop. I started to see myself differently. I found I was quite an interesting study. I had never found myself interesting before. I liked being interesting. This was the first taste I had of my inner richness. It was exciting.

The books I read became a form of traveling. I have traveled not only into other worlds, but I used my books to travel into my own uncharted inner world. I was learning about who I was, who I wanted to be, what I aspired to, and what I might dare to dream. Through my books, I learned the difference between good and bad qualities, the difference between being neurotic and character disordered, the difference between insecure and secure, the difference between positive thinking and negative thinking, and the difference between punishments and lessons. I learned about God and choices, I learned about life, I learned about the inner world. I learned it was up to me to create it and design it.

When I was reading and writing, I felt such a comfort in my solitude. I would enter a parallel universe where I was getting the secret answers to living a better and more fulfilling life. Hours upon hours could pass and in that time I felt focused, unafraid, and content. The hours spent reading and writing took away all of my loneliness and isolation. My world felt at peace.

My books helped me understand that life actually has a process, a unique design. It was not haphazard. It was a series of life classes designed only for opportunity. I began to see I was safe in this design as long as I used self-reflection. *I learned a positive outlook and a focused mind left little room for anxiety.* I learned the emotions were going to be a large part of my life for the rest of my life, and anything that made me uncomfortable could make me move and grow. I learned life is all about change. I could feel my energy beginning to shift and change.

Reading and writing became the pathway to my inner world, and as I read, my inner world became rich. As I applied what I learned, my relationship life became rich. I had a lot more to offer, and I began to like myself. I began to feel more hopeful, positive, enlightened, and understanding of the world I was living in. I had mostly been afraid of all of my emotions, blaming them for the circumstances of my life. My books taught me differently.

My writing is the way I became my best friend. When I write, I am essentially writing from a higher self to a more vulnerable self, one aspect guiding the other, one needing the other, one taking care of the other. The higher self is the part of me which understands what I am reading and it educates the more vulnerable part of me just like a parent to a child. I began to love myself through this process. I began to see things in my Self I had never seen before. I loved my paper parents.

Life Class Lesson:

In this section, you are moving directly into *conscious and purposeful healing*. Healing takes conscious, intentional work, effort, commitment, and attention. If you were to live in a house and never pick up after yourself, your house would become messy and chaotic. However, if you commit to picking up after yourself daily, your living environment is clean and peaceful. Self-esteem requires daily, conscious attention that is consistent and long term. Many actually prefer unhappiness to daily effort. In this class, you determine if you love yourself enough to put daily effort into your healing. Healing leads to becoming a healer. Just your example can be enough to inspire others to grow.

Reading is one the healthiest ways to put conscious effort into your healing. Reading is incredibly empowering. It helps you gain knowledge and learn skills to help solve your current problems. It helps you to explore yourself and to explore life. The more you know about yourself and how you function, the better your decisions will be. Better decisions mean less time spent cleaning up the unwanted emotional messes you have in your life.

**How committed are you to your healing?*

**Is your healing worth the commitment of reading and writing each day to transform your life?* Example: Absolutely I am worth it! I write and read the most when I am in emotional pain and need grounding and guidance to get out. It helps organize and calm my chaotic mind and to let the emotions flow through me with the least resistance. I use both books and writing to help me see the bigger picture and find solutions. Solutions bring me a sense of emotional safety. The solutions I find through this commitment to myself have saved my life over and over again.

Healing takes consistent effort to recondition the way we think. Our minds tend to focus and hold onto negative thinking more easily than they strive for positive thought. To keep the mind positive, you have to make sure you are replacing habitual negative thinking with its positive opposite. The minute you think you have positive thinking down and stop focusing on it, your mind will likely shift toward the negative. A focused mind has very little room for chaos. *I have to make a loving, conscious effort to keep my life happy and positive.* I find this type of work rewarding – not arduous – because the results make me feel so good. I do not enjoy being in fear, anger or sadness on a chronic level. I prefer to keep my chronic state of mind feeling positive.

**What life changing books have you read?*

**What did the books teach you about you and your internal world?*

**How did you apply what you read?*

**Do you live it out consistently?*

**If you have not been a reader or a writer, would you be willing to try, if it meant happiness and fulfillment?*

Extra Credit Advantage:

Healing reading for home-work

In the Meantime (Iyanla Vanzant): Ohhh, did this book ever inspire me. I slept with it in my bed at night for comfort, hope, and direction. For quite some time, this book and I were inseparable. With simplicity and love, this book cleared my confusion about having a relationship with myself. I cannot tell you how powerful getting clear feels. This was a book I read over and over. I lived this book, made Iyanla's information my own, and in many ways, now teach it through my role as a Psychologist.

You Can Heal Your Life (Louis Hay): This book contains positive affirmations as well as information about how to heal your past, your inner wounds, your health and your finances. There really is no issue not covered in the pages of this book. The most profound experience I received in reading it is that it made me feel safe. It made me feel I was exactly where I needed to be, learning perfectly what I needed to learn. It was something I could turn to and feel immediately uplifted.

Friendship with God (Neal Donald Walsh): This was such a fresh and interesting concept. So many times in my life when I was in utter desperation, God felt non-existent. In reading this book, I learned how to have an actual relationship with my inner life or my inner world. I learned I could be in constant conversation with the higher aspects of me that were unafraid, that were available at all times for advice giving. After this read, I did not feel so alone in my human experience; rather I felt that all was happening just as it should, comfortable or not. I started to believe I was not just abandoned on this planet in my human form. All of Neal's books have offered answers to questions that had been unanswerable for me. Having answers helps us make sense of our lives.

Seat of the Soul (Gary Zukav): This was a book that was hot because of Oprah, and it is why I purchased it. Not all parts resonated with me, but the things that did were incredible. I just needed pieces and parts from this book. It helped piece together the process of life and showed me that life is not haphazard in its design. There is form and structure underneath all chaos.

Differentiating Opportunity:

Suppose through conscious daily effort – reading and writing – you can uncover your true self, your unconditioned magnificence. What if you discover that purposeful healing is not limited to self-improvement but is actually geared toward self-discovery? The benefits of reading and writing clear much of the confusion that exists in our lives. Healing requires pure intent, daily commitment, and inspiration with the ultimate goal being the individual expressive freedom of who you really are. Suppose through your reading, you were able to find solutions to your problems that were totally in your control. Because reading is private and solitary, it is totally in your control. When you find solutions in this manner, they are the best solutions because they did not come from a dependency on another. They came from your in-sight and commitment as an individual. As you experience this, you are able find your own solutions. When you find your own solutions, you are differentiating.

I believe books to be your unique teachers and externalized parents. Books are a place to call home and feel at home. Home gives a feeling of being heard, loved and understood. The books I would choose were unique to my newly budding differentiating Self. They may not be the books you need. Your unique Self will find the books which speak to you. There is book out there for everyone open to the change opportunity.

Books do not necessarily make your life easier but they make life more understandable. This is your way out of your inner critic poison. It takes an open mind, the courage to change, and the ability to commit and do your best. Mostly, books bring awareness and understanding. Awareness brings transformation.

In the boat,
I am enraptured.
The me then
her life…
she wanted to capture:
her happiness,
she was going after.

As I sit in the boat
I remember…
this time for the me then
was so precious and tender.

As I become aware of
my surroundings,
I realize I am not nearly as cold.
My bones are not aching;
my teeth are not chattering.
I am comfortably sitting in this boat.

I am full.
I feel so proud
of the me then.
She was committed to
her search for meaning.
She was at a time of
a new beginning.

It is still somewhat chilly
as I coast along in the boat,
but the light is peeking
through the ceiling
of the white puffy clouds
up above me.

My eyes are adjusting
to the light.
I see color now.
The scenery is no longer
black, grey and white.

I embrace this new place.
Its beauty has
a much different face.
I am overwhelmed with
this colorful, vibrant space.

The water below is crystal blue.
The river is encased
by rolling mountains
so full of color.
It is astoundingly beautiful.

Feeling warm
as the boat moves on.
Up ahead a new destination…
a new lesson.

I see her.
She is busy.

She is journaling and reading,
learning at God-speed.
She is becoming aware
for her life to work
she has to understand her…

Sometimes when you are traveling a river you not only notice the different speeds and different levels of danger but you also see how deep the river is. When you feel fear, you may not know where the bottom is. We look at the fear, and it is dark; it seems to go on forever and has an ominous feeling to it. In this part of your travels, you may need to hold closely to your in-sights, or your insides. This place has the culture of duality because it is dark and it is light. As you observe this place, you will see that the light always follows the darkness. You will see the inhabitants here start off in the dark feeling small and as they pass through the darkness, they are expansive and full of light. What you will witness as you tour this land is that fear has a good intention. Its intention is to keep the river of change moving so you continue evolving. Evolvement brings maturity and with maturity comes the increased ability to love yourself. So hold on and let's take a dip into fear.

Fear

For as long
as I can remember,
fear was closer
to me emotionally
than any family member.

My fear,
unlike them,
was always there.

Its presence I could
always feel within.
Its darkness would
come from behind
and take me in.

Without my sight
in its darkness,
I was blind.

My fear was clearly,
for so many years,
the ruler of my life.
It had the power
to control me
and eat me alive.

It held me back
from living my life.

In this time alone
I knew…
my relationship with fear.
I had to get clear.

I had to befriend my fear.
Its seeds were planted

within me somewhere.
Its roots I had to discover.

For many days and nights,
I looked at my fear
and cried.

I got to know it.
I let it whisper in my ear.
It had things to say
I was ready to hear.
My fear,
it did not come
from nowhere.
It had been with me
since the first
emotional fracture.

It had been with me
since my first mistrust
that occurred in infancy.

My fear's intention
was to protect and warn me
of what was up ahead
that would hurt me.

In my discovery,
I felt compassion
for this mechanism.
My fear had good intentions.

I now had a very
new and unexpected
understanding.
My fear was not there
to paralyze me.

My fear was my ally.
If used correctly,
it could motivate me,
instead of engulf me.

My fear had new meaning.
I could let my fear
signal me
when it was time
to face something.

I knew fear would
always be there
to invade my psyche.
But….now I knew
I could use it
to help me.

For behavior to change
it must first be understood
by insight…

I think I am on my way.

Here, you have arrived and passed by the land of Duality. Fear, you saw, always brings on the darkness, and once you have passed through and gathered up some of your in-sights, you can clearly see that the light will always follow the dark. This is a culture which embraces the God of Fear, as this God is often the most powerful force to get you to move. Some, in the land of the Lost, crumble and do not want to travel to a place like this. If you get stuck with the Lost, you can be doomed forever. But here, the fear is temporary whereas, through fear, you have the greatest opportunity to evolve. Fear and intuition are co-leaders of this culture, one being of the dark and the other of the light. They are not at war. They work in harmony to cultivate the land to feed the people. The light usually begins first. If you have such distorted eye-sight that you cannot see the light, then fear will step in with its booming energy to bring you to the light. It may be a bit nerve wracking to disembark and be in this place, but this understanding of fear and intuition is mandatory for seekers. No matter the fear or how dark life can get, you will educate yourself on how to make the transition into the light where the eye-sight is clear and unobstructed.

Eye-Sight

For me, fear was an ever-present darkness. I felt the shadow of fear around me at all times. My life became a matter of trying to escape. I used to feel a looming dark essence come from behind and wrap me in its clutches. Fear sucked my soul out of my body. I felt at any moment the bottom would fall out. Unfortunately, for me the bottom did fall out many times. That thought was a reality for me. I was so vulnerable that even the slightest mishap in life would cause me to panic. The more I feared something, the more I panicked about that situation. My panic would start my adrenalin system, and I would be awash in my primitive brain chemistry. This adrenalin rush totally detached me from the thinking part of my brain.

My fears often made a mountain out of a molehill. Because of this, I developed some social-insecurities. I saw from the reactions of those around me that my instant panic button could be annoying. The reaction was automatic. I had no control over it. I lived this way for a long time. In my time alone, however, I decided to study fear. I began to feel proud that regardless of my fears I still kept up with life, school, grades, and friends, and could get out of my comfort zone. Something in me kept driving me forward. I believe I have a natural drive to survive. Or maybe I didn't have a choice.

As I began my study of fear, I learned a lot about my enemy. I learned it had a good intention for me. Its intent was, of course, my survival. In my studying, I was awakened to the news that fear had a silent partner: intuition. I think most fears start as intuition. Fear speaks for intuition when we do not listen to our guts. The more you ignore your intuition, the louder fear begins to speak. In learning fear was not here to paralyze me, I figured out I had to learn to listen to my *first knowing*. For me, the louder fear would get, the more paralyzed I felt. I liken this process to why people yell. Most people yell because they feel they are not being heard. When your intuitions are not heard, fear will step in. The more you ignore it, the louder fear gets. Unfortunately it is harder to listen because you become more afraid.

This all made sense to me. I began to take a look at my unnatural panic response, and I could see *it was my response to fear that was the problem, not the fear itself.* My intuition was sending me answers, guidance, and *knowing*. I have figured out my own desires to control my life are what silenced my intuition. I had made many wrong turns using my mind instead of my gut, and this is where fear would step in. Fear would begin yelling at me, in an effort to tell me I was headed in the wrong direction. I can always look back and see that I knew what I should have done the whole time but did not listen to myself. Learning is learning, however, and my hindsight would soon turn into foresight.

To imagine I was built with a perfect internal guidance system was amazing. I could reflect and see the times I listened to my gut, and I could see the times when I overrode my gut and made a decision I felt was more safe or secure. Each time fear would have to step in. My task was to learn the difference between fear and intuition. At times, this is still a confusing process. However, I have learned *there is always time to make decisions*. You may feel life is demanding an answer, and if you don't answer, you will lose something or someone. But all you have to do is be brave enough to take the time.

If you don't know, don't act. This has been something which has helped me to use my insight. In-sight is based on intuition. Intuition lives within the body; fear and panic live within the mind. I have learned that the courage to keep going is the cure to fear. Just keep moving and do your best. *If you avoid your fears, you cannot grow.*

In-Sight: Fear is our most evolutionary response. It is designed to fuel growth.

Reflections:

Fear was my state of being from my very first memory. With fear ever present, I felt paralyzed. I felt completely in its grip. Sadly, repressed fear turns to panic, and panic is not a natural state. When fear turns to panic, all the darkness of life slips in and takes control, which makes movement extremely challenging. I remember feeling scared beyond what I could handle, and my fear sucked me into my old programming. I would either avoid the fear at all costs or try to use some kind of force to control it.

I typically used anger as a way to force things, but whatever I chased, ran away. Sometimes I provoked abandonment or rejection out of my fears. It was a never ending battle. I did not have a strong enough inner world to understand that sometimes the most powerful thing you can do is turn away from a person and/or situation you are trying to control. I could not trust that things would find their own natural balance.

I have learned two things about fear: *Fear equals change, and change is uncomfortable*. The more afraid of change I became, the more chronic my state of panic. Panic creates the feeling of emergency, which was the environment I was raised in, and it was this feeling I tried to avoid. Coping with fear requires an open mind, surrender, and flexibility. Its intended purpose is movement, personal growth, and expansion. As I learned to become more flexible, I became empowered and aware. When I was rigid, I could not move with the flow of life, my emotions, my relationships or my achievements. To become healthy I had to learn to feel the fear and face it.

Facing fears requires introspection, strategy, flexibility, and creativity. Fear is typically created by the friction between where you currently are and where your growth path is taking you. You may struggle to stay with what you know, even if it is not healthy for you. Familiarity is security, however, familiarity breeds stagnation. When you resist and avoid, you are essentially stopping your forward movement. All of life is pulling you to change, grow and become more open. *You are here for expansion and transformation for the purpose of experiencing more and more of who you are capable of becoming.*

Fear has let me know there is danger everywhere in this life. Danger has a purpose. It helps you know what you want and what you don't want. There are always going to be hostile people, destructive relationships, and other unpredictable life circumstances. It is best to allow your fears to surface and to confront them. Let each fear whisper to you. Each whisper is a golden guide to the next place. Therefore, when you repress because you do not want to change, you create a state of panic. Panic comes from knowing a fear exists, wanting to avoid it, and then experiencing the build-up of more fear. When you choose not to face fears, they grow in intensity and size.

This is when the imagination takes over. Fear thrives on the unknowable. Once the imagination sets in, you lose your presence of mind, and you freeze. *Remember, the imagination and the spinning of all negative outcomes are no more real than a hallucination.* Work through it, face the fears, grow in confidence, feel successful, and just do your best! It will always turn out better than before.

The only way to break free from this dynamic is to confront it. Fear has a protective and self-preserving quality. It makes you so uncomfortable that it pushes you away from the people and circumstances which no longer serve you. It is also designed to bring you into a closer relationship with your Self. *The quickest and most effective way to build confidence is to face your fears.* When you are in fear, no matter your supports, you still have to face that fearful emotion on your own. Therefore, each fear you face brings you into a more trusting and accountable relationship with your Self. Each time you face a fear, you feel success. You have achieved something you questioned that you could achieve. Happiness is a byproduct of achievement. This is how fear brings you to inner connection.

Fear requires one companion: faith. You need the faith that all things always work out in the end, that life is not haphazard but designed perfectly for you to grow in your unique way. Most people are low on faith. I had to learn to embrace my fear as a life partner letting it push me, tug me, and catapult me to the next most beautiful chapter of my life. Faith, it was all about faith.

Life Class Lesson:

It is time to take a look into fear, the most important emotion you have. If taken advantage of, fear is the emotion of movement and evolvement. Present in some form on a daily basis, fear feeds upon the unknown, and life shifts and changes constantly. If you get stuck focusing on your fears, you will create more fear. Fear is usually your darkest hour, but if you can find evolutionary purpose and meaning here, you will find reservoirs of strength and fortitude you never knew you had.

You can show yourself you are stronger than you ever believed you could be. Fears are here to be faced in order to grow. Fear is the bridge you walk to get from the old to the new. This is the character building aspect of fear. The true caliber of a person is revealed under stress. Fear helps you take action and do the scary thing. You do not normally face your fears willingly. In fact, if you are preoccupied with your fears, the 'what if's,' and your imagined worst case scenarios, fear becomes a problem. It will take its toll on you, if it is running your life. It will keep you up all night, and it will make you have a low frustration tolerance during the day. Let's take a closer look at fear.

**Do you trust life?* Example: I love this question because the temptation is to answer, "Yes, I trust life; life is a loving, beautiful process." But that is only part of life. Here, is what I really trust about life. Life is all about duality. It is about the good and the bad. It is never going to be one way. For instance, it is never going to be all peaceful because we live in a constant process of change, and change brings uncomfortable times.

Life does not always provide ease and comfort, so at times, we can trust the predictability of life and at other times, we will feel as if we have nothing solid underneath us. There is value in not trusting life because when we get out of the belief we have something to rely on, we are forced to rely on our own facilities to get us through. The point is to learn to trust your *responses* to life will get you through.

**If not, list all the horrible events that caused you to lose faith. If you can now examine this list and think "these situations did not happen to me, rather they happened for me" can you find the gifts in each of one?*

**Write the gifts now.*

**Has fear every held you completely back in your life?*

**What was the result of not facing that fear?* Example: The result of not facing a particular fear has been delay. I cannot move forward until I face whatever fear is in front of me. I have also learned that when I do not face a fear, it just pops up again in some other form, and it is even bigger than it was before. This is always the way. I may get some relief in the moment for ducking a fear, but it is just harder to face later.

**Can you think of a fear you faced, and how it made you feel about yourself in facing it?*

**What did you learn about yourself that you did not know before you faced the fear?*

**How much a part of your life is the emotion of fear?*

**What have its gifts been for you?*

**What do you think your fear's purpose in your life is?*

**How do you work through your fear?* Example: The first thing I do when I am in fear is ask my Self, "Is this problem solvable?" When I ask this, I can instantly breathe better because *there is always a solution*. Once I start thinking about solutions, my mind is engaged and focused. A focused mind has little room for fears/anxieties. I begin brainstorming and writing a list of all the possible ways I can work through my fear. This gets me focused on the things driving my fear that are in my control which takes my focus off of the things I cannot control.

Once I have my list down, I make a plan of action to address my fear, one step at a time. This helps me to develop courage. I am most afraid when I allow my mind to feel like the fear is insurmountable, and it becomes bigger than it really is. When I break it down into finding a solution or solutions, I start to feel composure right away. I remind myself there is always a solution. It may take me time to find it, but once I start brainstorming, I am no longer stuck in the fear. I am moving through the fear.

**Do you tend to avoid things you fear?*

**If you avoid these situations, do they cease to exist?*

**Or, do these avoided issues get bigger and more difficult to face?*

**What is the value in facing your fears?* Example: The development of self-confidence has been my most meaningful benefit. In facing my fears, I pulled myself out of my comfort zone and was able to show myself that I can achieve and/or conquer things I previously viewed as completely out of my reach. It is difficult to feel the value of fear when you are in the midst of having the fear experience. However, you can evaluate how you changed upon facing the fear.

When I am in the middle of my fear, I am not open. Rather, I have learned from hindsight that *fear leads us to over exaggerate the dangers we are facing*. Things rarely turn out as badly as we imagine. Fear creates immediate distortion; we begin to imagine all the worst outcomes possible, and we cannot function in amidst of being overwhelmed. When I am overwhelmed, I, in effect, tip toe toward the situation with shaking knees, but I do face it.

Once I face it, I come to the conclusion that my anticipation of facing the fear is worse than actually facing it. My worst case scenario has rarely ever happened. It is my mind getting out of control that makes my fears what they are. Each fear I face, I gain confidence, and each fear I pass through, I become more aware of what I need to do to fight fear and I am less overwhelmed the next time.

**Can you feel your intuition underneath, driving the fear?*

Extra Credit Advantage:

Healing books for home-work

Feel the Fear and Do It Anyway (Susan Jeffers): More than a book, this became a mantra for me. The title alone was a complete inspiration, offering simple direction. When we're in fear, we are so overwhelmed, it is hard to think in an organized fashion, so this title became my mission statement. Like it or not, I would have to feel the fear and do it anyway. The book teaches you to transform your pain to power.

A Course in Miracles (Dr. Helen Schucman): This is one of those books that I read one page at a time in random order. I can open up to any page in this manuscript and gain something to contemplate for the week. This book, along with Neal Donald Walsh's books, differentiates between love and fear. I call love the harmony maker and fear the chaos creator. Without one, you cannot experience the other. The most important thing to come of studying fear is to understand its purpose is evolutionary. It is designed to push us all to wake up in our lives so we can experience harmony.

The Dance of Fear: Rising Above Anxiety, Fear, and Shame to Be Your Best and Bravest Self (Harriet Lerner): Fear is a universal feeling, and this book put me at ease because if we all feel fear then none of us is alone in the fear experience. It is a natural emotion, and this book gives clear direction how to accept and deal with fear. A great education.

The 33 Strategies of War (Robert Greene): This is one of the most brilliant books on the patterns of behavior. I devoured the keys to warfare and the interpretations. I reference this book constantly, and I use it with patients all the time. It provides amazing information and usable strategies on how to deal with topics such as fear, knowing your enemy, knowing yourself, thinking patterns, silence, patience etc. It studies some of our most brilliant leaders. Facing fears is a lot easier if we have strategies to apply. This book is all strategy.

Differentiating Opportunity:

Suppose fear is the key to your freedom, that fear is the elemental emotion in life that takes you from one place to the next new place. Remember that even little bits of courage have the power to dismantle fear. If you apply courage to your life, you are bound to have success. Fear has an upside and can be a great motivator. It can drive you to greater heights of achievement and self-sufficiency. As you learn to work through fear, you increase your skills in becoming an effective problem solver. Not only will you find solutions, you will also find you are more creative and resourceful then you ever knew.

This increases self-esteem. Increased self-esteem means increased courage. Increased courage means less fear. Less fear means a peaceful life. This will take you to deeper levels of trust within. As you work through your fear, you get more in touch with your intuitive process as well. When you problem solve you calm the emotions that block your internal guidance system. As you work through your fears and you engage in problem solving, you, in essence, learn to ride the emotion to the arrival of the perfect solutions.

Fear is a universal feeling. The way I feel fear is the same way another feels fear. What makes me fearful may not be what makes another fearful, but the feelings feel the same way. Fear is here to be our mentor through life. When I fear something, I examine it, typically get a book on the issue, and do what I can to face that fear. I know when I am in fear that it is time to clear something. I have also learned the only way out is through. I see fear like a chisel, and I am the marble. It makes me the unique form I am meant to be. Without my chisel, I would be a blob of marble just like any other. Undifferentiated. When I face my fears and I carve away at my emotions, I am creating myself into a unique and individual piece of art work. An original. Use your fear to create yourself anew each day and let your unique Self take form.

As I gaze at
the me that was then,
I feel a gentle breeze,
its softness so caressing
I expand my chest
to soulfully breathe.

From in the boat,
my heart feels at ease
as I look into the window
of this memory.

I watch the me then
embrace understanding.
Learning about her fear
was her mission.

As I look at that girl
on that adventure,
I feel so proud.
She was committed
to examining her desire.

She learned her fear
had the potential
to take her higher.

I could feel the breeze
rustling my hair
as the sun was peeking
through the spaces
between the clouds
up above me.

My skin felt the warmth
of its rays;
my heart felt so clear,
I finally understood the
true purpose of fear.

The warmth on my skin
pulls me in

to the scenery I am sitting in.
The water is so sharply blue.
It is still as glass.
I can see my reflection as I pass.

Below me, at the boat's edges,
I hear the sound of water
trickling ever so gently.

The colors in this place
are so bright and full of life.
The yellows, pinks, blues...
My eyes begin to cry.
The beauty of this place,
it is some kind of paradise.

The smells are so
fresh, crisp, and clean.
The birds in the trees,
touching my soul
as they sing.

I embrace the me
that was then.
Her hard work and
determination...
I sit quietly and
take them in.

The boat begins to move again.
I sense up ahead
something transforming.
This girl,
before becoming a woman,

she must first embrace her...

Up ahead is a voluptuous land. This land is full of color, texture, sweet smelling wind, the warmth of the sun, and the cleanliness of the rain. This is the land of the Feminine. Femininity is not just a female experience. Men also experience feminine qualities within themselves.

On the whole, this next scene is about embracing the body and not fighting it. The inhabitants here embrace their shape, their looks, and their curves.

It is also about embracing sensitivities, emotional twists and turns, and deep intuitions. I have yet to meet anybody who feels in total contentment with their bodies, their emotions, and their sensitivities. As the boat begins moving, allow your feminine qualities, desires and preferences to surface as you read and see which parts of you, you can love better or be in better acceptance of. To love yourself, you have to accept yourself and turn what you view as flaws into gifts. In this scene, you will see that beauty is external and internal in balanced harmonies. When the external and internal are in harmony, Self-love can thrive.

Femininity

Femininity
in my time alone,
I had to discover
and recover this mystery.

So many mixed messages
from family and society.
This topic so complex,
to this part of me.
I was divorced.

My femininity,
I confused with my body.
I focused on the outward
projection of me
and what I thought
I should be.

My outer shell clothed
in my insecurity.
I used this body
as a false sense of security.

Underneath the body
was a me that was weak.
The next person on the corner
would be skinnier than me.

Putting all my efforts into this shell,
my happiness was a
temporary hell.

In examining my fears,
I rediscovered an essential part of me:
my vulnerability...
It had been cut off from me.

Inside my body,
hidden to the world,
was my authenticity.
There lay my femininity.

A power in my bones,
my strength was my
vulnerability.

It was not weak.
It was the pure expression
of my femininity.
I learned to love
my emotionality,

I embraced this power.
I felt it overtake me
like a rush of water.
It washed over
the landscape of
my insecurity.

With this power enveloped
I began to nurture me.
From bubble baths,
hair, clothes, and make-up
to five-hour girl chats
with my female companions.

I embraced this strength.
My soul's desire:
to be a woman with grace.

Through this transformation,
so much about me
was changing.
My body was now just
a canvas for expressing
the vibrant, soulful woman
within me.

My outsides no longer
used to mask
my insecurity.

My intention had changed.
Now, when I went to decorate
I would ponder....
what clothes, colors,
styles, and scents
would most
authentically express
the light within me.
My outsides were now
just an outlet
for my soul
to express itself
as a woman who felt whole.

I found the inner feminine.
This essence in me
so strong in intuition.
A strong woman,
this part of me
full of passion and conviction.

The emotions...
they make me a woman.
I have to navigate them
like a sailor would the ocean.

My emotions,
like any powerful woman,
they oscillate like currents
pulled by the moon.

The power of
love and strength
I embraced.
They, as a woman,
would keep me safe.

How incredible
this coming of age.
I dance and I sing.
I exude a woman's being.

For my feminine essence,
I am so blessed.

In my transformation,
I was introduced
to that whisper within...
my intuition.

My intuition and fear,
close companions.
Their love for each other
so dear.

They are so much
the same,
and yet so different,
but they operate with
the same intention.

One is just louder
to human ears.
My intuition so quiet
I have to really listen
to hear.

With my spirit, consciousness,
Softness, and nurturance
I was learning so much
about the qualities
of being feminine.

My feelings of a new,
budding love for myself,
my identity grounding itself
into the strength of my femininity.

No longer a slave to
being what I thought
others wanted me to be:
quiet and meek with
no voice to speak.

This discovery – my vulnerability,
an essential part of being a woman.
I feel so free.

Being a woman,
a man could never teach me.
It had to be my own discovery.

I embrace me.

What a beautiful countryside you have passed. The sweetness of it and the rawness of its earth make it so deep and special. It is time get out and observe the culture of the Feminine. Men and women live here. This is not a culture of only female occupants. To be feminine is to be complex, to be emotionally available, to be interested in conversation, and to be into exploring the deeper and more metaphorical meanings in life. It is a place of dirt, of breath, of new life and the birth of new images and ideas. It is fertile with fresh ideas, creative adventures and imagination.

The people here are comfortable within the emotional world. They have nothing to hide and seem to walk in an unhurried manner. They are nurturing, life giving, sharing, and their signature way is soft, direct and pleasure oriented. It is another place of much duality, clarity, and patience. The inhabitants here know their inner worlds well, and they are sympathetic to the emotions of others. As you observe them, you need to be open to the depths that once frightened you as the people here are not afraid of their emotions. They will teach you of the ebb and flow of the life-death-life cycle, and you will learn here how to heal your broken bones. When you leave, you will understand any belief you had in being weak was of conditioned eye-sight. You will leave with love's embrace and with clarity on your own divinity.

Eye-Sight

Being a woman came with so much pressure. My eye-sight was I had to be perfect to be lovable. I felt I had to hold up a vision of perfection because the inside of me felt so imperfect. I put a tremendous amount of pressure on myself to be thin and beautiful. Focused on this, I did not work my emotional self. I felt I had control over my external appearance and very little control over my inner world. My outward appearance always got a response, but for a long time it was the wrong response. People liked me for the wrong reasons. I was sending the wrong message about myself. I was letting the world know I did not see myself as a person of value. As I started my internal journey, I saw the outward projection of me had a very small part to play in attraction, people liking me or not, and/or happiness. *I started to learn my attitude about myself was what attracted people or not.* When I feel good inside, I shine. I attract opportunities, friends, relationships, jobs, and positive events. Like attracts like.

I was gaining insight into the superficial world versus the emotional world. I began to see my inner richness was what people were drawn to. The outside of me became secondary. I do believe when you love yourself, you naturally want to take care of yourself physically, so your insides and outsides match. I have noticed when I am happy internally, I see myself completely differently in a mirror. I am kind to the vision of the me I see when I feel good. I am critical of my reflection when I am unhappy.

Inside, you have depths of love, beauty, passion, conviction, and purpose. When these qualities are nurtured, a vortex of energy surrounds you with love of self and love of life. This floods your life with all you need. I now celebrate my curves, my emotions, my depths...my femininity. It is the most powerful part of me. It is the difference between being centered-on-Self and Self-centered. To be centered-on-Self means to grow, to look within myself, to love myself, to put myself first, to honor myself and to speak my truth. To be centered-on-Self means my inner world is my treasure. To be self-centered means to stay focused on the superficial outer me.

When I am happy, I stand taller, walk slower, and I can feel that I feel good. If I feel good inside myself, I feel good about the outside of myself. It is all connected. I have also learned when you are happy, you are much sexier. A smile is one of the most attractive attributes you can possess. It has little to do with good looks. Attraction is an internal state of being. When I am happy, I am more composed, patient, aware, interested, and interesting. There is nothing more attractive than being interesting to the other. The more I grew, the more interesting I became. It was beautiful. The more you clear out all of the dark places in your life, the lighter your energy becomes.

Femininity is imbued with shedding. You shed each month, you bleed, you rest, regenerate, and renew. You are an emotional creature, an intuitive being, designed to renew each month. There is power in this. You can carry life, create life, nurture, and love. You are round, soft, voluptuous, and creative. You are also lunar. Your cycle follows the moon. Your moods, your psyche, and your body follow gravitational pulls. The feminine is powerful. You can multitask, commune, gather, and enrich. When you enrich the lives of those around you, you have come into your femininity in all its essence. To rise into the essence of being a woman is to embrace self-acceptance. There is nothing more beautiful than a happy, confident, deep woman.

In-Sight: The truer I am to myself, the more attractive I become

Reflections:

Until I had an eating disorder, I was ruled by my reactive emotions. I was highly sensitive, expressive, and intuitive about the workings of my world. But I was told I was too sensitive, too emotional, and said too much, upsetting others. My truth and my inability to pretend my life was normal were punished, killed, criticized, and shunned. My inner world was not allowed expression because people didn't like it. What that means is that people did not like me.

You are an expression of your emotions. The death of my emotional world occurred the day I decided to stop eating. When I stopped eating, I stopped feeling. All of my emotions became black and white. I projected everything onto good foods and bad foods. Food became the reflection of my emotions. If I ate good foods or didn't eat at all, I was a good person. If I ate bad foods, I was a bad person.

I felt better this way than I did being emotional. No one rejected me for being thin. No one rejected me for being perfect. No one rejected me for being pretty. The restriction of food made it possible to always be good. Further, I did not think at all about my family and its dysfunction, and I did not face daily rejection by trying to express my sadness and anger. It all went away when I stopped eating.

It was the death of my femininity. I was totally obsessed with the superficial. I was completely out of touch with my emotions, with the destruction I was doing to my body and mind through starving them. It felt good not to think so much. It felt good to have power over my food. It felt good not to feel sad all the time and to focus only on how many fat grams or calories I was eating. It felt good to be divorced from my anger, from yelling and screaming about the hypocrisy in my family. It all stopped when I got lost in not eating. I was no longer afraid. I was no longer too sensitive because I divorced myself from all these qualities. I even stopped having a menstrual cycle. I felt with this moment that I had won. I had gotten rid of my feminine.

I lived this way for a couple years. A teacher stepped in and put me on a program to gain weight. It took me seven years to mend the damage I had done to my body. The problem was that upon starting to eat again, I developed a fat/thin disorder. I went through many years after regaining my weight, feeling fat. As I grew as a person, the fat/thin disorder lightened up. I had to transition back into my emotional Self. I had to be open and flexible with being a woman. Being a woman became an interesting study for me. I had to define what a woman was, what my essence was.

In my studies I learned of the gorgeous complexity of being a woman. I studied femininity through two wonderful books: *Women Who Run with the Wolves* and *The Rent Tent.* As I researched my emotional world through my paper parents, I began to see beautiful as external *and* internal. I realized it was always going to be important for me to be thin, to enjoy fixing my hair, wearing clothes and make-up. But I needed to enjoy them for *me*, to let how I expressed my outer appearance be reflective of the inner feminine essence that was uniquely mine. It was no longer about having an image; it was about *being my own woman.*

I loved creating my femininity. I loved composure, emotionality, intuition, introspection, and softness. I love the creativity and duality of being a woman. I gave my Self the creativity to poeticize my presence. I loved that my emotions were round and voluptuous and sometimes moody. I loved that I was able to love without end. I loved that I learned to set boundaries for my Self like a mother would a child. I loved being pregnant with the new budding love of myself. I was out of the chaos of my body and into exploring my feminine energy. I began to love having my menstrual cycle and I paid more attention to the moon. My cycle follows the full moon. . I loved the idea of being earthy, raw, sexual, and communicative. This is all in the power of being feminine.

The feminine was something I had to define for myself. I had to figure out how to express what I was learning through my own idea of it. I came to love softness: the softness of my skin, of my curves, of my feelings, and my sensitive emotions. I learned to notice the softness of my voice, my walk, my style, and my life-approach. I realized the feminine has *needs* but was *not needy.* Femininity brought with it a sense of self-sufficiency. I also saw worry as essentially feminine.

I stopped punishing myself for worrying. It came with the hypervigilance of being a mother and nesting. It was part of my DNA. As long as worry was about Self-preservation and the safety of my environment, it was not coming from insecurity but rather instinct. Every woman, whether a mother or not, has the need to nest, nurture, and protect. For the first time, I was experiencing motherly feelings. I was mothering me. I was nurturing my Self in a way I had always needed to be nurtured, and I was becoming less needy. I was learning to meet my own emotional needs.

I stopped punishing my Self for being too sensitive. My sensitivity was my power. Sometimes it had a dark quality to it, but light always follows the dark. I had a unique ability to read people and instead of getting into self-doubt about my instincts, I let them guide me. It was at this time I took inventory on who I kept company with. I began to cut poisonous people out of my life. It was liberating. I was setting myself free of needy relationships which no longer served me. I was also embracing the relationships that felt meaningful to me. I had girlfriends who were as interested in growing as I was. We would gather and engage in growth promoting talks I found endlessly interesting. Each woman is feminine in her own unique way, and each woman expresses their own elements. There is not one feminine energy unique to all women, rather each woman is her own unique expression of the feminine.

Life Class Lesson:

Learning to love, accept and/or take care of your body and your image of your body is what will be analyzed in this lesson. Let's be real: nothing impacts your self-esteem more than not liking what you look like. When you are in conflict with your own skin, you are at war internally. Often the result is rigidly controlling your body in an abusive relationship to try and stay thin and beautiful or neglecting it all together. I have gone through every type of poor relationship with my body into finding my way to health. With health I have found peace. Health is about balance, and balance is what the mind, body, and spirit need. The body houses an internal emotional world and the health of this world is what essentially determines your outer beauty. My femininity is only complete if my inner and outer worlds are in sync. Femininity is that gentle, tender quality found in a woman's appearance, manner, and nature. A feminine woman gives the impression of mystery, depth, strength, delicateness, competence, intelligence, and worry. Let's find your feminine.

**Are you okay with your body?* Example: I am in a good partnership with my body. I say partnership because it is a two way relationship. If I am not good to my body, my body will not be good to me. I personally eat an alkaline diet, and I am committed to exercising weekly. Let us be honest that many of us feel inadequate when it comes to our looks, our bodies, and our physical flaws or ailments. We live in this body, and we cannot get away from it so why not treat it with the upmost respect. Poisoning the body cannot create good self-esteem. Starving the body is about trying to kill your Self. It is important to understand that happiness is an inner thing *and* an outer thing. I am all for changing your outer appearance if you feel it is not a true reflection of your inner.

I have come to accept that no matter how happy and content on the inside I am, if I am not happy with my body, my insides are no longer happy no matter how much I deny it. I am happiest when my outer world and inner world are in sync. For this reason, I am committed to my body nutritionally, with exercise and also with the acceptance that my body has its own right to be what it is genetically. I am in a constant balancing act maintaining the relationship; it has been one of the keys to my happiness. All things that bring us joy and reward are usually backed up by commitment and hard work. When we feel good about our bodies, we will naturally stand taller, have composure to our posture and we will attract more people, events and opportunities our way. Why be in a poor relationship with something you will never be able to get away from? You are stuck with your form so give it your all, and your life will change.

When I was anorexic, I was really happy. I was happy because I was committed to my body, and I liked the way that made me feel. I enjoyed putting thought, focus, and effort into being thin. I never found a diet that provided me happiness and structure like anorexia did until I was diagnosed with acidosis and learned I had to eat an alkaline lifestyle. In having a new rigid way to eat, I again began to feel happiness and control. Now, I have to eat for health and the benefits are being thin which is great, but I can also say eating this way gives me a sense of purpose.

My body naturally wants to be acid so to be alkaline I have to work hard and eat in a specific way. When I have a structure in my relationship with my body, I have happiness. Structure on all emotional levels was missing for me as a child, and I believe I found my first form of love and structure when I stopped eating. In the structure, there is freedom. When I feel positive physically, I feel positive emotionally, mentally and spiritually. Eating an alkaline diet, I feel smarter; I feel completely alive and with unstoppable energy. The lesson is *whatever we really commit to will bring us joy.*

**If you are not okay with your body, what do you not like about it and why?*

**Can you see the flaws you listed above as essentially feminine?*

**Do you allow yourself to love your body and to decorate yourself with your own unique style? Example:* Dressing myself, picking out my scent, and choosing my hair style are passions of mine. I enjoy having my own sense of style and using clothes, make-up, or other beauty regimens to express myself. It's creative, feminine, and wonderful. I love being a female for all these reasons. I can find endless ways to express myself through my style choices. I love putting things together. When someone says that is such a *Sherrie* outfit I know I have been successful in expressing my internal essence externally. There are so many ways in which we can communicate who we are and a really creative way to do that is to find your own style. I love that my style is not the same as others or even modeled directly after anyone else. I simply have found stores and places to shop that express exactly me. When I say this, I mean these stores fit how I feel emotionally. I walk in and I say *this feels like me.*

**How do you feel about your emotions?*

**Are you comfortable talking about them and working through them?*

**Do you have girlfriends you can count on to be vulnerable with?*

**Do you see feminine energy as powerful?*

**What about your sensitivities?* Example: I love my sensitivities because they make me empathic. They also let me know what and where my limits are. My sensitivities give me depth, they add color to my life, and they make me interesting. This is a gift. My sensitivities are what make me dynamic, complex, and different from others. My sensitivities are the answers behind my questions. As long as I am okay with them, what others think, feel, do, or say is more about their sensitivities than mine. I see them as things that I can draw upon creatively. I see them as motivational tools to dig deeper into myself, and I see them and accept them as essentially *me*. The self-acceptance aspect of my sensitivities is what drew me into a balanced relationship within myself. If I am balanced, then I can serve as a balancer for others. How wonderful to be able to use my sensitivities to do that!

**How are your sensitivities feminine?*

**Can you be okay being alone and counting on yourself to mother (nurture) yourself?*

**Do you have good girlfriends who can mother you?*

If you are a man:

**How do you feel about your more feminine qualities?*

**What do you find uniquely interesting about women that you admire?*

**What is the most feminine quality that you have?*

**Do you feel good about your body?*

**What about your clothing, hair, and makeup style?*

**How well do express your emotions?*

**How do you express yourself differently than the women you know?*

**What can you learn from women about expressing emotions?*

**What do you feel women can learn from you regarding emotions?*

Extra Credit Advantage:

Healing reading for home-work

Women Who Run with Wolves (Clarissa Pincola Estes): This is one of my all-time favorite books. I can't describe how deeply this book took me into my inner world or just how totally transformational it was for me. It took me to the depths of my pain and into the unlimited heights of my opportunities to be powerful. It is soft, nurturing, guiding, glowing, illuminating, raw, earthy, and essential. Clarissa touches upon the very nature of how women give themselves away, how women tend to put themselves second, and how women are creative, smart, resourceful and deeply psychological. This book continues live in my essence.

A Woman's Worth (Marianne Williamson): At the end of this book, on the very last page, I actually wrote "thank you." This is a simple, deep, great read about being female. It addresses the duality women live in, being soft on the outside but strong on the inside. I read a little, put it down, and feeling refreshed, read some more, put it down again and daydreamed. It was beautiful.

The Red Tent (Anita Diamant): This is a book I begged not to end. I actually had anticipation anxiety as I was finishing it. This is such an extraordinary book on the life of women. It is largely about nurturing, loving, being invisible, being visible, liberation, aloneness, togetherness, birth, sharing, sacrifice, letting go, life and death all wrapped within the psyche of the feminine. I was moved to tears and laughter.

Succulent Wild Woman (SARK): This book touches upon every aspect of being a woman from aging, to sex, to body parts, to the relationship we have with our bodies and the pride of being independent and strong, while also being vulnerable. The colorful and playful way in which it is written, along with the seriousness of the topics, made this book resonate with me and everyone I have gifted it to. This is another book you can open to any page and leave with a contemplation topic for the day. This book is inspirational, wild, fun, and deep. It shows by example the complexities of the feminine energy.

Differentiating Opportunity:

Suppose getting emotionally healthy created a natural response within you that attracted you to a healthier outer world lifestyle. If you were committed to being healthy physically, emotionally, mentally, and spiritually, how much deeper and enriching your life would be. Your sensitivities are exactly the elements of you that make you the unique being that you are. Love of self would change all the ways in which you carry yourself in the world; unlimited opportunities would flow in your direction. Suppose you lived your life in an unhurried manner, as if you had all the time for pleasure to come your way, and your posture communicated your self-esteem and your intelligence. Your femininity is the raw strength which carries you through life guided by intuition and creativity. Your worry is a strength.

The strength of the feminine allows you the ability to see the positive and the negative in all situations. Seeing all sides is a form of nurturing the truth. If the feminine within you allowed you to express your emotions with complete precision and detail providing a clear, efficient picture of any given situation, how much more power would you feel? The feminine allows you to consistently and specifically foresee which emotions and behaviors will arise in any given situation. The feminine allows you to experience and process a multitude of emotions at once. Imagine the power of embracing this part of you and allowing it to bring you unlimited success.

To differentiate, think about how you can be creative with your femininity. Focus on your posture. What do you want to communicate to the world with your posture? Laugh a lot. Find the joy in the life of the emotions. Cry it out. Break down. Get up again and keep moving. There is always something positive waiting to bump into you.

Your own needs must to be met in order to focus on someone else's need. As a woman, make it your responsibility to meet your needs. You know your needs better than anyone else, thus, you will know how to meet them. Communicate from a place where you have a dignity about yourself, and people will listen and hear what you have to say. No one wants to listen to an emotional child. It takes a certain level of maturity to listen well. Listening is feminine. To listen is to nurture, love and hear. *There is nothing more powerful than to nurture the growth of another.*

Coasting through
this memory
in the boat,
I feel empowered
and soulfully happy.

I close my eyes
as I lie back in the boat
to take in the me
that was then.
The part of her she embraced
was her feminine.

Opening my eyes,
I take in the scenery.
Everything around me
is voluptuous
with feminine energy.

The mountains
full and round like the female breast,
creating peaks and valleys
for the trees to rest.

The sky so deep,
the water so nurturing,
the colors so vibrant,
symbolic of feminine complexity.

The dirt on the banks
of the water
is the soul skin
of mother earth.
I realize I am her daughter.

Birthed through her beauty,
she gives life.
She is the light of
new beginnings.
Knowing her enlivens my feelings.

Gliding along
I feel so relaxed.
I become aware
I am so comfortable
lying back.

This boat, its surfaces not hard.
They are soft like a pillow,
like the catkins
of a mother willow.

So mesmerized by these feelings,
I do not open my eyes
to examine what this boat looks like.
So relaxed, I just continue
to glide.

I take in the
me that was then
into my soul.
I embrace my feminine.
The first part of my venture
in becoming a woman.

The me now knows
how important
this memory will be
on the rest of this life's journey
even beyond –
to the now that is me,
and to the future
of the me to be.

I feel movement underneath,
I sit up,
my consciousness
aware of what the
memory up ahead
will bring.

With excited anticipation,
such knowledge

the me then
was honing.

It was with this transformation to
becoming a woman
that the me then
would learn the
formula to a balanced life,
requiring her to embark on
the process of…

The land you are about to enter is the land of the Individuated Self. This is where you learn about love and relationships. The inhabitants here know of discernment. This is a good place. As you love your Self, you should naturally begin to see which relationships help you feel good in your life and which relationships serve to bring you down or away from Self-love. To have Self-love, you have to have people in your life who also reflect that back to you. When you do not feel good about yourself, you are not a good relationship chooser. As you develop more love for yourself, you have to take a deep look at how people make you feel. The more Self-love you have, the more independent a thinker you become, and this offers you objective clarity on how you are negatively or positively influenced by the people in your life. To make leaps and bounds in Self-love, you may have to separate from relationships to protect the relationship you have now developed within. As you observe this upcoming scene, take inventory on how your relationships impact you and allow this poem to give you in-sight on what to do with those who impact your life negatively.

Individuation

Separation,
so necessary for me.
I could no longer
tolerate the pain
of Disney.

In that place,
I have a script
and a character face.
I play the 'bad kid' role.
The one, who so long ago,
was the disgrace.

That role…
always available to me.
That was how they needed me to be.

With my fear understood,
and embraced in my womanhood,
I know inside I am
inherently good.

But Disney
wants to be right about me.
My changes they cannot
authentically see.

I still get filtered through
their old perception of me.
The 'bad kid' role,
I have no control.
When I don't react accordingly,
that is automatically
my label.

I can no longer fit in.
So, I am on the outside
looking in.
With this perspective,
I understand its operation.

Disney's fuel
is the gossip game.
With each other
talking bad about the other,
they are looking to blame.

Too much pain,
I had to individuate.

With my ice pick,
I went into each relationship
and cut out all the
backstabbing and gossip.

That meant...
I also had to stop
the drama.

With this individuation
I am free...
Yet,
I sometimes yearn
to fit into Disney
because it is my family.

But in fitting in,
I cannot be me.
Separation...
so necessary for me.

I keep all of my
relationships separate.
Outside of me and
the other person,
other relationships
are none of my business.

Without gossip,
there is actually room
for depth and something
authentic.

If Disney entices me,
I set boundaries.
I now have to be
my own stability.

I have to provide myself
my own good parenting
to protect the vulnerable one
that resides within me.

In this way,
I am starting to feel complete.
My individuation is
my gift to me.
It is the hard earned pearl
to come of this journey.

In its own way…

a sort of alchemy.

The individuated, who are natives to this land, bring an awe inspiring quality of clarity to those who visit them. This culture is all about cleanliness and emotional health. They have what is called selectivity, and this is what you will learn from them as you visit. To be discerning or selective, you will learn, is about being clear about who and what is healthy for your life and who and what is not. You will learn to see people for who they are rather than who you would like them to be.

This land is pure and does not allow in the drugs of hope or gossip. They will check you at the gates. As you exit the boat, leave hope and gossip behind. When you enter into a relationship in the hope that your partner will change or to be different, you are usually getting stuck in a poisonous relationship. When that person does not change, you get angry and begin to complain behind their backs, still all the while feeling they should change. As you sit with the people in this land and they educate you on discernment, you will learn to be aware of how you feel towards other people. If you feel badly towards somebody, then that is the Omen that that person may be a poison you need to rid your life of. You cannot have clear eye-sight as long as you are engaging in unhealthy relationships.

Eye-Sight

Individuation is the beginning of becoming a separate Self, an individualized Self. This was a powerful moment of my understanding. I had to become *me*, and that meant I had to begin to separate emotionally from all I had been through and also from patterns of behavior I had developed from my upbringing. I was ready to take a journey into my individuation by establishing personal/emotional boundaries. I had achieved much transformation but was still perceived, at least by family, as the bad kid. I embraced my growth and began to take all of my relationships to a one-on-one level. I got rid of relationships which did not benefit me. I began to see through the eye-sight of responsibility to my Self.

I cut out all the gossip and made each relationship about me and the other. I cleaned my relationships up, and like the phoenix, I rose out of that old perception of me. Many people in my life still live the old story. *But the only perception of me that matters is the perception I have of my Self.* It is here I have found freedom. Differentiating was offering me the opportunity to practice knowing who and what was correct for me and who and what was not. This allowed me to set the boundaries in my life I needed set. In setting boundaries, I was beginning the process of taking care of me. I was no longer invested in what others thought of me.

The only person that can change your life is you. Setting boundaries takes courage because people outside of you do not like them. Boundaries are a form of saying "no." Most people do not like to hear "no." If you have people invested in keeping you in the old story, and you begin to say no, expect some chaos. In time, the chaos ceases as the others see you are now in charge of your life and your decisions. They may not like it but eventually will have to adjust to it. You are treated by others at the level of respect and love you have for yourself. *Saying no is a powerful expression of Self-love.*

Sometimes, you have to love yourself enough to separate from those you *should* love. Separation does not necessarily mean a literal break. Yet, sometimes black and white separations are the only way. Your internal, emotional world is your guide, and it will guide you to the right decision in each relationship. Black and white splits are about letting go, releasing the other to be whomever they need to be without contempt. Each soul has to walk its path. As you let go, you are set free and blockages of emotional energy are released. With this release comes more freedom to be yourself. The more genuine you are, the more efficiently you will live life.

In-Sight: Who is in my life is the most important decision I can make. One wrong person can destroy my life.

Reflections:

By this time in my healing, I had begun to carve away at my childhood and past. I see things metaphorically, and I saw my family like Disneyland. Each person had a character-face and a ride they controlled. Each person wanted their ride to be better than everyone else's. The family was set up on competition and comparison, which created a minefield for gossip. The gossip in my family got so intense, it was unbearable. Everyone talked behind everyone else's back. This set up separation and division: one person couldn't be happy for another, one person was elevated above the other, and someone was always being picked on.

This was my entire life. It superseded my nuclear family. My grandmother and her sister were at war, and my mother and her sister were at war most of my life. The back stabbing was relentless. It was the gossip game held in the arena of verbal warfare. If I entered Disney, the rides, the music, and the drama would start. I would get eaten up and spit out every time. My family structure is still set up this way, and it always will be.

Gossip is the most evil form of communication because nothing is based in truth. Gossip is based on reaction, bullying, being right, and insecurity. The emotion that creates gossip is envy turned into jealousy. Envy is an inspirational emotion based on our wanting to be better individuals. If it is repressed, it turns into jealousy. Of all the emotions, jealousy is the most violent. Containing elements of rejection, low self-esteem, comparison, and lack, this emotion creates separation and division. *When jealousy is present, there is no room for love or being happy for another person and their success.*

When anyone said no, Disney blasted into full drama operation. It was a crazy-making, no-win environment, where emotional games, instead of truth, ran the operation. I did not want to be a part of this any longer. I wanted to be different and stop the patterns which were deeply ingrained in my psyche.

It was my mission to develop my own sense of my Self. My inner awareness of who I was and how I, as a unique individual, fit into the world became my creative mission. I was certain I did not want to recreate what I was raised in, or emulate those I was raised by on an emotional level. I wanted to experience myself as a person who had a place in the world, who had a right to express herself and the power to impact and participate in what happened to me. I wanted to develop an awareness of myself as a separate person, to know where my needs and feelings stopped and the needs and feelings of others began. When my life was imbued with gossip, I was carrying so much emotional baggage that I could not separate my own feelings from the gossip. I spent so much time defending myself against untruths I couldn't connect with my own truth.

The process of separating and individuating would take me years to accomplish. But I began by peeling back the layers of my Self, sifting through what was thought about me, what I was conditioned to think about myself, and what I so deeply believed about myself. The Self is the inner core of every person. This Self is unique and pure. It is the *you* that you know you have always been but could not previously express or reach. It maybe the *you* that no one approved of, so you kept it hidden. I have always known my inner core was there, and now was my time to go into that part of me and discover who that was.

In my discovery, what became clear were all the conditioned family roles: my brother, my hero; my mother, my savior or the victim; my father, the villain or hero, and me, the bad kid or scapegoat. As I began to separate, they all just became people to me, people I loved but did not necessarily like. I became okay with loving people and not liking them. I became okay with not pleasing them and not wanting to be around them. As I gained space and perspective, I became clear on how dysfunctional the family system. It was as if I were sitting on the fence watching Disney. It was painful, sad, enlightening, and freeing.

To leave everything you have ever known is to take a drastic jump into a relationship with the Self that may at first feel intensely lonely. I wasn't jumping ship in a complete way, and throughout my life, I would have to undo the habits and seductions of Disney, but I was starting. The new life I was pursuing would be seductive in its own right. The new life was uncharted, and would take many, many years and mistakes to perfect.

Life Class Lesson:

This class is going to examine the nuclear family and individuating. The nuclear family holds the old programming which created the poor eye-sight. Fear is the vehicle which takes you through the unknown as you individuate and find solid ground within yourself. Most families are poisoned and consumed with gossip. I have found I have needed different levels of separation from family members throughout my life. At one time or another, I have had complete separation from each of them as I was working to decondition their impact upon me. Some separations were short; others have been long term.

I have needed each one of the separations to help me decide which relationships I could enter back into and which ones I would need to stay out of. Individuating gave me clarity as to which aspects of people were unhealthy for me and which, I could love and accept. My nuclear relationships have been my greatest teachers. In these primary relationships, I learned who I wanted to be who I did not want to be. This helped me define myself.

**What is the poison of your nuclear family? Is it secret keeping, denial, gossip, enmeshment, superficial closeness, judgment, or competition?*

**Think about how this has impacted you. Can you see its impact on your sense of Self?*

**Are you self-conscious?*

**Do you care too much about what others think and say about you?* Example: This is an interesting question because really, who does not have some attachment to what other people think? We are all concerned with our reputations, how others perceive us, and what is said behind our backs. I do not think any of us is ever immune to these concerns, but it is important not to let what others think paralyze us and rule our lives. At times in my life, I did care too much about what others thought. I expended a lot of effort defending myself against what I perceived to be an untruth about me.

Here is what I have learned: people are going to think whatever they are going to think and no amount of my explaining or defending is likely to change their opinion. When I feel myself getting caught up in someone else's opinion of me, I work to narrow my focus onto myself and living my life. As I practice this, my outer concerns decrease. I realize I have *let go* to truly embody this. I have learned that when people start talking about me, I must be doing something *right*!

**Are you sensitive to criticism?*

**Do you please to fit in?*

**Do you really know who you are?*

**How would your life be if you decided to cut out the gossip?*

**How would you feel inside?*

**Gossip breeds a lack of trust; are you someone people can trust?*

Do you want to be someone people can trust? Example: Yes, and to do this I learned not to gossip. I learned to share my feelings directly or to keep silent. Trust cannot be developed if there is gossip. Even listening to someone else gossip, you are directly involved. So, even if you just allow yourself to be a receiver of the gossip, you are suffering the ramifications. It will block intimacy in the relationship you have with the person being gossiped about. We all gossip because it is human nature, but what you have to be clear about is, would you tell the subject to their face what you say behind their backs. Most people answer yes to this question but don't really mean it.

Being trustworthy is essential to all bonds if they are to be healthy. Staying out of gossip is hard work. It is important to learn when you need feedback about a relationship and when you are just gossiping. I always question myself if I am genuinely looking for feedback and support or if I am just venting in a harmful and nonproductive manner. I catch myself doing both. This is another thing I love about journaling because I can vent there and then ask for feedback later if I need it.

How would you go about being that?

Extra Credit Advantage:

Healing reading for home-work

Boundaries in Relationships (Charles L. Whitefield): This book was an incredible education for me because setting boundaries is difficult and often confusing. I learned about the structure of boundaries, ways to know where my boundaries are or should be, and why boundaries are mandatory. This book was written with love and sensitivity which made it a gentle guide into doing something very difficult.

Dealing with the Crazy-Makers in Your Life (David Hawkins): I read this book cover to cover and over and over. I have never felt more a sense of understanding or belonging. I had been around people who made me feel crazy most of my life and

I would get confused about whether I was crazy or them. In this book, I was able to get very clear on the character of the crazy-making people who plagued my life. I would not have near the skills to deal with these people without this information. Amazing read.

Emotional Vampires: Dealing With People Who Drain You Dry (Albert Bernstein): Amen to this book! It gave me direct advice and skills in how to deal with these types of people. I was able to understand why I left interactions with these people feeling exhausted, infuriated and defeated. There are so many people like this in the world, and they are incredibly tricky and hard to recognize until you have been lured in and become prey. The gift of these people is they have taught me self-control, silence and patience. This book is a necessary read. Oh, how it helped me.

Differentiating Opportunity:

Suppose you can use the primary relationships in your life to help you decide who you want to be within yourself and in your relationships. Imagine with this change how much more beautiful your life experiences would be. In order for you to fulfill your greatest potential, life will require that you differentiate. As you differentiate, you become your own unique personality and you feel your independence from others. If you can be independent from others, you can have true intimacy with them and rid your relationships of abusive tendencies.

In order to differentiate, you have to love your life more consciously and with more awareness. Choosing to do this, sets you free from living your life as prescribed by other people. You get to determine your values and live according to what you believe. *When you love your life, your life will love you back.*

As you take more responsibility for your choices, you can begin to escape the webs of your family ties and conditioned eye-sights that have led you astray. Imagine being no longer bound and a victim of your past. The most magical aspect to intimate relationships is you can learn exactly who you do not want to be. This is a great gift. Your don't-wants lead you in a new creative direction into Selfhood. Analyze all the poisonous relationships in your life and see if you either have or do not have those same traits. When you are around people who are poisonous for you, you often change who you are. How can you change yourself to be different? Knowing who you do not want to be is a creative opportunity to be more uniquely your Self. Examine what you do not like in others and be what feels like a better version of yourself. Be a person who is more authentic and grounded. Be someone you can love.

When you change your fundamental conditioned approach to life, those who conditioned you may not like it. They may not like the new you, they may cut you down, they may talk behind your back, and they may be angry with you. *If they are not happy about your changes, and they cannot see the beauty in the shifts you are making, then they do not have your best interest at heart.* When you change, you challenge the old story and your role in the drama. This threatens the whole system.

Some people are just going to fall away. People who once made you happy are no longer going to make you feel happy. Things that once inspired you will no longer inspire you. Events that once made you excited will feel uneventful. This is the process of differentiation. Things that used to fit, just no longer do. *To try and a squeeze yourself into people and places that are now too small for you is to shrink your soul.* It is time to give thanks for differentiation and rise to your next level of expansion. *You are now doing things in your own way.*

As I sit in the boat
and take this memory in,
I am drawn to a sensation
in my left hand.

I take my gaze away
from the memory.
I take my eyes toward
my hand.

As I open up my hand,
I begin to cry
as I see the light
of what is there
in my hand.
I am holding the most
magnificent pearl.

The tears streaming
down my face.
Being separate,
I am now truly safe.

All this hard work
has had such a
beautiful purpose.

I have built
the love of me…
Up ahead I see
my crystal palace.

I see it up in the distance.
It is shiny, pale pink,
and majestic.
It looks like a place
where love would live.

As the boat glides on, I am in tears.
I cannot believe I have made it here.

My crystal palace,
so symbolic in its singularity.
It represents a me that is...

You have reached the end of the journey at a land called Unique. You have traveled through the land of the Unexpected, of the Unbelievable. You visited Human Angels and Special People. You traveled through Shocking and Angry territory and spent some time with Despair and feeling Lost. You saw what war was like when you passed through Authority. You stopped to sight see with Dishonesty and observed the life of Secrets. You have walked the land of Surrender and used your Books to Find Meaning. You traveled on through the land of the Fearful and found amazing treasures there to help you evolve. You touched down in the Feminine and let your feet feel the rawness of your inner soil. You learned in the Feminine Land of the emotional and intuitive nature of your soul. You came through the land of the Individuated and saw the freedom and cleanliness of lives that do not take on poisonous relationships.

Now, at your final destination, take a deep breath before you visit with those who know they are Unique. Once you have Individuated, you have carved your Self away from your old conditioning. You have separated from who and what does not work for you to be happy. Now, you are Unique. You are each an original, and you each have a print to leave on this life. You are here to live your dreams, to be all that you can be and to do this you must continually love yourself and maintain being Unique. As you read, embrace all that you are in your complete magnificence. Romanticize your Self in all your shining divinity. You are here to touch people, to make a difference and to live out your own legend. Let your mind open to all it means to be you.

Unique

I am but just one cell
in this vast cosmic divinity.
I must embrace

all that is unique about me.
I have to do this
to fulfill my God given destiny.
My small part is necessary
for the cosmic working
of this "life thing."

No more trying to fit in.
In doing so, I lose
my unique expression.

I must use my five senses
to express outwardly
my soul within.

There is only one of me
in the sea of divinity.
That is why I have a body.
To be separate
allows for the unique
expression of my individuality.

On a higher level,
we are all connected.
Each of us having our own
unique purpose.

To be the same
is to be deaf, mute and lame.
Yet we are all a family.

Each person
has a contribution.
It is lightness or darkness.
Whatever he or she chooses.
In each moment, we have
to choose this.

We will all get caught up
in bad choices,
but the point is
to make your contribution
mostly lightness.

To be unique is to be free.
I have to embrace my power
to experience and express
this journey deep into
my singularity.

I chase this life at God-speed.
Each person's part
I realize is of equal necessity.

Each of us having a body
to use as the vessel
for our divine creativity.

I embrace this process.
Through it, I have built
the love of me...
brick by brick.

It is not about being narcissistic,
not for me.
For me, it's about embracing
this life's offerings.
On the other side of pain
is a glorious possibility.

Undock your boat
and embark on life's journey.
Know yourself
and give to this world
your unique being.

The cosmic divinity
pines for your beauty.

The people of the Unique have something precious. They are free. They feel free to be themselves. As you get out and watch them move, you see they hold their heads high. You can see their necks long and lean, their throats open, showing they are always ready to share and relate. They are no longer worried about what others think of them. Why? Because they love themselves, flaws and all.

They know themselves. When you love yourself, and you really know who you are, there is not much that can take you off center for too long. I want you to get out and be in your own full expression in this beautiful land where you know you are loved for being exactly who you are.

Eye-Sight

Experiencing, uncovering, discovering, and creating my uniqueness was and continues to be a beautiful process. I chipped away at a shell which was no longer suited for me. I did not need that armor anymore because I felt confident enough to be fully expressed as me. All the growth I did made me feel empowered and in control of my life. *Unique* shows I feel in control not with ego, but with a deep sense of self awareness. The experience of me has become soft and loving on the outside, but I am like steel on the inside. I have done enough work on myself to have a balance. It is liberating to feel my uniqueness. I feel I can now celebrate who I have become knowing deeply I have a huge and unique purpose in this world which can only be expressed by me.

I want you and every reader to be inspired to go through your darkness, clear those traumatic experiences, embrace them with understanding, and clean them up. The goal is living your full expression. You have throats because you are here to share with others who you are, how you love, how you work your way through life, and how you feel. You are unique. You are needed, you have purpose, and your gifts are important to the whole. You have something special to contribute

In-Sight: There is only one me. I am special.

Reflections:

Once I had really gotten to know myself through examining my journey, I began to feel a certain peace of mind. I could look back and realize that I would not change anything I had been through. I would keep my life just as it was. I did not want someone else's life or someone else's stuff. Resolving and coming to understand and accept my own deck of cards, I developed the feeling that I had arrived at a level of self-esteem that was good enough; I found my direction and was no longer being forced down life's river. Instead, I became a willing participant.

The journey through life is amazing. Looking back, I was able to see where my childhood left me with gaping holes in my self-esteem. Those gaping holes caused me to make many self-destructive decisions. However, each place of being lost opened up a place in me where I could commit and do some internal work. Even though I was like a piece of Swiss cheese I was able to take the journey. Your holes are crazy-making or they can make you interesting. If you leave your holes gaping and do nothing to fill them, you will remain a product of your old programming, but if you are inspired and curious about these holes and have an interest in how to fill them up, you will eventually become whole. *You will go from having holes to feeling whole.*

The journey of life has been full of pain, uncertainty, and fear. It has also been full of excitement, interest, opportunity, depth, and individual creation. The journey to gaining my self-esteem was rocky. I had to learn to withstand the discomfort of life's challenges. There were so many times along the way that I not only wanted to give up, but actually did give up. I experienced levels of frustration that I could not tolerate; many times, I felt like life was hopeless and a never ending series of battles. Sometimes, I didn't think I had it in me to fight each day, each minute, each second. I looked ahead and just felt tired. When life is dark, you cannot see. I have learned the only way to have sight in the dark is to have in-sight, sight from within. This sight within is what helped me along in my journey. One thing I never did was stop traveling. I may have taken rests along the way, but in spite of myself, I kept journeying down life's unpredictable flow.

In my journey, I felt hopeless, mostly about love and relationships. We are here to love and be loved, and I just couldn't seem to get that down. I was angry, hurt, afraid, and deeply insecure.

Yet, somehow, I just knew to hold on. The current stressor would pass and I would wait for the next one. This is how I lived for a really long time. As I was going through my pain, I wasn't able to find the meaning in it. All I really wanted to do was survive it. That is what I did.

The more mature I got, the more self-reflective I became. This self-reflection later led me to my healing. As I began my journey in Self-Reflection, I began to find significant people who would help me. Each person in my life played the exact right role for me to be exactly who I am, and for that, I am grateful. Some of the most painful experiences and relationships that I have had have led me to my unique self. By my nature, I have always been driven toward the depths of life. My deepest pains have turned out to be my greatest gifts. Those pains created scars in me that I can own and transform in any way in which I choose. I can either let my pain turn me off to life (and in moments it has) or I can make the choice to embrace my scars and learn to live an even bigger and better life in spite of them. Being Self-reflective is the path to living authentically.

I do not feel I was a *victim*. I simply understand I am *human*. Being human means that we will face challenges throughout life that seem insurmountable. You are not immune to the challenges. The other part of life is learning that nothing, absolutely nothing, is insurmountable. Each situation you successfully overcome, you become a more unique and expanded person. You find fulfillment and purpose in each challenge you successfully face and put to rest. You develop confidence as you allow your life challenges to carve out your uniqueness. Your life pains are your chisels creating and carving you into the unique human being that you are.

You are here to be individual. You may be similar to others, but you have the opportunity to put your own special touch on every ounce of life you come into contact with. You are not here by accident. You are supposed to be here. You have a unique purpose if you can commit to being the very best, differentiated Self you are supposed to be. Mind you, not everyone is interested in growth, not everyone is interested in being a unique Self. That is okay. That is the choice they choose and that is unique to them.

If you are a seeker and want the very most out of life, if you seek to deepen and ever-expand your purpose, you set yourself apart from others and realize that you pine for your own magnificence, you yearn for your success and independence and you realize you will be forever seeking and expanding your life with total commitment and focus. How beautiful is that! There is no end, so there is no let down when one goal is reached, there will always be another goal to seek, and the excitement in life will again begin. Being unique is about embracing that you are the only one who can add your flavor to life.

Life Class Lessons:

In this final class, you have arrived at individual uniqueness. In this lesson, you have the opportunity to embrace your unique, singular self. As you grow through your journey in life, you may feel you are weird or different from your families or peers because you do not take in the world through the same filters. You do not see things as they do. Because of this, you go through stages of feeling like you don't fit.

Because you are an individual, the goal is to fit within your Self. This places you on a quest to find yourself and create your own place in the world. You start to see the qualities of you that don't fit as something right about you rather than something wrong with you. You embrace your power to put your own unique twist on everything you do. As you meet new people with whom you fit, you still put your own creativity into the ways in which you approach life. This is how you cultivate and nurture your individuality. You incorporate your essence into everything, giving it the breath of personal touch.

I have found that my successes are what have set me apart from others. Successes come from the journey. Successes come from differentiating. Successes come from embracing who you are on all levels and searching always to continue to uplift and create your life.

What qualities have made you feel different, weird, awkward, and like you didn't fit?

How are those exact qualities gifts that you can nurture?

How do you see yourself as a unique individual? What makes you different than others?

In what areas of your life do you express your unique qualities the most? Example: I express myself uniquely everywhere, in my work, in my writing, and in my relationships. There is an inner part of me that is highly creative, equipped with my own language and expressive relationally. I have grown to love me and to be excited about who I am. I am fully inspired by all my insecurities in that I find them to serve as creative avenues for further growth leading to wellness. I don't always love the uncomfortable times in my life, but they are opportunities to creatively transcend. I embrace the unique take I have on my life's process and that I somehow find a way to live it through the comfortable and the uncomfortable. I love this about me.

What do people most compliment you on? Example: The compliment I get most often from patients, friends, family, and strangers is that people feel better after spending time with me. This is something I feel so grateful for as there is no better compliment than to know that just being me has a positive impact on others. This is a direct acknowledgement of my inner being and how the inner essence of me has a positive loving impact on the world. If you have had these types of compliments, you are on the right track. If you love your Self, you will have a positive impact on others. There will be nothing off-putting about you. Loving yourself will draw others to want to be around you, because being around you will make them feel good.

What do people most criticize about you? Example: The people, who genuinely love me, do not criticize me. They give me feedback. Feedback comes from love, and criticism comes from competition. I look at criticism as the idea that I am on the right path to being my own individual. The more people talk, the better of a job I must be doing. Those who have an agenda with me or a need to control my choices will get a heavy wall for a boundary. These people consider me disagreeable. Why settle to fit if I am naturally a miss-fit? I only need to be my own fit!

**When you wake up in the morning, do you immediately see yourself as unique and exciting?*

Extra Credit Advantage:

Healing reading for home-work

Soul Prints (Marc Gafni): There is no better book to help you define and see your uniqueness. This is a kabbalah based book, an invitation into your Self. I accepted my invitation, and I hope you do as well.

The Alchemist (Paulo Coelho): This is one of my favorite books of all time. This is about finding your personal legend. We are all here to create our own personal legends. This is all about uniqueness. When you are on the path to Self-discovery and you believe with all your heart in your dreams, the Universe will conspire for you to achieve them. This book also talks about Omens. It teaches of following the signs which are divinely given to help you achieve your personal legend.

Differentiating Opportunity:

Suppose the things about you that you used to regard as insecurities, issues, and deficits are really the things that successfully separate you from the crowd, and being separated from the crowd is where you thrive. As you embrace being individual, you will see this as your greatest blessing, rather than a curse. And the more individual you are, the more miracles are sure to come. Being individual means being cleansed. This means being cleansed of negative people, cleansed of persistent self-defeating thoughts, and cleansed of living out old programming.

You are given a unique set of life challenges to survive. No one human being has the exact same life experience as another.

What if these life challenges were given to you to assist you in creating your highest potential? The more individually you approach life, the more different your approach makes you from other people; it will help you to reach higher than you could have ever imagined reaching.

Unwanted fears and insecurities, which bother you, do not have to hold you back. Try looking at these fears and insecurities as assets and not liabilities. The goal is to accept yourself, insecurities fears and all. You are here to accept and embrace your individuality, your awkwardness, your difference. Suppose you can learn to use and incorporate all of who you are in ways that can serve you and allow you to become more differentiated. The more you differentiate, the more peace of mind you will have because you will be living authentically. To live out the false-self is to live a lie. If there is a lie, there can no peace of mind.

In living out of your differentiated best-self, you find ways to use your insecurities to fill your holes and find your ways. You are here to be the beautiful differentiated Self you are, and you are here to leave your print on your families, your friends, your communities, and the world. Give love, energy, light to the very core of how special you are. You are here to shine.

Sitting in the boat,
caressed by mother earth's breath,
her breeze is gently touching
beneath my hair
on the back of my neck.

I clutch tightly to my pearl
and I breathe in the fact
that for now…
I will stop here.

I feel so proud.
I have reclaimed
the most essential memories
of the me that was then.

Up ahead, I will soon get out,
and I will venture into
my crystal palace.

As the boat pulls toward the shore,
I feel a peace inside,
so much pride for the journey,
I have thus far survived.

The light and the darkness
are just a part of life.
They will put, from time to time,
some gray in my life.
But now I feel stable.
I can be flexible.
This life I will certainly get through.

At the shore, the boat has stopped.
I begin to step out.
I have the insight…
this boat I have never been without.

In fact, I have never taken
the time to examine
what this boat looks like.

As I step out,
I look back at the boat.
That happy sadness once again
pushing itself into my throat.
I realize I have never been alone.
What I had been traveling in
was not a boat at all.
My heart feels so full.

I start to weep.
This whole time
I have been traveling
in an angel's wing.

Its luscious white feathers,
so soft and tender,
they nurtured me
on this guided journey.

So consumed with my pain,
I did not see
something higher
has always been guiding me.
This whole journey
has been divinely inspired.

As I approach the door
of my crystal palace,
the wing remains docked.
It will be there forever.
Its whole purpose is to take me further.

As I open the door
and see the beauty within,
I am consumed with passion.
My heart feels alive.
I love this life.

My palace is not fully decorated,
but it is my home,
inside, lie the healing of my bones.
As I look around,

I am gazing at the
start of the interior decorating.

To my left I see…
the love of me on the mantle.
That decoration,
my most prized possession.

I need the love of me
placed in the center
to always have it as a reminder.

My other prized possession
is the love for my family.
Its presence in my palace
seeps through the smell of
the burning candles.

Of course, there are also
my hard worked for boundaries,
but with my parents
I love them completely.

As an adult, my view
is not so singular.
I know they both have suffered
their own fair share.

The aroma of their presence is so sweet.
For their love, all I have to do
is breathe…
Their love will fill me.

In my palace, there are also
my wonderful friends.
Each has their own decoration,
symbolic of their unique essence.
Each one of them is a God send.

They teach me so much.
For them, I am passionate.
So nice to look around this palace
and realize that I have them.

Over in the living room is
a picture of He and She.
In a living room long ago,
they told me
they would never stop loving me.

To this day they show up
for every defining moment I glean.
I celebrate them,
and they celebrate me.

Then, there is the picture
on the wall of Laynie...
She so helped me.

As I sit down in the softest chair
to take in all that life
has had to share.
I am wrapped in the blanket
of my spiritual angels.

They keep me warm
and help me to receive.
This way, they give me
something to give back
to humanity.
In this palace,
I sit and relax.
As I look around,
I feel so proud;
the thoughts in my head
as I begin to fall asleep
are thoughts only of peace.

I trust me.

For this journey I am so grateful.
I cannot wait to see
what is up ahead for me.

Thank you for inspiring me.

Until next time....

I will be chasing life at God speed.

Blessed be...
this amazing journey.

You have now landed upon the shore of your own individual island. You have built yourself slowly, deeply, and carefully a Crystal Palace for your new Self. You have reawakened your spirit from deep within. You have purpose and value as gained through the heroism of your travels. You have been through many places and visited different landscapes. You have collected in-sights as you watched your own personal movies unfold. You are as rare as the snowflake, and you are here to express your Uniqueness. You have a new experience up ahead inhabiting your own Crystal Palace (Self). This is where you continue to grow and evolve throughout the rest of your life. Before you enter, you must first take a deeper look at finding the meaning in your suffering. This will serve as the pathway to the door of your Crystal Palace. Once you travel this walkway, you will get the keys and enter. Here, you will learn life maintenance.

Part II

Finding the Meaning in the Suffering

As you have finished journey, it is time to make sense of your travels. You have answered many questions and have received direction on differentiating; now, you need to find the meaning in your suffering. Finding meaning is about finding the gifts and learning opportunities that your pain provides you. Inside the core of each painful experience is the light of growth and opportunity. How do you find the gifts in your pain? For starters, you have survived your pain, and knowing how to survive is a gift. Good survival skills will take you very far in life.

Learning to see that all parts of your life can be useful is another gift. I learned anxiety early. I love my anxiety in that it keeps me moving. The one cure I have found to my anxiety is movement. I see anxiety as a fuel. I use this fuel to drive me toward getting the work done of ten people, because success feels good. I would never be as successful as I am without this fuel.

This story was about a boat traveling down an unpredictable river. A river always flows between two banks. This is why the poetry was flowing down the middle of each page. It is symbolic of the river and also, the grey area. The grey area is where the pain is. The banks are solid ground, static, stable, and secure. The river is all about the unexpected, the unpredictable, and the uncertain. It is always in motion. When you are in the river you are in the middle where life really has no form you can count on. It is the space of the unknown. It is impossible to stop the river so you end up traveling whether you like it or not.

Growth and meaning come through surpassing your fears

When you are in the river, you are growing. The river is always in movement. It twists, turns, and has shifting speeds as you travel along it. Because it is always in motion, you are always bound for a new destination. *When you grow, you find new destinations*. Arriving at a new destination means you have grown to a new level. You get to stop and rest for a while as you practice living out the changes in your new level of life. Then life will change again. Back into the emotional river you go until you hit the next new level of learning and living. Life is continually shifting from solid ground, into the river, then onto new solid ground and back to the river.

Fear and change are the pressures which push the current of the river. Facing fears on the journey is the path to growth. If you are feeling, you are growing. It is the path to expanding your ideas about yourself and your life. Each new situation you face and each new issue you confront or solve in a new way gives you improved skills to be an ever fuller expression of who you are. The act of facing fears creates the building blocks for self-confidence and self-esteem. With a little courage and faith, you show yourself you can accomplish far beyond the limited views or eye-sights conditioned into your mind and automatic behaviors. Whenever you are in fear, you are in uncharted territory. You are breaking away from the old and creating the new. In between the old and the new is where fear thrives. Here, many turn back.

The old eye-sights cause you to fight the river. To fight the natural flow life takes is to shrink from your own evolution. The more you fight the river, the more friction your life will have. You may not want to travel the unknown to get to the newer, happier place. But when you stagnate, you become a collector of emotional baggage. If you resist change, you will acquire more and more of this baggage. You become more unconscious and emotionally out of control. The more baggage you collect, the more effort it will take to get you moving where life wants to take you. When you are weighed down by your emotional baggage, you end up letting your emotions control your life.

In this book, I use the metaphor of Bricks to represent the weight or gravity you accumulate with your resistance to life's flow. You become immovable. Your unresolved issues, old habits, ideas of being a victim, blame, resentment etc are what you become. If you are full of Bricks, you are too heavy to move and you never get in the river of transformation. Rather you go against the river, you do this by simply not moving. If you are not moving with life, you are moving against life.

Alchemy as your transformation process to deeper meaning

The goal is to turn your Bricks to Crystal. It is your life's purpose to transform. You are the alchemist of your own destiny. Alchemy is a magical, transformational process of metamorphosing an average or common substance, usually of little value, into a new more magnificent substance of much greater value. Turning your Bricks to Crystal is the process of looking for the meaning, learning, gifts, and opportunities in all of your suffering. When you are suffering over your own suffering, you are living out your conditioned eye-sight and missing out on the opportunities your suffering offers.

When you resist the movement of the emotional river, you stop your forward moving progress, and you halt your growth opportunities. If your attention is stuck on your suffering, you will continue to suffer. You become non-productive, immature, and an unconscious dead weight to yourself and the relationships you have with other people. Because emotional reactions are rather unconscious you end up at a great risk for allowing your emotions to control your decision making. To heal and find the gifts, you have to jump in the river.

Your darker times need to be utilized to find new avenues of inner strength. You have to remember that pain always occurs at the precipice between old and new thinking. Differentiating is about forcing yourself to think in new and more expanded ways. Can you imagine the possibilities that would come as a result of thinking in new ways and forcing yourself to change ingrained, dysfunctional behavioral patterns? Can you imagine pulling all the gifts out of the pain you have accrued? Can you see how useful these gifts are to you as you approach the newer places in your life? It is about developing and adapting to the circumstances of your life. Each new phase will require you to develop newer, more improved skills.

Each phase of the journey is stretching your idea of yourself beyond your comfort zone and into new levels of living, loving, and expressing.

Emotions are vehicles for meaning

The emotions are the vehicles that transform your life, so you may as well surrender to the river. Feelings are never wrong. When you are in the river, your emotions direct you to the places you need to heal. They are there to guide you. When you are traveling, you need to trust the emotions and their truths. If the feeling is true for you and it is an honest reflection of what you feel, then it is not wrong. Your emotions are your experienced truth of your circumstances.

How you take in the world is unique to you. Everyone has their perceptions and they can be as unique as a fingerprint. Your unique perceptions are what make you interesting and differentiated. It is silly that we try so hard to be the same as others. The very process dims how interesting we each really are.

What I love about the river of growth is there is so much to gain out of life, so much life to live, and so much opportunity for the grandest, most amazing living experience possible. It is all opportunity, the opportunity to undo what you learned about yourself and to decide who it is you choose to be. This big universe needs each and every person to play their part. When you see or know of someone who is actively not growing, understand that is their choice. It can be used to inspire you to continue on your own growth path because you will see how miserable not growing is from observing them. Many people love their misery; they can become addicted to it. Sometimes, misery has the payoff of negative attention.

You learn through self-awareness. To gain self-awareness, you need to give yourself permission to feel. You learn by examining why you did the things you did and why you felt the emotions you felt. It does not matter who agrees or disagrees with you. *You are the only person living your life, and your understanding of your Self makes you unique.* Forward moving people are alchemists, and they live in Palaces. These people have the ability to change and to deal with change. They accept the facts of their circumstances and then decide what do about them. They are aware that most in-sights come from the emotional ups and downs of life's flow.

Pain is opportunity

The greatest insight I ever received set me free: *Painful experiences do not happen to me, they happen for me*. Each painful experience in my past was perfectly designed for my evolvement. Each experience, if re-examined with new in-sight and openness, had a lesson for me. A beautiful lesson. Anything negative I learned about myself was a conditioned belief. You evolve and learn more from your emotional pain than any other life event, so jump in the river. If you can see nothing is happening to you but rather your experiences are happening for you then you have an opportunity to find the higher purpose in everything you experience in this lifetime. This absolves you of blame and from taking things personally. Everything that happens is in perfect design for your next level of living and loving. You cannot reach those next levels without challenge. When you are challenged, you are sloughing off the parts of you that are no longer effective.

Blame is the glue that keeps you stuck in your problems, in problematic relationships, locked into poor decision making, and out of the river of change. If you no longer connect in love, you often connect in blame. In order to absolve yourself of blame, it is important to look at the concepts of accountability and responsibility. The conditioners, who hurt you, are absolutely accountable for their actions. However, whatever hurt was caused now belongs to you and is part of what pushes the current of your river, and you will have to take responsibility for resolving the hurt within you. Blame sucks life dry of meaning and purpose.

The way you make your conditioners accountable for their transgressions is through setting firm boundaries on your relationships with them and or getting rid of the relationships all together. You have to decide if people treat you in accordance with your value. If not, then you need to use your boundaries to limit your emotional connection. Setting boundaries on relationships is how you take responsibility for your emotional world. If someone treats you poorly, you make them accountable by limiting or eliminating their closeness to you. In doing this, you offer yourself freedom, and you offer them an opportunity for growth through the loss of the relationship.

If you pull the word resent apart and you look at it as re-sent, you can see every time you blame someone, that blaming emotional energy is re-sent back to you. Chances are you are the victim of a victim. If your parents were parented to believe they were magnificent and lovable, they would have parented you the same way. Blame keeps you stuck looking in the rearview mirror, living the old story, and keeping it alive. This gives you poor life-eyesight; you cannot see the divinity in all of your experiences. When you cannot see, you bump into everything, get hurt, and repeat patterns. You are destined to live out these negative messages until you can correct them and clear them. Your negative experiences are instrumental in creating distorted eye-sight which leads to incorrect behavioral patterns. As you live out these patterns you create more pain to help you evolve. Some people continue to live the old story, and they do not evolve, but the evolving opportunity is always there.

Relationships will provide you things, opportunities, resources, time, and energy in direct proportion to the amount of love you have for yourself. As you grow and examine the relationships in your life, you will no longer want to keep the people who drain you. You will see your desires for better treatment grow. You begin to leave your source group to start new relationships which are more in line with your new sense of value. When you do not value yourself, you will choose people who do not value you either. How you let others treat you is the great mirror for how you feel about yourself. Relationship pain often starts you down the river of transformation. *Nothing can cause you more pain or more beneficial learning opportunities than your relationships.* You can't live with them, and you can't live without them. You can only accept, evolve, and learn from them. You have to appreciate every relationship experience because each offers you more than it takes if you are focused on healing.

If you do not like the way you are being treated, it is time to reflect on your current state of self-esteem and see what improvements in yourself can be made to attract more fulfilling relationships. You cannot change another person. When you are afraid to be alone, you often get high on the drug of hope and think with enough feedback and coercing, the other person will change and the relationship will be happy. Hope is a drug because it can keep you hooked to the wrong relationship patterns. As painful as it may be, you may have to love yourself enough to separate and face being alone. I have learned *you have to be the change you want to see in the other person.*

The gift of pain is it is as creative as you want it to be. Pain is such an inventive emotional state because when you are in it, you desire to get out of it. Pain creates the opportunity for movement. Pain drives the river of change. This is when you can get resourceful and begin to self-examine. Pain makes you question your life, the people in it, yourself, and your directions. All of these questions are new in-sights derived from living with incorrect eye-sight. These in-sights teach you what is correct for you and what is not correct for you, who is correct for you and who is not correct for you. Sometimes you may find even members of your family are not correct for you. These feelings/in-sights act as guides to the kind of life you want. Pain is your gift to let you know what you don't want. Remember, your don't-wants give you perfect vision for what you do want. This is how you assign meaning to your suffering.

Letting go

Your experiences are here to lead you to your next level of learning and evolving. Evolving often requires letting go: letting go of people, letting go of blame, and letting go of the picture of the life you think you should have. *When you let go, the perfect picture will appear.* In-sights at each new level give you new and improved eye-sight for decision making. You have the opportunity to continue pushing upward and onward to your next form of evolvement. It is life's way of helping you rise up to the next new form of who you are. You are always rising, rising up and up with each issue you uncover and with each forgiveness you embrace, with each humble moment, with each breakdown survived, and with each insight gained. You rise to expanded levels of life, love of Self and joy for life. You are unique. Embrace who you are uniquely and trust your process.

Self-acceptance is the one ingredient necessary for finding the meaning in suffering. Acceptance is your ability to embrace the facts and to decide what you want to do with those facts. When you can accept who you are, you become clear in those facts and you then have the ability to see what you might change. When you have self-acceptance, you can differentiate yourself from others. You have to be able to love yourself regardless of other people's opinions. You will learn that many of the things you have been conditioned to think about yourself are far from true. You will see that often, what others told you was wrong with you was simply an expression of your own individuality. Maybe, the quality being criticized is actually one of your most important gifts. What appears like rebelliousness to others may be your strength and courage.

Asking questions leads to meaning

In each part of the journey, I asked questions as part of life class lessons. The power of asking questions helps you to see where you developed your issues. It helps you see what aspects of your problems need more work. Asking questions allows you to understand where you are still held back. Asking questions is powerful. It is how you discover answers to your own questions. *You were conditioned to believe others know better than you do.* You have to learn that nobody knows you better than you know yourself. As you look inside yourself for meaning and validation, you see that all of your answers can come from within. You discover that you can answer your own questions efficiently and that your answers actually work in the world. You are able to develop self-confidence and trust in your own abilities to navigate your life with your own answers.

Fear and discomfort are necessary parts of the human experience because these emotions drive the river of transformation. When you are feeling, you are transforming. Fear is your most evolutionary response. All other negative emotions are born from fear, and they all serve as catalysts for change. When you are feeling feelings you do not want to feel, you become very clear on how you would like to feel and thus, you have instant direction and goals to strive for. What great knowledge!

What I want you to take from this personal story is that each of you is in this life doing essentially the same thing. You all live on the dualities of hope/pain, loneliness/togetherness, and kindness/meanness. Each part of your life is designed perfectly for you to learn, grow, and evolve. You can be victimized, yet, you do not have to be a victim. Survival and the inspiration to keep moving are the ingredients to a successful and rich life. Like the snowflake, you are a distinctive individual. You may not be in the same human process as other people, but you are a unique expression of the process. You are all doing life in your own way. Doing life in your own way gives your life a deeper importance and commitment. When you do things in your own way, you have to be responsible in your decision making.

As you search for meaning in your life, you must remember that you are not here on planet earth by accident. You have a reason to be here, a unique reason only you can fulfill. That reason becomes clearer as you use your pain to allow you to differentiate. Your pain is what chips away at your don't-wants in life so you can become clear about who you are and what you do want. This process gives you direction, and direction leads to the depths of meaning.

Looking back at the painful times in my life, I can see that the pain was momentary. It was up to me how long I chose to hang on to it. Usually when I am in pain, I am there due to fear or not feeling good enough (another form of fear). This fear is usually centered on a personal weakness or an insecurity that I did not feel was up to par for the situation at hand. When I felt put-to-the-test, I became afraid of failure or felt afraid of being vulnerable in some way that felt threatening to me.

Life is a series of classes

As an adult, I am now able to look at fear-provoking situations as life class pop quizzes. Life is offering me an opportunity to strengthen a current weakness. When I look at it like this, I feel like all I have to do is pass the quiz. There is no real harm or threat except not passing the quiz. If I don't pass this quiz, another similar and even more challenging quiz will be given to get me to face the fear I am afraid to face. Taking this perspective on life keeps it from feeling like a personal attack. It feels better to look at it as classes and quizzes designed to teach me I am stronger beyond what I could ever imagine. This also helps me clarify the exact insecurity being targeted, which gives me presence of mind and I can see how it would be useful to do what I am afraid to do to pass the quiz. All pop quizzing is designed for my growth and evolution. Each quiz successfully passed has given my life more direction, meaning, and significance.

Meaning in life does not come from changing anything in the external world. It comes from the changes you make in your internal worlds. The changes you make internally have the power to impact your experience of the external world. *You are here to create for yourself a genuinely empowered life.* All that power comes from the changes you make within. Finding meaning or the search for meaning is a choice. Many do not search. Many passively wait and feel entitled to have meaning given to them. They stay at the starting line of life with their bricks refusing movement.

Meaning in life comes through the emotions. Having meaning is the emotional experience of feeling fulfillment. You may be surprised to learn that work, hard work, is what creates meaning. The harder you work at something, the more meaningful the experience. Most certainly, the path to finding meaning in life is the ability to work through and define your feelings throughout life's journey.

If you allow yourself to feel life's pain, you will be able to deal with life's pain. If you can deal with it, then you can heal it. Healing brings more meaning into all of your experiences because with each healing you are more complete as a person. The more complete you are, the more meaning your life has.

When it comes to finding the meaning in your suffering, you may want to consider there are no real tragedies in life and no real victims. There are only opportunities to learn from what feels like a tragedy or to learn from a moment where you feel victimized. Underneath those feelings are opportunities to develop strengths you never knew you had. The gift of pain is that you often learn more from your pain than your joy. You cannot always have control over what happens to you in any given moment, event or relationship but you can learn to control your responses to whatever is happening. *There is a positive outcome waiting to be discovered in all adversity.*

The most beautiful aspect to finding meaning in your life is that each person's idea of meaningful has its own colors. Meaning is individualized. Certain basics for meaning are common to the human process but as you expand yourself, meaning becomes very individualized. This is why the process of differentiating is important; it is the process of becoming a complete, separate, and authentic person. Finding meaning is part of that process. In other words, there will be the struggle and desire to find the meaning in each day. You are likely to be most fulfilled and inspired when you are on your way towards a goal. You find meaning in the process or journey each day.

Have you ever noticed that once you achieve a sought-after goal, a certain depression, feeling of loss, or let down follows? The excitement of the journey gave the goal its meaning. This is why you are excited and re-inspired to reach even higher goals. This is what I love about personal growth: we are always on the journey that makes life interesting, exciting, emotional... and meaningful.

Time provides the space to find meaning

You are built with an innate sense that there is a higher purpose to all the chaos. You may feel that higher purpose to be obscure or unavailable when you are in the midst, but *time* will always bring you a sense of the higher purpose. Any and all tragedy seems to get better with time. Time gives you the opportunity to reflect back on your experiences. Sometimes, the further away from an emotionally charged circumstance you get, the deeper your learning and understanding become. Time brings with it emotional clarity and the ability to see the bigger picture. In the bigger picture, always resides the higher purpose of what occurred. When you are reactive, you are too flooded with emotions to analyze, and so this is the gift time provides you. As the heightened emotions subside and you regain your presence of mind, you can begin to find the meaning in the pain you experienced, and you can see all you learned as a result of it.

Time also provides another beautiful emotion: the emotion of gratitude. Yes, you can feel grateful for the pain you have endured. You can see that you would not be exactly who you are without the pain of your travels. Gratitude provides the opportunity to be inventive, creative, and courageous as you travel on. Gratitude gives your life the positive twist it needs. Gratitude offers meaning to your pain. *To stay in continued suffering is a choice. To work toward a meaningful life is a process.* Therefore, if you have started your healing process, be grateful. If you feel you are well along your way in your healing, then you can be thankful for all you have to share with others.

I believe it to be in your very nature to seek fulfillment. Gratification is not fulfillment. Gratification is an immature need that requires immediate short term attention in the now. When you are gratified in the short term, it quickly passes through, and you quickly need more gratification. Gratification is usually a demand requiring someone else's effort. Fulfillment, on the other hand, is the result of a long term process of personal growth and expansion. It is the reward for personal effort. When you differentiate, you are stepping onto the path of being fulfilled by becoming all you are capable of becoming. You will realize you have *opportunity* all throughout life provided by each and every experience you have.

Each opportunity affords you a chance to expand your capabilities which puts you in a true commitment to your journey. As you expand, you are open to new things. You no longer cower from the novelty of your journey. You see change as an opportunity to develop your potential and reach outside your comfort zone. This allows you to be creative, intuitive, imaginative, and ingenious in your life rather than staying stuck in your old suffering. When you are experiencing new things, you are growing. When you are feeling, you are growing. As you grow, you find new meaning and purpose for your life.

An internal life force energy drives you through life with an intelligence that is far beyond your limited human mind. Meaning comes through having faith in this life force intelligence. Faith is a requirement because this intelligence is obscure and indirect. *Patience often brings faith.* As I stated in the beginning of the book, patience is the ability to endure under difficult circumstances. If you are patient, you give yourself time which can open the door to cohesion, understanding, and meaning.

Be true to your Self

When you choose to find the meaning in your suffering, you are able to rid yourself of the humiliation and shame of being a false-self. The false-self dies, as you learn to be true to yourself. As Shakespeare says, "To thine own self be true." The more you examine your life, the more meaning you can discover in all of your challenges. You can begin to find peace of mind. When you have peace of mind, you minimize the stress and anxiety in your life and are filled with inner calm and serenity. When you access peace of mind, you can live with a sense of freedom.

Your challenges help you arrive at this more meaningful state in life. You have learned through your pain that you need to be flexible with life's inconveniences. You learn to eliminate feelings of jealousy as you differentiate and fall in love with your unique Self. You learn to forgive and to see your conditioners as human just like you. You stay away from negative conversations and people. You become so Self-assured that you no longer take everything personally, and you move through your emotions quickly.

When you are searching for meaning, you have to invest deeply in yourself and the process of your life. If you are not willing to make this investment, what does that say about how much value you assign to yourself and your life? Why would others want to invest in you, if you do not find the meaning in your life which gives it value? Any investment starts with the emotion of love. When you do anything from love, the finished product will always reflect it. If you love something, you will focus on it. If you love yourself and desire to find the meaning in your life, you will invest in yourself with commitment.

As you begin investing yourself and consider all you have accomplished thus far in your journey, take a minute to really look at all you have accomplished. When you can see what you have accomplished, you can also see what adjustments will be needed to keep you on track. *Most likely, you are overly focused on your mistakes. If you are to find the meaning in your suffering, you need to give equal attention to your accomplishments.* Just surviving a bout of being in the midst of a life challenge is an accomplishment. Give your Self credit! When you focus on your accomplishments and you find the meaning in your mistakes, they become necessary learning experiences. When you can do this you are able to stay positive in life and continue with your forward moving progress.

The destination is a clear sense of Self, which is exemplified by the structure of the Crystal Palace. The Palace is the Self you built along the river after travels that gave you form, structure and a strong identity. Life may take you in and out of tumultuous times, but once you have a solid Self, you have a Palace. When you arrive at your Palace, you are not finished traveling, but you have a place you can always come home to. You have a Self you can count on. You have given yourself everything you did not get as a child and have built your Crystal Palace.

As you approach all of life's pop-quizzes, challenges, and obstacles, you can go two ways. You can blame your outer circumstances, or you can go within and use your in-sight and creativity to find the meaning and larger purpose gifted by each challenge. If you can consciously put this effort into yourself and your life with passion and dedication, you are sure to develop significant resources and skills to help you carry out and illuminate your unique and individual purpose in life. As a result of this, you become a gift to the world. You become a person whose energy is full of richness, wisdom, and kindness. This will impact everyone, whose life you touch. This is the process of alchemy. It is time to enter your Palace.

Extra Credit Advantage:

Healing reading for home-work

A Man's Search for Meaning (Victor Frankl): This is a story about finding the meaning in suffering. I learned from this book that we are in fact compelled by our search for meaning in life. I learned that we have an incredible power within our choices to shape our minds and attitudes regarding everything we go through here on the life path. If we cannot find the meaning in our emotional pain, there are so many negative effects. The worst is giving up. I learned we need to see all our challenges as growth opportunities. People, who find the deeper meaning in their human existence, set themselves apart in that they are able to make their lives extraordinary.

The Alchemist (Paula Cohelo): This book is about living our lives with love and purpose. It shows that life really doesn't have to be that complicated. We are all unique and those, who embrace their uniqueness, do not give up on their dreams. It is very easy to settle and give up that dream. When that happens, we cannot enter or have a Palace. When we are committed to our dream and personal growth, the universe will conspire for us to achieve it. After all, this universe pines for our individual expressions of beauty and uniqueness. As we become individual and embraced in our uniqueness, the only place we need to look for our truth is within our Selves.

Tao Te Ching (Lao Tzu): I reference to this book daily. It is my manual for learning to just...Let Go.

Part III

Living what you have learned: The Interior of the Crystal Palace, A Uniqueness Operating System Designed for Self-Assembly

The Internal Operation:

At the end of the traveling story in this book, you arrive at the Crystal Palace. The journey, which took you to this destination, traveled through rough waters and undulating emotion. There were tumultuous experiences, loving experiences, experiences of deep betrayal, and awakening experiences. All along the way, you were able to ask questions, integrate answers, and look at new ways to use this information. It was inspiring to take it all in. This life is amazing.

Arriving at the Crystal Palace, is not a fairy tale ending where you live happily ever after. The remainder of the book will provide you clear direction in how to live here after. The whole point of learning is to change, to live what you learn. When you enter the Palace, you go within. It is reflective of your self-esteem and capabilities to date. When you go within, you transform. The internal operation of any business must be in working order for it to thrive and be successful, and the same applies to the business of your self-esteem. If the internal operations are in order and you have a step by step system to keep it progressing and growing, then your success is assured. Congratulations on making it this far.

Inside the Crystal Palace is the formula for Differentiating. Why is this important? It is important because differentiating is the defining process of a lifetime. It starts at birth, and it is supposed to flow all throughout life. In other words, it is the process of open-ended maturity/growth. It means you are in the consistent creation of becoming your own person. You are becoming an individual, who is a totally integrated and whole. You are driven toward experiencing your totality and full expression. In order to feel or experience this totality, you have to take care of yourself physically, emotionally, mentally, and spiritually. You need to have good physical health. You have the need to have an alive and active engagement with life. You need the resilience to be able to handle your stressors and set-backs. You need all of this to find happiness and significance.

This is why I say differentiating is the practice of a lifetime. Differentiating is the movement upon which life can rise and fall and ebb and flow. Encapsulated in this flow are your dreams, your aspirations, your ventures, your successes, your failures, and all of your faulty decisions that lead to collapses and crises – which are then followed by new beginnings. When one thing ends, another must begin. It is the movement of your life unfolding, phase after phase.

This process is all encompassing. It includes all of life's dualities. You cannot know success unless you know failure. Duality gives life a measurement system, so you can know all angles and ends of the human experience. The more you know, the more opportunity for growth and personal refinement you have. In this sense, you are always in the process of becoming your unique and authentic Self. You have to toss yourself onto the path of growth and live it bravely. You have to add courage and faith to your fears and struggles, and you have to fight the urge to shy away from uncertainty. In this way, you live a fulfilling life and not the unfulfilled lives of those who stay on the safe side with their Bricks.

As you differentiate, you are like a butterfly coming out of its cocoon. Aspects of you that were once discarded out of criticism or shame, now come forth to be acknowledged. Those aspects of you that were once fragmented, now desire unity. Those pieces of you that were once broken, now desire wholeness. Dreams and ideas which previously had no form now suddenly begin to take shape. As you differentiate, the miracles begin to happen in your life. These miracles are your self-created rewards. Your mistakes are your self-created learning opportunities. *Now, you can remember that on the other side of a mistake is a miracle.*

There is a voice deep within which is in constant conversation with you. This voice is the voice which holds your highest dreams and fantasies. If you are able to respond and interact with this voice, it will naturally place you on the path of differentiation. If you beat down, degrade and admonish the voice of your desires, you essentially get in the way of your progress toward inner totality. You get in your own way. This makes the movement of life rough and hard, as life becomes unhappy, difficult and debilitating. It puts you in conflict with this voice and its desire for development and maturity. When you get in your own way, you experience a lack of fulfillment, and yet, if the voice is strong enough, it will encourage you not to suffer over your own suffering and not to take a passive approach to life. You can go into personal therapy to alleviate suffering, look for appropriate books, or write out your feelings. As you take responsibility, you are back to listening and heeding this voice. You have re-evaluated and recalibrated. You now have direction, and you can get back to living the life of your deepest desires.

As you enter the Crystal Palace you are consciously entering taking responsibility for your life. When you take responsibility for your life, life is much more fulfilling. Arriving at the Crystal Palace means you have established enough of a sense of Self to give yourself a place in the world. You now have a place to do your internal work. For the moment, it is enough to go inside and rest. Welcome to the Crystal Palace. You are here to learn the magical process of self-assembly in a step by step fashion. How exciting! Open your door!

The Crystal Palace:

Cellar- *the place of humility*
Ground floor- *the place of maturity*
Second floor- *the place of letting go*
Third floor- *the place where everything makes sense*
Elevator and Stairs- *the process of evolution*

The Cellar: A New Beginning

The Crystal Palace is a transformational place. As you have been traveling down life's river in the *now* moment with each pain you suffered you were starting the alchemy of your Palace. As you enter, you have to start at the bottom in the Cellar and work your way up. First let's take the word Cellar apart to find its meaning. Within the word Cellar is the word cell. As biology would have it, each person starts off as a single living cell when the sperm and egg fuse. The cell then begins to rapidly divide almost instantly. Similarly, you are born pure, and you become rapidly divided from within due to your conditioning so you begin to change to maintain love. Your conditioners have a part in determining your function, just as the energy around the cell has the most impact on the cell's DNA function.

Loving Yourself at the Cellular Level

You go to your Cellar to reprogram yourself at the cellular level. You are here to get back to being your own single living cell in its purest form. You go the Cellar which is a small room (cell) designed for contemplation. The word, Cell is dualistic: You are here to return to your very beginning (that original cell), and you are placed in an enclosed space (a cell) in order to do so. The Cellar is like a chrysalis. The process of growth is to get back to that single living cell, your true self. The process is designed to help you find your uniqueness, to find your individuality, and to embrace who you are as a single entity. You are here to find who you are before all of your conditioning. Once you love and rediscover your singularity, your love will be expressed exponentially. You are here to start your deconditioning process so you can be reborn into your differentiated self.

For change to be permanent, it has be in every cell of your being. You need an enclosed space to block everything out to redefine your function, your purpose, and your energy. My work was started in the Cellar because the changes I was going to undergo would impact me down to every cell in my body. In the poem *Unique,* I talk about being just one cell in the vast cosmic divinity and how the Universe pines for my singular beauty. My whole person was in the process of change. I needed to be in an enclosed space to do this work safely. When you enter the Cellar you are being re-born, so to speak, into the new and into the vastness of the singularity of being your *own* person.

Cleansing by Looking at Your life in Review

The time of birth into a new beginning is always a critical one. Why? Because it involves movement, and movement can be dangerous. In other words, you cannot push the river, and if you make movement to stop the river, you put yourself in imminent danger. Life will naturally allow for the arrival of the new beginning. Movement that is timely and natural will lead you out of danger. When you are in the Cellar, you are in a cocoon-like state. You are enclosed, growing, developing, analyzing, understanding, changing form, and becoming more clearly defined in your own unique colors. The danger you are being led out of is the danger of continuing to live your old eye-sights. In this Chrysalis state wrapped warmly in your Cellar, you are going to change the very fibers of your being by looking at your life in review. It is both detoxing and redefining. You will use review to find and invent the new.

As you review, you will see that as young children you were not capable of experiencing anything beyond the now to make any kind of reflective sense of anything. You did not have a past, present, or future mind set. Pains turned to Bricks and as you kept moving, you began to put these pains out of your conscious mind; you did not fully heal them because you were being dragged through life into the next experience and into the next and the next. The Cellar contains all you were not able to deal with. You had the feelings, but not the time, mind-set or maturity to deal with them, so you threw them into the Cellar, shut the door and kept on living.

If you haven't already, you will come to see this past as a story. In the Cellar is the unexamined story. It was *experienced* but not *examined*. As you examine this story through self-reflection, you begin the process of emotional detoxification. The Cellar is where you start the process of restoration. Here, you begin building belief in yourself, in your life and in your spiritual beliefs. You start to develop trust in your Self. Love of the Self grows when trust is present. If you can develop trust within, you will approach other aspects of life with a newly focused sense of trust. Everything, however, must start with the very core of the individual.

When you begin your inner work, your problems are like bricks. They feel heavy and awkward. Bricks are tough to carry and hard to break. They are solid. With enough pain, you become hard. Typically, the Cellar is where you keep the stuff you do not want others to see. It is full of messy boxes, papers, and emotional noise. As you start your work, you are in the Cellar looking at a mountain of unorganized memories, emotions, heartbreaks, traumas, and tragedies. Here, you assume the position of *humility*, give yourself permission to feel, and get on your hands and knees to begin the examination of your emotional inventory.

Each brick in the Cellar has a box it belongs in. The first part of healing is to get all the right bricks in all the correct boxes. This is called emotional organizing. This is what writing this book was like for me. I organized many of my memories, my emotions, and broken pieces. Once something is in its place, you have the opportunity to examine it. When things are all over the place, some are seen, others are hidden or misplaced and some get so covered up you can hardly remember them. It can be hard, arduous, exhausting work to get organized! But, it is work worth doing. The more you organize the pieces of yourself, the more insightful you become.

Our time in the Cellar is very emotional. Remember at the beginning of the journey, we packed *permission to feel.* It is time to use this concept. When we are in the Cellar, we have to honor what we feel. Healing takes time. Lessons are difficult to learn and old programming hard to decondition. There is a lot of clutter. It's emotionally painful, because we are in the habit of not dealing with our pain. We have been in the habit of avoiding what we feel. When we come to this place we are faced with the reality of all we have not dealt with. This can be a daunting emotional experience. There is a lot of chaos to cleanse.

Working through resistance

As we first begin this work, and see all we need to clear, we may experience strong feelings of resistance. But the only way out *is* through. Resistance is an important emotion all unto itself, and I encourage you to experience it. It can hold you back in life if you hang onto it too tightly and yet it shows you where you are hung up and not moving. Resistance is meant to pass through. In other words, it takes you to the next level of healing. Resistance is like a door that is shut, and you need to find the key. Working through all your emotions is what breaks through your barriers and mental blocks so you can start your inner work.

It is your task to remain gentle with yourself, when you feel your emotions, knowing that all the information you need in order to heal has, for one, already been survived and two, is scattered about in front of you. Nothing is missing. It is not all put together, but it is all there, waiting to be put together. It will always wait. The objective is to start. Many never start. This is a time of the fresh start, and absolutely all you need to heal is available. This is a time of learning to be open and to no longer shut your eyes and grimace at the task at hand. It is a time to find the inspiration from within and clear your life of all unnecessary baggage. Remember to pull out the *Open Mind* you brought along at the beginning and repeat to yourself "I do not have to be *right* I have to be *open* in order to heal."

Willingness was another concept on your traveling list, and it never applies more than in the Cellar. Remember willingness is the signature fuel behind all growth. You are designed to expand yourself all throughout life to newer and newer levels of your potential. Willingness takes effort and commitment. If this is applied to any task, you are sure to succeed. *Permission to feel*, check, *Open Mind*, check, *Willingness*, check. Now, let us start examining all these broken pieces lovingly, gently, objectively and intelligently.

Putting yourself back together

The Cellar is your place to start remembering or re-membering (putting your cell or your Self back together), but you are remembering with a vision that is self-reflective. As I personally went through all my strewn papers, visual pictures, auditory memories, I re-experienced all the maimed parts of me – the parts of me I threw in the Cellar out of shame, out of not wanting to look, out of wanting to avoid pain, out of the simple need to survive. I also experienced the positive memories which gave me strength and resilience along my way. These are equally important as these are strengths to hold onto and to continue to cultivate.

The memories that will surface will be tragedies, amazing moments, loving moments, hateful moments…anything and everything that stands out as defining *who you are*. You can observe and understand the experience as if you were watching a movie. As an observer, you can clearly see the role each person played in your dramas, including yourself. The role you played is the most important one, because it is the only one you have any control over changing. This helps illuminate you with understanding. *Understanding precedes meaning*. Once you can find the meaning in all you have been through, you can create new images of who you would like to become.

The lasting objective is to see the divinity in all you have lived through. You can start to see that each experience was meaningful and necessary for you to become the highest version of who you would like to be. It is a place of truth. Therefore as you self-reflect, you will not only view and understand your conditioners but you will also be exposed to all of your weaker places. It is in the vulnerable places where your growth opportunities reside. These become your in-sights. You may have had your pain, but you also played a role in that pain. For instance, if you felt victimized, you may have learned to be a victim. If you learned you were bad, you may have become bad. These are the sweet vulnerabilities you can take responsibility for now and transform them.

As you sift through all the memories, you will start to see patterns of behavior created out of your rapidly dividing Self which started way back at your innocence. You will start to see the truth through all the distortion. When you are examining, you are taking a deep look at the truth. You get to see who you are, how you came to be that way and how you have hung onto a distortion as truth. *Any belief in being substandard is not a truth, it is a distortion.* You also receive the gift of understanding that your conditioners were probably doing the best they could with the knowledge and resources they had at that time. It doesn't mean it was correct, it simply makes them human. If they are human, then you do not need to hold them to blame. You can simply let them be human. In all honesty, I could not have raised two kids in my early twenties, when my parents raised me.

You will probably find that your parents did not receive the kind of love and nurturing they needed from their own parents. My parents never had it to give it. You have to use the *open mind* you packed in preparation for this journey to see that not all that happened to you was coming from a purposeful place but rather from an unconscious place. To get to these moments of clarity takes time and effort.

My Cellar was full of haunting old tears, intense anxieties, and horrible feelings. I could feel all the sadness I was never able to have validated, all the abandonments, the feelings of not being good enough, every fear that had turned to panic because my fears were not seen as real. I could feel all of the anger I had, all the times I said "no thank you," and I was not respected. I could feel how my anger had turned to rage. I could feel all the unrequited love I had to repress, and all the jealousy I had, as my envy had turned to jealousy out of never feeling good enough. It was all there in front of me in my Cellar. I sat on my hands and knees and looked at each piece of me and found the appropriate place for it to reside. I was removing blame and adding acceptance in order to organize my emotional traumas.

<u>Seeing the good</u>

My Cellar was also equipped with my moments of brilliance, but what I notice about my happy times is the boxes are nicely organized. I can feel them when I glance through the boxes and I smile as I see myself having those defining moments. Re-living those memories is inspiring to me and they fill me with hope. I can feel love when I look at these boxes because they are peaceful, in place, and solid. Looking in these boxes offers me a short rest in my review of my past.

I have boxes of pure joy, full of memories like the freedom of riding my bike. I have boxes of defining moments like attaining my Ph. D. or landing my first triple jump ice-skating. I have boxes of digging deep and succeeding when I thought I couldn't (this is my told-you-so box) and I have boxes full of social laughter, friends, and good family times. I even have a box of trust and faith. All of these boxes are full of love, my contentment with my Self, being proud of my Self, and feeling love for my Self. It is only my pain that is all over the floor in an unorganized mess. Why? *Pain is unsettling, and love is organizing.* You start your Self-love in the Cellar beginning with the detoxing of your single cell.

Doing my inventory was a process I can honestly say made me acutely aware of who I was as a unique emotional being. It also made me acutely aware of the damage and which parts of my singular cell would need transformation. I decided to take my time with each broken piece. With each piece, I was able to feel the emotions I needed to feel back then. I could feel it in the now, start the release process and put it in a place. Each broken piece of you has its own place in your identity. The organizing of the boxes is the development of the identity which makes you unique and different from those who raised you.

Each broken piece is connected to a memory. Each memory is like a mini-series and it is heavy with your Bricks. When you are in the Cellar you get to watch each mini-series as an audience member. Just like any member of an audience, the show you are watching can evoke powerful emotions: the tenderness of sadness, the fire of rage, and the ache of loneliness. The positive thing is these are your already survived memories. Because they have been survived, they can be watched with separation and perspective. This leads to the awareness of how these memories made you who you are. You get to view yourself from a distance. This is how you gain in-sight. You can, with perspective, see what you needed and what you did not get. You can see, in review, what you could have done differently, or how you were too beaten down to do anything differently. You can also see what parts of you are now are still broken like the person you were then. You can understand what parts of you currently still need work. You can see where you are still lugging your past around in your current belief system. All of this takes time.

Healing has its own timing

You cannot rush healing. Healing has its own flow and timing. When you are in the Cellar, you are on a different type of time. It is *spiritual time or inward time*. You will stay in the healing process until you heal. You will stay in your chrysalis-like state safely within your Cellar. You will know you are healing, when you begin to feel better and lighter. Every broken piece you clear is adding more love to your relationship with your Self. You are re-membering or self-assembling. When you first get thrust onto *healing's time*, you can feel worse than ever, partly because you are resisting the time it will take to heal. You can feel a loss of control because you do not get to determine how long you will be in the Cellar. There is a higher purpose to this, of course. *The purpose is to learn patience.* You cannot be successful on subsequent floors of the Crystal Palace, unless you have cultivated patience.

You will find you are the most content, when your heart and commitment are genuine and when you know what patience is and can still be patient. When you have been placed on *healing's time*, you learn that you must allow each step to take place in its own time. Patience is about fortitude and endurance to withstand what is uncomfortable without acting out in a negative way. Patience is the practice of perseverance. This is where you learn the difference between gratification and fulfillment. Gratification is having a pleasure or need met in the moment. Fulfillment is the longer path to lasting growth. The beginnings of fulfillment start in the Cellar. So, take your time, and trust your healing process. You are in the throes of beginning the new.

As you cultivate patience, it is worth examining how patience and frustration are closely related. These are great emotions to experience. The emotion of frustration can drive a cluttered mind to quit. If you want to love yourself, you can never quit. You were quit on by your conditioners, so you do not want to repeat that pattern. If you quit on yourself and your healing process, you abandon yourself. When you are frustrated, you are on your own agenda. When you are patient, you are on *healing's* agenda. When you have patience, you can see the whole picture. It will be a new art form to practice patience, but you have *healing's time* to give you whatever time you need to get it right. In the Cellar, you need to learn to use your frustration as fuel. There is a great energy that comes with frustration. If channeled correctly, it can keep you motivated to find solutions, and there are always solutions.

As you sit in your Cellar, make sure you take time to breathe. Cellars tend to be dark, without windows and underground. *Breathing helps you to integrate*. Each Cell needs oxygen to survive so breathe into the integration of all you are accomplishing. Integration is a process which needs love and time. Constructing a Self is the most important job you will do in this life. It is the only process that really matters.

Each mini-series has a life class lesson. Life class lessons provoke questions. One thing I know for sure about the inner world is if you ask it a question, it will formulate a response. This helps you avoid being the victim of your circumstances. You may have been victimized, but being a victim is a chronic state which does not promote healing. It is here in the safety of the Cellar, where you can transform your life and start the foundation of your Crystal Palace. The foundation is the most important part of any structure, because it is what stabilizes the rest. So, you have to take your time, do your inventory, and lift the bricks. There is much to learn at this stage.

Each mini-series holds a message of truth, the pearl inside the clam. What you will learn from each mini-series is *all you have ever really needed was love*. My parents needed it from their parents, and I needed it from them. The truth is you need to find love and stability from within. You cannot ever fully count on people for love, no matter who they are. You have to go within. All of your pain serves to take you within yourself, so you can develop love from your own control center, yourself. The Cellar is reflective of being within. It is the core part of the structure. When you are in the Cellar, you are converging with your core wounds. This is why you need the permission to feel. You are here to bond and develop a loving and accountable relationship within yourself. This all starts with looking at the truth. The truth is the best cleanser.

The Cellar, once it is cleansed and organized, will need a few things. Here is what mine looks like: I have a wall full of my boxes organized and in place. I have a throw carpet in the middle of the room with a soft and comfortable couch to rest on. Next to my couch is a small table with a lamp, my journal, and a pen. Draped over the back of the couch is a cozy blanket. Right next to the couch on the floor is a basket. You may ask why all this is there. After all, everything is packed up and organized. Oh, if it were only that simple. You will be in a process of healing and evolving your entire life because current day abandonments/rejection will trigger all other abandonments/rejections. When this occurs, the abandonment box will fall off the shelf and land in a heap on the floor waiting for you to come and reorganize it again. To reorganize and assimilate the current emotions, you will need to write and evolve your way through the now-issue as it triggers all the feelings of the many mini-series in that box. This is just how it works.

Whatever feeling arises as you examine all the materials in front of you, I want you to go to your couch and get out your journal. I personally write down the lesson each broken piece has to teach me. When I write, I contact the more evolved part of me, and let it guide me to take care of the feelings associated with each memory I review. In this way, I keep notes and document every detail of my journey. It is another way of making each memory real and another way to affirm the emotional me that was then. If I am able to be empathic with myself, analyze what I have been through with clarity, then I am on my way to Self-love. Many people who travel the world document their travels. I suggest you document your inner travels as you go through your darkness. This way you can always find your way out.

Getting to know yourself

I want you to write about yourself and all that you are learning as if you are the most *interesting* study. What a shift to transfer from feeling substandard into feeling *interesting*. You are all *interesting*, because you are all singular and unique. When you can find yourself interesting, you will begin to feel human again. So, take an invested interest in yourself and express that in your journal. Allow whatever feelings arise to express themselves by releasing them in written form. In this way, you solidify what you feel, your emotions begin to organize themselves, you are giving them form by writing, you are engaging in internal dialogue with your Self, and the intensity of what you are feeling will decrease because as you write, things begin to settle and make sense. Now breathe. At the end of the day, it will all fall into place. Writing gives us this advantage. This is why I strongly suggested you bring a journal on this journey.

This kind of writing will illuminate the negative patterns you have had, and once they have been illuminated, you have new in-sight. All the destructive patterns are your areas of focus and transformation. This is where you have control, because you can take full responsibility and transform them into healthier patterns. You may not know what that new pattern looks like, but you know you need to establish a new one. It is all about getting organized, taking the pieces of yourself and letting them find their place.

As you organized your Cellar, brick by brick, a staircase was built leading to the ground floor of your Crystal Palace. You built yourself a staircase out of your pain. You evolved in a step by step fashion. With each step, you built one more step out of your pain. When you grow, you rise to a new level. The stairs are there to take you up. When you are ready, you will rise step by step to the Ground Floor, knowing exactly what your pieces are and what you are made of. You will see how you were living out the beliefs of your conditioners and how poor eye-sight was misdirecting your life. In rising from the Cellar, you are coming up with in-sights (answers from within).

Traveling the river of my story is exactly what Cellar work looks like visually. It is like watching a movie. Each poem was an experienced but not examined mini-series. Each was a part of me, which needed integration, and each poem offered me an in-sight. I would like for you, my wonderful reader, to make a list of the unhealed Cellar memories that have impacted you and created your core wounds. Take your time, as you create this list. I want you to be sure that you do not miss anything. Each memory will contain an in-sight necessary for your growth on subsequent floors. Remember, you can only gain your in-sights by doing your Cellar work. You are in the Cellar to get reconnected with your divine singularity. You are here to experience your own, individualized single Cell. You are in the Cellar to learn humility. You have to surrender to your pain in order to gain the necessary in-sights.

In the Cellar, you have gathered in-sights, and you have now placed them in your in-sight basket next to your couch. They are outside of you in the basket because at the moment they are conceptual. Here is a list of the in-sights gathered throughout your journey:

**My reactions to the world and relationships are based upon conditioned beliefs which have nothing to do with me.*

**Each time I am people pleasing I am giving a little piece of me away.*

**A child's life needs form and structure*

**We all feel emotions the same way. The way I feel pain and loss is the same way another feels pain and loss. When we can connect in our pain we feel seen*

**Self-confidence is nurtured through mutually beneficial relationships.*

**If I am a false-self, then I am not my Self. I become false to fit.*

**Each insecurity has an evolving purpose. They are not meant to go away; they are meant to lead the way into healing.*

**We develop disorders out of our emotions. At the core of any disorder is the need for control.*

**It is okay to need help.*

**I am lovable enough to be chosen*

**I am at my best when in action. Always look forward*

**My answers live in my body*

**The truth can hurt*

**It is hard to let go*

**I am not by myself, I am with my Self*

**Everything I need to learn is available in information. I have paper parents.*

**Fear is our most evolutionary response. It is designed to fuel growth.*

**The truer I am to my Self, the more attractive I become.*

**Who is in my life is the most important decision I can make. One wrong person can destroy my life.*

**There is only one of me. I am special.*

When you get to the Ground Floor you will take these in-sights and begin to fill in your empty spaces and make them a part of your whole. As you give up old beliefs about yourself, you have to replace them with something new. In order to replace old beliefs, you have to release them, and let them be in the Cellar. You are now ready to move up, be receptive, and rise to the Ground Floor. You have gathered new information in your healing time to replace the old programming. You are at the precipice of the new. In your time in the Cellar, you have begun your change at the level of the Cell. Now, you need to spread your wings; it is time to learn to fly.

Extra Credit Advantage:

Cellar reading for home-work

Yesterday I Cried (Iyanla Vanzant): This is Iyanla's personal story of gathering her life and her identity. This was inspiring for me when I was first in my Cellar, because it was all very confusing and overwhelming emotionally. Reading other people's stories can serve as guides through our own dark times. If they can make it, so can we. They let us know, whether their struggles are the same as ours or not that we all struggle. The struggle and getting through it give us the model to follow.

A Million Little Pieces (James Frye): One of my favorite reads, this is about a man who is an addict, but is also trying to get his life together in a functional way. The message I took from this book is we can overcome anything if we can learn to *Hold On*. When you're in the Cellar you just need to Hold On and do your work. The pain will pass.

Emotional Equations (Chip Conley): This is a logical, grounded, linear book based on understanding the mechanics of all that we feel. If there is any one book to help you organize your boxes, it is this. It will organize all your feelings and help you understand them as well. This book is the greatest emotional education around. The understandings you receive from this book need to go in your in-sight basket, as they will be used upstairs.

Radical Forgiveness: A Revolutionary Five-Stage Process to Heal Relationships, Let Go of Anger and Blame, Find Peace in Any Situation (Colin Tippin): The Cellar is all about learning to understand forgiveness. This book makes the concept of forgiveness something doable and not in the way you would think. It lets you know that everything in your life has happened perfectly. It helped me to learn to let go and move forward without taking things personal.

Ground Floor: Getting Grounded

The Ground Floor is the space created to practice seeing yourself as worthy, smart, valuable, and lovable. You can practice rising as you embrace all the expansive changes you have made at the very core of your being. Your very fibers have already started the change; now it is time to learn to fly. This is the next phase of integration as you have successfully passed through gestation. On the Ground Floor, you begin the process of actively and intentionally dividing your Cell into whatever you would like it to be. Now, your function is determined solely from within. We prepared the soil in your Cellar, and it is here on the Ground Floor you become fertile, creative, expressive, and inventive with your singularity. You must cultivate and nurture your growth process with care. The labors of the Cellar had a long season so getting Grounded is a sure sign of your impending success.

The Ground Floor is the place where you become *Grounded*. In the Cellar, you were able to separate how you learned to see your Self through the eyes of your conditioners and how you would like to see yourself. In the Cellar, you were illuminated by your own in-sights as you reviewed how you came to be. Now, you have new thoughts about yourself. You have a more mature perception. The feelings have been released, lessons examined, broken pieces put in a safe place, and a robust understanding has developed.

The Ground Floor is a place of experimentation. Here, you take your first steps using your new in-sights. Bring your *open mind* to the Ground Floor as this is where all the change work happens. Also, bring your *willingness*, an essential ingredient to trying new things. Sometimes, the Ground Floor can be a struggle between slipping into old programming and staying current with our new in-sights. It can feel like a one step forward, one step backward process as you ground yourself. What you will learn on the Ground Floor is you are going to fall in life, no matter how emotionally healthy you are. On the Ground Floor, you begin to learn to fall with acceptance and awareness.

As you experiment with new belief systems, you become okay when you fall, knowing it is part of Self-development, rather than getting into fear and self-punishment. You can fall without having your self-esteem fall. This is how you become grounded. You have with you a sense of who you are, how you came to be, how your conditioners and other relationships harmed you, and how all of this happened perfectly to make you the unique Self you are becoming.

The Ground Floor has many rooms to assist you in your experimenting and practicing. It is equipped with a Kitchen, Living Room, Office, Windows, and a Front Door. All of these have important purposes. Rooms create boundaries. You cannot be healthy or grounded without boundaries. Therefore, the Ground Floor has the most rooms. It is where you learn emotional intelligence. To be intelligent emotionally, you have to learn when, where, and how you gain emotional clarity. One major project in getting grounded is to separate your emotional goals into different phases. Each room has its purpose and its lesson. Each room serves to make you clear about who you are.

The Kitchen: Examining your in-sights

You will start getting grounded in your Kitchen. Kitchens are full of excitement and transformation. It is here you will unpack the in-sight basket you brought with you from the Cellar. You will take these external concepts and make them a part of the new person you are becoming. The Kitchen is a place of gathering and blending. This is what happens chemically in kitchens. Things are being created and are changing form to become a complete new whole. What starts off as separate pieces becomes one. The perfect ingredients and temperatures make the perfect dish. Every ingredient adds something essential to whole.

Each dish requires a perfect balance to come out the way

a cook would want. I started to see the intelligence of the Kitchen as a metaphor for my own personal transformation. I would experiment and be creative with all the new in-sights I found in the Cellar. Each in-sight added to my sense of Self would have to be added to the whole at the exact right time. Each in-sight would need the perfect time to simmer. The in-sights would need to cool and marinate together, to blend to find the balance which would leave the creator pleased. The Kitchen is reserved for the process of transformation, creation, and experimentation. I love my Kitchen.

I started by examining the in-sights from my basket and how each would have to transform to help me get grounded. Each in-sight would serve as a tool to help me change, understand, and mature. As I stood in my Kitchen I first pulled out: *My reactions to the world and relationships are based upon conditioned beliefs, which have nothing to do with me*. How would I transform this into something usable in my life? As I studied this in-sight, I realized that I learned very early I was not as important to my parents as their needs for themselves. Nor was I a star enough to be the most wanted or prized like my brother. I realized this ingredient was a fundamental core wound that transferred into poisoning my sense of Self. I was conditioned to believe that spicy was not good and because of this conditioning, I felt insecure and substandard. I was certainly not as good as the others in my life according to my conditioning. They all seemed to blend so easily.

I was the one ingredient that gave everyone in my family a disgruntled face growing up. I now see that I was just spicy! Deliciously spicy. It is not *my* issue that others don't enjoy spicy food. I could see how many benefits there were to my spice, such as having a determined way in the world. This determination aspect of me could only bring success if used in the most flavorful way. I would now embrace my spiciness. On the Ground Floor, I would learn all the varying ways to express my spiciness that would bring beneficial results. How exciting! I could finally embrace and change my mind about who I was rather than trying to dull my spice to make others comfortable.

In my Kitchen, I could see how embracing my spiciness would be important and also highly creative. I would have to test out how to marinate it, what to mix it with, and what other ingredients could enhance and balance it. I would want each dish to have some kind of spice, since in the Kitchen I was utilizing my in-sights to provide me the right ingredients to cook up the best me I could possibly create. Spice would now be one essential part of me added to each and every dish in some beautifully creative way. Spicy is exciting; it makes people alert and interested, and it even has cleansing properties. Spicy is about movement and energy. I could see my spice as an essential part of me and one that did not need to be taken from the whole.

It was so inspiring transforming in-sights in the Kitchen. I found that experiencing that transformation was also connected to self-acceptance. I was seeing through the in-sights that there were aspects of me that did not necessarily need changing; they just needing some adjusting. The next in-sight I reached in and pulled from my basket was: *Each time I am people pleasing I give a piece of me away.* For starters, if I continued to give my Self away there would be nothing to transform. There would be nothing of me to bring to the Kitchen, nothing to add or take away. When you give some of your Self to someone else and they take it with greed, it is gone forever. People-pleasing is like emotional prostitution. You are giving your Self away for no return. It is loss. This was not a way for me to live anymore. I would have to figure out what to do with this ingredient. It would have to be removed from my ingredient list and transformed into *me-pleasing.* If I am pleased and happy and I add this to the creation of my Self, I will likely not pick people who need pleasing.

As I looked at this people-pleasing in-sight, I saw it was liquid, leaky, and messy. When I consistently bent to make other people happy, I lost my Self. I was too leaky, too liquid, and too messy. The end result was being empty and without any real form. As I stood in my Kitchen, it came to me, I would have to take a liquid substance and turn it into a solid. I would have to bake. What I knew of baking was it was always related to something sweet. The intention behind people-pleasing is to be as sweet as one can be to keep others happy. I would have to take the batter or the liquid of who I was and bake it into a more solid, substantial, and beautiful form. If something has form, then it has boundaries. When you people please, you have no boundaries. Cake batter is delicious, but if you eat too much of it, it takes away from the cake. I would not give too much batter away, just like I would no longer give my Self away. I would save it all for the cake. The cake would have form, and only special guests would be invited to share in the end result. This is how I would transform this part of me in my Kitchen.

The next out of my basket: *A child's life needs form and structure*. My early life never had any structure or predictability. Therefore, my new growing Self would need a menu. Menus prepare you for what is available. They give you form and structure. Menus also have many different sections offering different types of foods. A menu of *me* would begin with light starters so I am sure to have light feelings in my life. I would have main courses so that I could feel full and rich and I would, of course, have desserts to make sure I would have sweetness in my life. These would be the main three sections for me to work with. As time went on and I practiced using these in-sights, I would make adjustments to my menu.

As I reached into my basket for the next in-sight, I was feeling invigorated. It felt like getting new clothes, so many new parts to try on. The next in-sight: *People all feel emotions the same way. The way I feel pain and loss is the same way another feels pain and loss. When you connect in your pain, you feel seen.* You can connect not just in your pain but in all of the *flavors* of your emotions. We all *feel* the emotions the same way. This in-sight was about flavor.

In order to maximize this in-sight, I would have to decide who I would relate to and who I would not. I had learned that some people were not interested in connecting emotionally, and I had become someone who really desired to connect emotionally. My palate finds some tastes savory and others, bitter. In the same way, connecting emotionally is not to everyone's taste, and I could empathize with those who did not desire that taste. I had experienced all sides of all feelings and tasted all their flavors. My tastes had changed as I matured. I would simply stay in line with those who shared the taste for the deeper flavors of the emotional life experience and respect those who do not have that same palate.

Flavor is important in each dish. The emotions are the flavors of your essence. I would start a new understanding of the emotions based upon flavor, tastes, and how well they agree with me. If I ingested a relationship that did not fit for me, I was going to want to get rid of it, just as if I was going to avoid a food that did not agree with me. I would have to learn which flavors I would want to entertain in my life as I became more grounded.

Self-confidence is nurtured through mutually beneficial relationships. As I stood in my Kitchen at my island, and pondered this in-sight, it came to me that two parts put together would create a whole. Two people in a balanced give and take relationship would create a deep connection. In Kitchen terms, the perfect marriage of two ingredients according to my taste would be peanut butter and chocolate. There is a sweetness when things work together to make a whole. Each individual ingredient is delicious on its own but when you put them together, they create a deliciousness only achieved through combining. On my Ground Floor, I would have to learn about mutually beneficial relationships which would mean I would need to learn to receive as much as give. I could only imagine how rich with sweetness my life would soon be. Being given too would nurture my Self-confidence because it would show me my value. When you give and it is appreciated, you *feel* your value. This would be the joy of combining flavors. Each in-sight built upon all other in-sights.

I reached in the basket and held the next in-sight gently in my hand. Before I looked at it, I closed my eyes and had a moment of gratitude for each and every in-sight I gathered on my journey. These would be essential ingredients for my transformation. I opened my eyes and saw: *If I am a false-self, I am not my Self. I become false to fit.* Being a false-self is like being a fat free food. There is nothing real about fat free food. It is completely chemically altered. It is altered and then advertised as healthy. As a false-self, I was unhappy advertising as happy. I was always trying to fit and altering myself to appear better than I was. This is how fat free food is. It is not better food, and it is much worse for you than whole foods. The body can assimilate and digest whole foods with ease and efficiency. On the Ground Floor, I would transform from being an altered-self into a whole Self. No more fat free foods or low fat foods would be in my Kitchen. I would no longer alter myself to be what I thought others wanted me to be. Life would now be lived from being whole.

I could see how all these in-sight would be 100% necessary for me to become a more mature and grounded person, and I felt hopeful and at peace. The next in-sight lifted from my basket: *Each insecurity has an evolving purpose. Insecurities are not meant to* ***go*** *away, they are meant to* ***lead*** *the way into our healing*. When you feel insecure, you feel substandard, and you want that feeling to just go away! Yet, insecurities are like the aging of a fine wine. Wine is aged so the consumer can experience its greater value. Your insecurities tend to revolve around your core wounds, meaning they tend to carry a theme. There are many core wounds each with their unique flavors, just like there many types of wines. My core wounds would always be what they are. They are alive within me and reside in my Cellar. Just as wines are aged in Cellars, so are insecurities. I go to my Cellar to age my insecurities. I am there to mature them, massage them and grow from them into my greater value. I am not there to get rid of them. Wounds leave scars, and scars don't disappear. Scars, if massaged and nurtured, are there to build character.

A wine that has aged has a fuller, deeper, richer flavor and experience. This is the same process of the aging of insecurities. Each time, one of my core wounds was triggered, I would go to my Cellar to further age and mature my perception. In this way, each core wound led to more maturity and promoted the healing process within me. As a wine ages, it becomes a more elegant experience for the palate. The flavor deepens.. As my insecurities aged, I became a person of deeper character. I became someone who would be embraced in the essence of her full expression, her elegance, and the poetic nature of her presence. When you age your insecurities, you emit depth, intelligence and richness. This was a profound in-sight because you do not need to get away from what your core wounds. If you let them lead you, you will see the unlimited layers of growth they could provide.

It is an enriching process to examine each in-sight and to see the larger value each in-sight offers to our maturity process. The Ground Floor was where I would get to live this new level of my aged maturity. I reached in the basket and pulled out; *We develop disorders out of our emotions. At the core of any disorder is the need for control.* There is nothing worse than walking into a messy Kitchen. It is disgusting to see dishes everywhere, counters not cleaned, a disorganized refrigerator with outdated foods, and a messy floor. This is who I was as a person before I stopped eating. I was a mess. I was dis-ordered or not in order. I was emotionally unorganized, out of control, sloppy with anger, sad with loss, and frustrated with outdated family systems which did not work for me. I was a disaster.

When I chose to stop eating, I did not truly organize my emotions, rather, I organized my control over *something* and that something was food. In Kitchen terms, I went from being dis-ordered to too orderly. I had a Kitchen that now, no one would want to be in again but for different reasons. Now my Kitchen was sanitary to the point of being uncomfortable, and there was no food in it. I would now have to learn on my Ground Floor the flexibility of having structure and comfort at the same time, so my Kitchen could become a place for gathering, sharing, laughter, transformation and connection. My need for control was at the center of my structure and now this need would have to age and mature.

The Kitchen on the whole was an emotional place for me personally because in the Cellar I had survived so many issues with food. Food had the power to make me good or bad. In the Kitchen, I learned we all need good nutritional habits to be emotionally well. My relationship with food had to go through some changes in order for me to find physical health. I had been so averse to food that I had become aversive to cooking. I had the fear if I began to like food, I would not be able to control myself. Food had always been related directly to body or self-image. Now with my new in-sights (ingredients), I was ready to learn and practice new ways of being.

One thing I learned in the Cellar was when I was sad or emotional I would restrict my food. At any major life loss, I would restrict. Restriction meant cleanliness to me. On the Ground Floor, I would learn to be responsible for my body. My self-esteem was tied into what I ate. I would need to find the middle between being too sloppy and too rigid so I could be a flexible chef and be the most efficient me I could be.

It is okay to need help was the next in-sight pulled from the basket. I looked at it and took a deep breath. It is a lot of work being human on this planet, and it is even more work to be a conscious human being on this planet. When I looked at this in-sight, I breathed a sigh of relief because countless times, I had felt isolated in my emotions and in my experience of life. As I looked at this ingredient, I understood no person is here to do this life alone. You are biologically drawn to be in relationships with other people, and you are biologically drawn to grow. You are all singular, yes, but life is challenging, and you will need others added to your growth process so you can discover who and what works for you and who and what does not. If you don't try different spices, you will never know your likes and dislikes. This is why it is important to have *recipes* to follow in your Kitchen.

A recipe is like a food therapy session. It gives direct guidance (with individual creative flexibility) to help you when making a new dish. In this way, you are not starting blank, without guidance and creating something that tastes as if it started without direction. There is no point in floundering around in life without a guide. The form of the guide can show up in numerous ways. Emotionally I have always sought out guidance, whether it was from a therapist, a book, my journal, friends, family, mentors, bosses, managers, or my spouse. Each person or book has helped me know the exact right spices to add and take out in my life. Often times, the trial and error of my own experience has been my most brilliant guide. When you learn in this way, you add things to the recipe so you don't forget when creating future meals.

There should be no shame in needing the guidance of a recipe. It doesn't mean you cannot be individually creative as you get better in the Kitchen, but it is nice to have guidance at times. You are likely to need the most help when you experience your more painful emotions, just like you most need a recipe when you are learning to cook an unfamiliar meal. Just because you need help, does not make something wrong with you. Just because you need a recipe, does not mean you cannot cook on your own. In fact, reaching out for help shows humility and that there is actually something right with you. You like to perfect the dishes you make in your Kitchen, so why not put the same effort into your own personal Self.

When you have guidance you increase your rate of healing and when you increase your rate of healing, you find that you like yourself more and more as you continue. The whole goal of this book is to teach you how to develop a relationship of love and trust within your Self. Let us see what else the in-sight basket has to teach us. *I am lovable enough to be chosen.* Being chosen is a direct reflection of your value. I see this, in Kitchen terms, as being the choice of your favorite foods. When you actively love a certain food or meal, you will always have the taste and craving for it. You will think about having it throughout the day with anticipated excitement. When you become lovable as a person, this is how other people will feel about spending time with you. More importantly, when you love who you are, you also will look forward to spending quality alone with your own energy. I can sometimes look so forward to my solitary time that I have it all planned out before I even get home. I will choose movies to watch, foods to eat, and will think about what books to journal about before bed. It is a beautiful feeling to know that happiness can equally be created alone or with another.

As you become the chooser and lover of yourself, you will begin to find yourself fantastically delicious and so will others. You will use your in-sights to deepen your presence. As you deepen your presence, you have an enriching impact on those around you which will make others find you interesting, calming, funny, and light. This is when you have increased your energy potential. When others choose you because they feel better after they have been around you, you have come into knowing your own value. It is the same experience of calm you have after eating a lovely meal. You have become 'gathered' emotionally and people are able to have the whole experience of who you are instead of experiencing fractured parts. You have become emotionally nutritious. Being chosen by others or through your own desires, you are on the way to the deepest experiences of love that life has to offer.

Life is about change, and this is what Kitchens are all about. The next in-sight to add to my growth was *I am at my best when in action. Always look forward.* Kitchens are the one area in a house full of action. Any time you are in a Kitchen, something is being worked on and its form is changing. There is absolutely nothing inactive in a Kitchen. Kitchens are where you create new dishes, parts are being made into a whole, temperatures are changing, and all things are periodically in transition. The same is true for your personal growth. You cannot be thoughtless and inactive and expect transformation. Your work on yourself will take focused attention, great effort and then, a period of waiting for the finished product to manifest.

When you are in the Kitchen, you do your work and then step back and look forward to the result of your effort. Personal growth is the exact same process. The greatest reward of your action is the enjoyment of the new wonderful you that was created. Action = results. This is why you start your grounding process in the Kitchen. You are here to do your prep work, to get clear on the current recipe of the new you being created, and then to combine all parts into a whole to then look forward to the outcome. This is the chemical process of becoming a whole.

The best action always comes from your internal guidance system which makes this next in-sight incredibly important. *My answers live in my body.* When I say that I eat Alkaline what this means is I am looking to balance my body Ph level. Ph is about balance. To live efficiently you need emotional and mental balance. You literally are what you eat, just like you are what you feel and think. If you want to live a healthy long life, you have to pay attention to your core Ph level; if you want to live a healthy emotional life, you have to pay attention to your emotions and thoughts. Negative thinking impacts my emotional life just like junk food lowers my body Ph. The basis of all disease starts with an out of balance Ph, meaning the body is too acidic. If you pay attention to Ph and eat life giving foods, your body will stay more alkaline or more alive.

At the core of the emotional being is intuition. This is a lot like your body Ph. You rarely do pay attention to your intuition, and you end up letting your thoughts and emotions become acidic. They eat away at you. If you have too much acid in the body, the acid will eat away at your organs. When the body is acidic, it does not have enough oxygen. When you are emotionally and mentally acidic, you cannot think straight to make good decisions. You create too much anxiety and can't breathe. Again, you are low on oxygen. Your intuition is your life giving guidance system, and like the blood Ph, it must be nurtured.

If your body Ph is acidic, you will have disease. If your emotional and mental life is acidic you will experience dis-ease. Both the Ph and intuition are compasses for going forward. In my Kitchen, I will have to learn to eat foods which are life-giving. I will eat lots of greens, sprouted grains, eliminate meat and dairy, and fill my body with oxygen. When I am balanced physically, I am immediately balanced emotionally and because my body is not wasting time on digestion, my intuition will be more alert, life giving and ready to guide me with emotional and mental clarity into my best life decisions. This is about balance.

The in-sights pulled from the basket are the greatest treasures of my journey because they help me feel safe and grounded in life. There is nothing more profound. The next in-sight I examined is *The truth can hurt.* When I ponder the concept of the truth, I see it as the great awakener. In Kitchen terms, it is like your morning coffee. Coffee wakes you up. The truth also wakes you up. I don't particularly like my coffee black, and the truth in its rawness can leave its own bad taste. But I have learned in my Kitchen that there are ways to work with the truth. I add the two ingredients of acceptance and humility to my truth to make it a more manageable process rather than a bitter event. This is like adding cream and sugar to my coffee to make it more drinkable.

Because the truth can be painful, and black coffee's taste is bitter, I think it is important to manage your emotions around the truth. As you add acceptance and humility to your cup of truth, you are letting all the flavors of the truth blend together and set. Once all the ingredients have been added and they have had time to set, you can then start looking at the truth with patience and a contemplative mind.

As you look at a truth in this way, it gently pulls you out of your distortion or old eye-sights, and you are placed into reality. Reality is truth. Truth is the one and only place you can truly heal from. You cannot heal from distortion. Distortion creates only more distortion. Truth is like the cream in coffee in that it will eventually rise to the surface. The truth is patient but pushy in that the truth's drive is for an awakening just as coffee serves to awaken the mind and body. There is no point in avoiding it, nor do you need to begin any kind of action when you are in the shock of the truth. Just add acceptance and humility, and start your day.

Most of you typically start your days in your Kitchen with a cup of coffee. In the Crystal Palace you will start each Ground Floor day with a cup of truth, so you can venture out and live that truth with acceptance and humility. There is no better way to start the day. The great awakener is something to embrace not to avoid. The more it is avoided the harder life becomes. So, take your cup of truth and let it run sweetly down your throat into the essence of who you are. The truth may hurt at times, but always remember on the Ground Floor, the truth is the only way to feeling grounded. The truth literally puts your feet on the ground.

Being in the Kitchen I could see that my new life was beginning to become more clear. I had certain objectives to follow and to learn as provided by these in-sights. The in-sight placed on the counter next was: *It is hard to let go.* Letting go would be one of the major growth opportunities for me to embrace on the Ground Floor. My old programming gave me the illusion that I had to control my life, or else my life would unexpectedly take directions and turns that I would not like. I controlled out of the desire to feel safe in an unpredictable world. In living in this type of worry and anxiety, I did not realize it, but I was *spoiling* my life. If you control life, you will spoil it; if you learn to let go, you keep everything fresh. In trying to control everything, I did not know when enough was enough. I was too scared to step back because I did not believe that life would fall naturally into place. I was trying to eliminate change.

In the Kitchen, it is all about change and transformation. It is the open ended process of creativity and unpredictability. You never truly know how anything is going to turn out and each time you cook something, it always turns out slightly different from the last time you cooked it. In the Kitchen, I would have to learn that all things change, so there is nothing to hold onto. I would have to learn to be open and patient.

If I am worried that the dish I am cooking is not going to turn out the way I want and I continue to add spices, I am likely to overdo it and spoil the dish. This is how my old programming had me living my life. I was clutching for control, and it did not allow for any open creativity in my life or for any real joy. Joy comes in freedom, and this is what letting go provides. I would now have to learn to do my work and then, step back and trust that all things would fall perfectly into place. In this way, I would add the ingredient of freshness to my life, and I would no longer add the ingredient of anxiety to my dishes and spoil them. The fresher something is, the better it tastes. I had much practice to do on the Ground Floor in learning to let go.

The next in-sight to come from the basket made me smile. When we realize *we are not by ourselves that we are with ourselves,* we have really come a long way in our healing. This would be something valuable to practice on my Ground Floor. The love of me. In Kitchen terms, this is the process of melting into a new relationship in your perception of yourself. When you perceive that you are by yourself, you feel extremely alone. You may feel unattached to anything deeper or more plentiful. In the Kitchen, I did not need to find other ingredients to combine with. In other words, I did not require other people in order not to be alone. I needed to take one ingredient and change its form. This is an emotional change in perception. This particular in-sight would require *melting*.

In this situation, I would have to take a solid fixed perception of me and melt it into a liquid more fluid perception. When you feel alone, life feels cold. If you take an ice-cube in its solid form and let it melt into a liquid, you are still dealing with same substance. I needed to melt my fixed, cold state of mind and let it transition into a more liquid form by adding warmth. Love and acceptance is warmth. The whole intention of the Crystal Palace formula is to learn to love your Self. It is to learn to melt into the essence of who you are. Ice cubes are hard, difficult to hold for long periods of time and are at their best when placed into a liquid. You can achieve a similar effect by adding warmth (love) to your hard cold parts.

In the Cellar, you become aware of your colder qualities, and you can see they do not serve you in your personal transformation. When you become awakened within, you warm up, and realize that you are a very special person. You are not so hard and cold as before. As you warm yourself up, you become warm with love, knowledge, skills, compassion, friendliness, confidence, and expansion. When you love yourself, you are never by yourself; you become with yourself. You like who are, and you like your own company. Your old beliefs have become liquid and flexible. As you warm up, you transition into being someone *you* love. The lovely thing about liquid is its fluidity, its softer edges and its ability to move with a current. This is how you should love yourself. You should love yourself with flexibility. You should have a poetic essence to your edges, and be able to trust the flow on which life takes you. When you have warmth, you will melt people with your presence and draw the right others to you, but this can only happen once you thaw into your singular liquid form.

Learning to love yourself does not come without direction, and this is why the next in-sight is so important. *Everything you need to learn is available in information (paper parents)*. Every Kitchen needs to be equipped with Cookbooks. Life is the open-ended process of creativity and personal re-invention. You are here to re-invent yourself over and over again all through life. Cookbooks are full of ideas, guidance, recipes, Kitchen information, and nutritional information. Cookbooks are your guides to enlighten your mind and your palate. Books are your emotional guides to enlighten you in life.

In a Cookbook, you choose what you want to eat, and you will have guidance to create each dish. You do not have to follow the guidance directly but use your own creativity to enhance the dish. When you read personal growth information, you get much of the same. Not every book out there will be the book for you, but you have plenty to choose from, and you get to choose which recipes or parts of recipes most authentically match your palate. Information is guidance. You need guidance in life. You are here to be inventive, creative, and inspired to make your life extra-ordinary. If you are here, why live an ordinary life? If you are going to cook something, why not make it the perfect expression of your palate on that day.

No one is really alone or without hope because there is too much information out there just waiting to be utilized and put into action. If there is a question, an uncertainty, a pain, an issue, or a fear, there is information and guidance out there to help. Self-help books are life cookbooks full of recipes you can sift through. You need to find which one works best for you. It will come down to motivation. If you have lost the motivation to cook a dish, you are not going to have an extra-ordinary eating experience; if you lose motivation in life, you are not going to have an extra-ordinary living experience. You are the most unmotivated when you feel alone and without guidance, and this is why it is necessary to have cookbooks to guide you. Information is the vehicle which leads us from the darkness into the innovative.

Having a guide connects you to something grounded which

you will need when you practice this next in-sight: *Fear is our most evolutionary response. It is here to fuel growth.* When you are in the Kitchen and you are looking to chemically change the capacity or intensity of any substance, you add heat. When heat is added to any substance, the particles within the substance all begin moving rapidly creating a greater degree of separation between the particles. This greater degree of separation between particles is what causes the substance to expand or to increase in its capacity. In simplistic Kitchen terms, when you heat things up, they increase in volume.

This is similar to what fear does. Fear is designed to increase your capacity; it adds intense heat to life. When you feel fear, you undergo a chemical change which causes racing thoughts and anxiety. Your system gets turned on, your body becomes adrenalized (energized), your breath quickens, you become acutely alert, your heart rate increases, and you become ready to move. Your whole internal system is moving rapidly just like the particles in a heated substance, and this movement creates an increase in your volume.

In this way, you have completely expanded on a neurophysiologic level. This is why fear is your most evolutionary response. Without fear, there would be little evolvement. On the Ground Floor you will now understand fear's intention, as you practice turning up the heat in your Kitchen. You will know when fear is present, because you will expand and you will be prepared for new action. New action is what gives rise to confidence. You learn through facing your fears that you are not limited in your capacity in life. Each new level of fear you face is a new level of growth and expansion achieved. In other words, with each fear you face your life expands. You break through all your limits and open up more and more life to enjoy.

As you are on the Ground Floor spending time in your Kitchen, you are learning to be true to yourself. I cannot be really true to myself, if I am not facing fears. The benefit to being true to yourself is you expand to possess a greater attraction potential. The next in-sight read: *The truer I am to myself the more attractive I become.* What a fun creative in-sight to play with. I can't wait to decorate. When I am true to myself, everything I create becomes imbued with my essence. The outer is what you first see, but it must be combined with an inner quality to have any depth or attraction potential. In the Kitchen, you work the inner and outer. The Kitchen is about transformation. Since I just left the Cellar, I made my Kitchen cocoon-like. Yellow is my favorite color because yellow is the color of wisdom, light, life, and happiness. My preferred shade of yellow is called warm cocoon. I painted my Kitchen walls in this soft, deep, powdery yellow to begin my new life full of light, drizzled in wisdom topped with happiness.

The crown molding, baseboards, and cabinets are white. White is the color of purity. In my Kitchen, I am transforming into my purest Self. The cabinets all have paned windows; my dishes are white and my glasses are tall and clear. The sink and eating area are framed with an expansive paned glass bay window. The window lets in a maximum amount of natural light. The natural light is reflective of the natural expression of who I really am. Beautiful bouquets of deep red flowers are all around the Kitchen to remind me of the blood of the birth I lived through in the Cellar. There is no birth without a little pain and discomfort, and the red flowers I have are in honor of the painful passages I have taken in my life. I have dark hard wood floors and an island in the middle of my Kitchen for cooking and preparing. My counter tops are earth toned in color to remind me to keep my feet in the dirt and on the ground in the rawness of who I am.

In my refrigerator, are all of my alkaline, life enhancing, powerfully green vegetables. In my pantry, are my sprouted grains. I only eat whole foods which are unprocessed and unrefined. Whole foods are non-toxic and have inexpensive healing properties which provide me a deeper quality of life. The purpose of the Crystal Palace is to learn to feel whole; therefore, I choose to eat whole foods. I can learn a lot about myself from whole foods. Whole foods are pure in their form. The truer I am to myself, the more pure in form I become. The more pure in form I become, the more attractive I am and the more miracles I attract.

In the Cellar, I started my detox from my old eye-sights (artificial processing). The amazing benefit of lack of artificial processing is the energy saved. With whole foods, my body can use all of its energy to repair rather than digest, which makes me more efficient physically, emotionally, mentally, and spiritually. When I do my inner work and detox old-programming I also have more energy to love myself and love my life. It is all the same process. If I detox my old programming, I can come to life focused on repairing and adding to the quality of my life. My energy will no longer be wasted in being a false-self, which is similar to a processed food.

I have found that when I eat whole alkalizing foods, everything I put into my body is life (light) giving. I am eating live foods, which are not processed. As a person, I want to be alive and not processed. I want to be whole and have a glow. I have no junk food in my Kitchen, because I am not junk. I have found ways to love natural sweetness and the crunch of life and this is my essence. I started my processing of learning to be whole in my Kitchen. Being whole is a beautiful thing. It is internal and external. The healthier I am within, the more attractive I become externally, and the glow of my essence becomes a magnet for miracles. You have to protect your wholeness not just with diet and décor, but you also have to protect yourself from poisonous people.

The next ingredient I pulled out of my basket is probably one of the most important because it is about selectivity, knowledge, and discernment: *Who is in your life is the most important decision you can make*. This in-sight is about ingredients. One of the essential decisions when creating any dish in the Kitchen is what ingredients will be necessary. Each relationship in your life is one ingredient in your emotional soup. In your dish, as you select your ingredients, you have to make sure everything can work together in harmony and that each ingredient will blend with and enhance the flavor of the others. In this way, you create a working whole where each part positively impacts all other parts. This is how you should also look at your relationships.

Having the wrong people in your life is like adding too much salt to a dish. If there is too much salt, the dish is not repairable or eatable. It is ruined. If you keep the company of even one person who adds too much salt to your life, your life will be deeply impacted. This person can cause you to veer sharply away from who you normally are and has the power to color your view of the whole world you live in. Their salt ruins your whole perception. Why? Because your self-esteem is largely tied into belonging with the people you have close bonds with. One person can literally take your life down a dark and negative path and bring you so far away from who you know yourself to be that it will feel like you have been ruined. Therefore, you have to always be selective.

As you practice the art of discernment of your life ingredients, you create a life that has simplicity and peace. You have to honor yourself, and discernment is the start. The final in-sight: *There is only one of me. I am special.* This may be my favorite in-sight. This is about the uniqueness of me. I am unique, and I am dynamic just like my Kitchen. I love how my Kitchen is set up and decorated because it was done by me. I love all the in-sights that came up with me from the Cellar, because they are expressive of what I need to learn as a single Cell.

In cooking all these in-sights up in my Kitchen, I see that I am special and I am intrigued by me, by all the growth I will learn and have learned already, and by all that I can and will accomplish. It is nice to be leaving my Kitchen with the idea that I *am* special in my totality. I have come to accept and love that I am imperfectly, perfectly me. I feel ready to take the in-sights out to the Ground Floor to see just how expansive my life can be. There is only one of me. I like that there is only one of me. It inspires me to be as fully expressed as I can possibly be.

In the Kitchen, you are unpacking and understanding the work you have to do on this floor. As you become better cooks, you become more wise and attuned in your knowledge of ingredients. You learn what you like and what you don't. You learn what blends and what does not, and you learn what enhances and what spoils. This is the same with choosing your relationships. You have to learn who works in your life and who does not. You have to learn who you like and who you do not, and you have to learn who gets you lost and who enhances you. As you become grounded, you will practice making healthy, mutually beneficial, harmonious relationships so you can live a life…delectable.

Now, you are blessed enough to leave this Kitchen for a while and head out to your Office to figure out how to make all of these new concepts work in the world of your active life. It has all been hands on learning in the Kitchen; examining all the transformative processes available to you has been creative, inventive, and innovative. In your office, you will get a more linear or left brained focus on these in-sights. You will begin to measure your Kitchen ideas and see how you can put them into a live setting. It's time to practice living your new knowledge. Welcome to the Office, the place of focus.

The office: Staying on track and measuring success

The Office is the space that allows me to focus and stay on task. Having a space to use my conscious effort enables me to learn the exact elements necessary for a successful journey into the building of my personal growth and success. As I consciously focus on my Self, this focus allows me to understand how my actions have a direct impact on my results. Understanding how my actions determine my results is powerful knowledge, as it gives me direction and understanding. Understanding this relationship helps me see what adjustments and adaptations I need to make to live a more fulfilling life. Knowing this puts me further down the path to realizing my dreams.

As I become conscious and focused in my Office, I realize that when I am purposefully loving my Self, I am on the path to accomplishing more than I could ever dream. All possibilities open up when I am consciously focused and concentrating on *my inner life*. This allows me to understand the causes of many of my mistakes, and having this understanding, helps me not to repeat the same mistakes over and over again. I love how my Office brings me into such deep concentration and contemplation. Things become more positive as I look at them head on. In some way, having a focus decreases the fear of the unknown. My Office is where I am *smart* about my life.

It is where I understand each ingredient in the Kitchen and how each can be successfully utilized for my personal advancement. It is where I take the time to measure my progress and my ability to have self-acceptance on my new journey. I like having a work-space full of rulers, pens, graphs, papers, calculators, glue, tape, pens, and highlighters. The Office is where all my work is put into measureable goals. Goal setting is a fundamental part of healing. Goals achieved help me to see my progress. If I can measurably see I am making my goals, then I am inspired to do more work. *This space is where I find inspiration and motivation.*

I learn about creating visions boards, and I hang them up on my walls tracking all my dreams. I write my affirmations on index cards and repeat them morning and night. When I achieve what I put in writing I file it away and create new goals. It is in this space I begin my dream work. In this space, I have the focus and commitment to keep my dreams clear and concise in my mind. I write them all down to solidify them. In this room, I have an intense commitment to the dreams for my life. This allows me to dream and to find the ways to make my dreams into a reality. Because my dreams are such a part of me, the details of my path become crystal clear and alive with meaning and energy.

My visions boards are the first place I see my dream in pictures. This Office contains the energy and vision of forward progress to date. It also helps me see where and when I need to go back to the drawing board and try a new mix of in-sights in my Kitchen. It is good to measure progress. It gives you the ability to analyze where you are, where you have come from, and where you dare dream to go. For dreams to manifest, however, you have to put them in live action. In the Office, they are in thought form. Actions follow thoughts and so this is why the next phase of dreaming transitions into the Living Room.

The Living Room: Learning to live

The Living Room is the created space to practice *living*. It is alive. I had survived as a child but not lived. If you are living, then you are not hiding from life, fighting life, fearing life; you are living life. This took much practice for me, as I am so naturally fear-based, but my Living Room has a bay window which is where I learn the process of Self-imaging. Self-imaging is the intelligence of this room. This is the room where I have the freedom to fully express myself. This is the room of day-dreaming. It is where you practice all you cooked up in the Kitchen, and the goals set in your Office. It is the room of *being* and *becoming*.

My bay window is where I do my Self-reflection and Self-imaging. In my bay window, I of course have my journal, but accompanying my journal are books I am studying to become more and more of the Self I would like to become. I choose to self-image in my window because in my window, I can see out far beyond where I am as I sit and write. Imaging is the same process. It is about seeing beyond the you that you are right now and daydreaming about the you in the making. For this reason, I could read, write, and sit in my window for hours on end.

Staring out the window in my solitary time is enchanting. I love to watch the weather whenever I am in my bay window. I love all four seasons, each bringing me into a completely different feeling state. I am also able to see the weather as symbolic of how everything is changing and moving all the time. I do not prefer one season to the next, as each season or each shift in weather just gives me something more to write about. My emotions are similar to the changes in the weather. I find them interesting material to explore, observe, and grow from. On the Ground Floor, dreams of who you can become begin to develop. *Dreaming and Self-imaging are the seeds of all greatness.*

In my bay window one day, I defined what I thought an adult was, and I wrote the following list: *Composed, smart, discerning, emotionally in control, open, able to listen, able to speak slowly and intelligently when emotional, disciplined, firm, powerful, self-sufficient, standing firm in personal beliefs, responsible, clean, and mature.* Wow, what a list. This is what was missing from my parenting and largely what created many of the painful memories in my Cellar. I wanted to be what my conditioners were not. So, I took one word per day and tried to *live* and embody the energy the word communicated. I tried to live its meaning. I ran to my Office and measured my results, and cooked up new ingredients in the Kitchen. This was a deep and impactful process for me. I began to like myself. I began to realize and think about the fact that I could become whatever I wanted to become.

Living life offers a sense of comfort and freedom never felt by me before. I find that solitary time is my most productive, creative time when my dreams begin to show themselves. In my Living Room, I step into the courage to live. I find that living often means the ability to relax and tune out, to not be so work obsessed. This is a place to relax, laugh, and escape into movies, TV, cozy blankets, a good book or a place to take a nap. To live means to enjoy. I have learned to enjoy life, so I am grateful to have a *Living* Room.

Windows: Seeing inward and outward, light

Another aspect of the Ground Floor is Windows. Windows bring in natural light and fresh air. Within each of you, is a natural light. You are all born with this light. It exists in all of you. It is the essence of who you really are. Each of you is here to express this very part. It is your guiding force and the untainted part which never left. When you open your windows, you let in fresh air. There is nothing more that can make me take a deep breath than natural light and fresh air. You all have your own essence, and when you heal, you become clean. Your aura becomes clean. You become a breath of fresh air.

Air, which is old, unworked, and unmoved, is suffocating, frustrating, and thick. This is how the aura feels to others when you are not well. You become repellent. You become like Pigpen on Charlie Brown. You carry your dirt with you everywhere you go. You become one of those people who have bad energy. You are someone who has not done their work. This is what they feel like. When you rise up from the Cellar, open the Windows, and let the light in! Be that breath of fresh air. This is what the Ground Floor is about, expressing your cleansed energy. When you really know who you are, people experience you as light, open, flexible, accountable, attractive, and positive.

Windows allow you to see inward and outward. You can see who you are internally and how you can impact the social world you live in. When you are able to look inward and outward, you can see the Self you are and the Self you would love to become. Any adjustments you see are new in-sights to take to the Kitchen. This exact dynamic is the ongoing process of keeping your lights clean. If they are clean, they can shine! If they shine, you shine. Soon people begin to notice there is something deeply magical about you, but they can't quite put their finger on it. When they leave your presence, they think to themselves, "Wow, I love being around that person. I feel so much better after I am with him/her." This is where you become a gift to the world.

The Front Door: Standing your ground with boundaries

Finally there is the Front Door. The Front Door is symbolic of being open and being closed. It is a boundary. I get to decide who, if anyone, can enter my Crystal Palace. I can also decide when I want to be open with the outside world and when I would prefer to be closed. The Door teaches me many lessons as I begin the development and interior decorating of my Crystal Palace. I learn many things regarding boundaries with the use of this Door. I learn from this Door never to give my Self away. I learn hard lessons about house guests. The Door teaches me I am the only one who can live in my Crystal Palace. My Door is where I stop and someone else starts. No matter what is going on my Door helps me to stand my ground.

You stand your ground with boundaries. You set your way with your Door. When you set your way, you are making a clear statement of who you are and letting everything else around that statement fall into place. When you set your way, you make a clear statement to the Universe regarding where you stand in any given situation. It is the Door never to kick down. The key is in your pocket. I am the only one who has the key to my Crystal Palace...to my Self.

The Ground Floor, as a whole, is demonstrating the process of becoming content within your Self. So, now that you have covered the Ground Floor process, you may be wondering what the beneficial result of becoming Grounded is. It sure sounds good, and it takes quite a bit of willingness, so what is the benefit? When you are Grounded, you live as an emotionally and mentally stable person who has a certain trust and honor for life. You become admirably sensible and realistic about yourself, life, relationships, and growth. Your cells glow with positive resonance, and you have a trust in life because you can trust yourself. You are more oriented to the now and not so consumed with future worry, as you know the Now contains the seeds for all future endeavors.

At this stage, you embrace and honor what you feel, think, and do, as you are aware all things are leading to your success. You become aware that with effort backed up with belief, you can have all you desire. When you are grounded, you have a trusting and accountable relationship within where you know what you know, and you know you can count on what you know to lead you correctly. You have become less stuck by being accountable and responsible for your own emotions, reactions, and actions. This is the essence of trust. Further, when you are grounded and you support and love yourself, you have developed into an individual who is never to going accept less than you believe you deserve. You are now embraced in practicing Self-love and you use your door firmly, when you need to keep out the "less than desirable" people, events and circumstances. In this way you stay Grounded.

Extra Credit Advantage:

Ground Floor Reading

The PH Miracle, Balance Your Diet, Reclaim Your Health (Selley Redford Young, Robert O.Young): Since we start in the Kitchen, I recommend this book. It is about Ph Balance. Life is all about Balance and reclaiming who we are. We need balance, when it comes to food in order to be physically, emotionally, mentally, and spiritually healthy.

Emotional Equations (Chip Conley): This book is all about mixing and matching parts and pieces to make a whole which makes sense. This is another Kitchen book, one of the best books written on emotions. It is simple, logical, helps us to bring meaning into our lives, dreams, and desires. Every line in this book is based in mathematics, and that is exactly what the Kitchen is about: adding, taking out, remixing, and creating a whole.

The Secret (Rhonda Byrne): This book belongs in your Office. It is the start of visions boards, dreams, finances, family, positivity, and spirituality. It is simple, practical, and applicable to everyday life, a must read.

Evolve Your Brain (Joe Dispensa, DC): An incredible Office book, this book is an education on the brain and how much power you actually have in changing your life by changing your thoughts. Changing your thoughts can change your feelings, and changing your feelings can change your thoughts. When you have positive thoughts, you are a beacon for attracting positive experiences and vice versa.

Power of Positive Imaging (Norman Vincent Peale): This belongs in the *Living* Room. This is the space in the house where you can daydream and image for the grandest most beautiful experience you want from your life. Imaging is such a powerful tool. What you imagine can come true.

Power of Positive Living (Norman Vincent Peale): In your *Living* Room, you practice living. Living, truly living, means enjoying. Life is not enjoyable if it is negative, so use this book to practice positive living. If you just like the title and want the book to remind you to live positively, that is enough.

Boundaries: When to Say Yes, How to Say No To Take Control of Your Life (Dr. Henry Cloud and Dr. John Townsend): This was the manual on my door in my Palace. With the knowledge in this book, I learned how to say no in a way that increased my love for others and decreased the chaos in my life. When I need to say no to someone, it helps me to have more love for them. If I am saying yes when I want to say no, I will be filled with resentment for them. This book is the instruction manual for the workings of your Palace Door.

Get Out of Your Own Way: Overcoming Self-Defeating Behavior (Mark Goulston and Philip Goldberg): This book was simple, sensible, and refreshing. I was able to devour this book and to easily see all my bad self-defeating habits. This is a must read for every human being who wants a straight shooting look at getting out of your own way.

Second Floor: Rest, Cleanse and Rejuvenate

The Second Floor is where you go to a higher level away from the busyness and rest. Rest is important for your cells. If you do not rest, you will not have the capacity to keep your shine alive. Without rest, you will impede your forward moving progress. Every cell in the body needs rest to function properly. If you do not get the rest you need, you will experience a loss of energy, anxiety, irritability, and the feelings of depression. You may experience memory problems and an impaired ability to think quickly and efficiently. If you allow yourself to get to this place, you will end up again in the old programming of negative and defeatist thinking. You need all your energy available to you to continue on the multitasking effort you have in your life. You come to the Second Floor to balance your energy.

The Ground Floor is always going to be a busy place because life is always going to change and get you off balance. When you are off balance or in a creative process, you go back to the work of the Ground Floor and get grounded. One thing I have learned about life is nothing is permanent. In order to be happy, you need a fair amount of flexibility in your daily life. The Ground Floor is where you go to learn flexibility and adjustment. At each phase in life, you will get to the place where you feel aware of where you are for the moment. This allows you a sense of calm because you have achieved the awareness this phase has required. The Second Floor is the place of rest. There are not as many rooms on the Second Floor as compared with the Ground Floor. On this floor, are a Bathroom, a Bedroom, and a Self-Preservation room.

As you have your physical and/or basic needs met on the Ground Floor, you rise up in your maturity. As you mature, you become more and more psychologically healthy. You realize *happiness is not an event it is a process*. You become aware some days are going to be fulfilling and some days are not. It is a place of reasonable expectations regarding life. The Ground Floor is busy, active, and alive with new thoughts, behaviors, and dreams. It requires constant attention, focus, and maintenance. You need a place to release and cleanse, you need a place for rest, and you also need a room to retreat to if rest refuses come.

The Bathroom: Prepare, release and cleanse

The Bathroom is the most important room on the Second Floor. This is the place where you release all unwanted poisons and cleanse. It is also the place where you first see your reflection in the morning and the last place you see your reflection at the end of the day. The mirror is where you see yourself from an observer's vantage point. It is here you can be reminded you love that person in that mirror. You are developing the love of Self in the Cellar and Ground Floor. You can rise up to the Second Floor feeling accomplished. *Happiness is a byproduct of achievement.* Cellar and Ground Floor work are where you achieve. The mirror is where it is reflected back to you. On this floor, I consent to feel proud of my Self.

The two most special times for me in the Bathroom are the morning and evening cleanses. My morning cleanse is consumed with getting ready for the new day. Each new day is essentially blank. You may have an agenda, but life will bring you a surprise or two. I cleanse in the morning as a preparation ritual. I start my day off with a clean slate. My mind is usually busy with thoughts of my Ground Floor work. I love getting up and welcoming the new day with a shower and getting beautiful. It is a respectful way for me to honor the day. I dress up for the event. I honor it with maturity and readiness. There is always mystery in each morning because I have no idea what will unfold. The unknown always brings angst, but I get up and suit up, ready to take it on. I remind myself that no matter what happens, at the end of the day the positive and negative will all average out.

The evening cleanse is signified by the bath I take each night assimilating all the new things the day brought. Every positive and negative emotion seeps in, as the warm water caresses my skin. I can sit and breathe. I add bubbles, Epsom salts, and a sweet aroma to my bath. Epsom salts are healing and known for sucking toxins out of the body. Those toxins include negative emotions. I take this bath in the dark and light candles. Once my lights are dim, I refrain from turning them back to bright after the bath. As you dim the lights, the natural melatonin in the brain begins its production. If you turn the lights on after it has been dim, you have to start that melatonin production over again. It is a settling time. I let go of the negativity of the day and the hustle and bustle. I relax my mind, my body, and my spirit in this bath.

This bath is meditative. I use this time to detox from Ground Floor work. I let this bath cleanse me of all the day's activity before I get into my bed. This is how I honor my Bedroom. I do my best not to bring activity into my place of rest. I close my eyes and picture all the activity leaving my body. I feel all the stress leaving my body. It can be very stressful keeping ourselves grounded, so this is where I let that part go. The warmth of the bath is soothing and helps me to get drowsy. I use this bath to find my balance. There are times in the bath that my mind will race with feelings, and I can envision them detoxing and leaving my spirit.

Once I am out of the bath, I put my favorite lotion on, so I can go to my bed feeling clean, fresh, and with a sweet aroma. When I bathe, I am cleansing my energy as much as I am cleansing my physical body. I see sleep as the time my spirit gets to leave my body and be free of the burdens of being confined in my human experience. Doing this little ritual helps me go to a peaceful rest. I believe you can either go to a good space when you sleep or you can end up in a bad space depending upon where you are in your headspace. This bath is about letting go. It is about having the emotional awareness of the things I cannot change or influence and the things which I can. It is on the second floor where I process letting go. My bath before bed is where this process begins. When I know I have done all I can do during a day, then it is time to let the rest go. The goal on this floor is to have faith and not worry about tomorrow.

The Bedroom: Rest and rejuvenate

Resting is an important part of any journey. It is how you let down, come to balance, and know you have had a day of productivity. My bed is significantly important to me, because it is my place of becoming unconscious. I do not have a TV in my room as I need my mind to be at peace. My bed is voluptuous and has all white covering and sleeping pillows. White is pure, it is quiet, and it is clean and the color of the clouds. I put splashes of color on my walls and in my throw pillows and throw blanket. I liken my bed to heaven, a place of purity and peace. I have also found gentle white noise in the background soothes my mind. I love ocean waves, the sound of rain, a stream, or even a thunderstorm. You spend a third of your life in bed. Eight hours a night equals a third of your day which equals a third of your life. Therefore, I made my bedroom a room I love. I suggest you do the same.

The worst predator of sleep is the Mind. The mind is active and worried about what is coming or what has happened. I try and remember as I go to sleep that in the present time, nothing is happening, and I am safe and okay in the *now*. When I get into trying to control my mind, my mind seems to rebel and get even more out of control. Sleep and anxiety do not go well together. Part of my uniqueness is my mind cannot let things go until the next morning. I am not the type of person who can push things out of my mind and get a good night's rest when something is stressing me. I know there are others, who can sleep like babies under the most stressful circumstances, and I am clear I am not one of them. So, I have to deal with my circumstances. Because rest is what happens on the Second Floor, it is something I have the opportunity to practice. My nightly routine is very helpful in getting me to sleep. Each floor has its opportunities. Luckily if I cannot sleep, there is a room I can go to for sleep medicine.

The Self Preservation Room: Finding resolve

My Self-Preservation Room is where I go when I cannot sleep. If my mind needs resolution or busy activity to wind down, and my bath, cozy bed and white noise do not work, this is my safe place. In this room, I realize I don't always need as much sleep as I think I need or as I was conditioned to believe I need. Sometimes, I need a lot and other times not so much. From being in the Kitchen, I have learned to listen to my body. I have learned my body is really smart, and it will let me know what and how much of everything it will need. I have learned my body and its needs are unique.

When I come to the Self-Preservation Room, I relax and find resolve. In this room I, of course, have a journal, but this one is my sleep medicine. Whatever ruckus my mind is creating, I get it all out in vigorous writing. Sometimes, I do research on the computer if I am worrying over an unanswered question or detail in my life. I have found once it is out, I can get back to sleep. I would rather sleep shorter hours with deeper sleep, then toss and turn all night long. It is amazing the crazy things I can stress about at night. It is also amazing how sometimes a good night's sleep can change my whole distorted perception of whatever worries creep up.

The Self-Preservation Room is reserved for my sleepless nights. It is always dimly lit, and in this room, I play soft music like Enya to continue to calm me. I am so grateful to have a room for everything. Once I have let it all out, I can enter my Bedroom and sleep peacefully and wake up with a renewed perception. I can preserve myself and my emotions by simply letting them out. The emotions just want to pass through. As nighttime comes, the quiet alone can give the mind space to erupt into anxiety. If this happens it's okay, just let it out and find some kind of resolve, so you can let it go.

Internal peace comes from rest and self-preservation. Each and every step of self-love leads you to more expanded forms of who you already are. The more you expand, the more of you there is to love. How wonderful is that! You are unique and will have your own designed floors based upon what your unique needs are. In order to know what your floor requirements are and what rooms are necessary, you have to do your Cellar and Ground Floor work. Sometimes on the Second Floor of my Palace, I can see things from such a different perception. After all, I am higher up, so there is more to see. It is also amazing what you can see when you have rest, when you cleanse and nurture yourself. This is what the Second Floor is all about. Rejuvenation.

Extra Credit Advantage:

2nd Floor Reading for home-work

A notepad or a journal. On the first page please write "Sleep Medicine." If you are restless, it is your mind. Release all mental clutter in your journal or notepad, and you will surely go back to sleep. It is healthy to release all negativity before sleep.

Tao Te Ching (Stephen Mitchell): This is the Tao written in simple short chapters. It is all about the art of letting go. This is the one book I use daily on my Second Floor. Each night before bed, I read one verse and allow this to give me freedom emotionally.

3rd Floor: Perspective and Understanding

The Third Floor of my Crystal Palace is still somewhat under construction, and I visit there but not for lengthy stays. It is a mystical place. It is where I am *up* and can see my life from an existential or more spiritual place. It is the floor where things make sense, no matter the pain. When I am on this floor I realize life is not haphazard. Its design is perfect. My visits to this floor bring trust that everything happens just as it should happen. It is a place of perspective and understanding. Here, I am aware that I am responsible for my individual life, and I am responsible for giving my life meaning. I am responsible for living it passionately and sincerely in spite of the many worldly obstacles life has to offer. Here, I am responsible for finding the beneficial meaning in *all* the obstacles I face in my life.

It is all windows, floor to ceiling, where I can see out, but no one else can see in. It is private, soft, gentle, and ethereal. Here I realize I am not alone, have never been alone, and will never be alone. From the Third Floor, I can see out of my Palace. There is no separation of rooms on the Third Floor because it is a place of being completely connected. It is where we are all *One*. It is just one room, no boundaries. When I am here, I also experience no boundaries. I am as expansive as eternity all from the single cell I have nurtured within me. Up here, it is clear and open. I have learned the most on this floor from looking out the windows. The most interesting aspect is the ability to see out and learn what parts of the outer world need boundaries and which parts of the outer world can remain. When I am up here, I have effortless insight into how the outer world operates in an unpredictable way. My task is to take care of my internal world and make it stable.

The Lesson of Perspective: The ability to see the bigger picture

When I look out from the Third Floor, I have complete clarity. I can see the outer world and its impact on my inner world. Because of this perspective, I have learned to manage the outer world with boundaries. This is the only floor where I get enough clarity to be able to *set my way* when I return to the ground floor. It is the floor of understanding and insight.

Looking Down: How to deal with love and relationships

With the gift of this higher perspective, I see my palace has an outer structure of boundaries. It has a Porch, a Front Yard, and a Fence. Each one of these places is significant in how I deal with *love* and *relationships*. From the Third Floor, I was able to observe the difference between Brick people and Palace people. I had had many Cellar experiences getting tangled in bad relationships and was not able to get real perspective on how I kept ending up in bad places with the wrong people. Here is what a Third Floor in-sight has offered me:

As I stand with my face pressed against the window and look down to the outside of my Palace, I can see everything. It is amazing what you can see when you rise above a situation. I could so clearly see from this perspective with clarity and understanding that Brick people do not look at their mistakes. Palace People, on the other hand, know they have made a mistake and recognize they have some adjusting to do. They understand they have to change. Brick people think the world should change. I can see that the Brick people feel life is unfair to them, and in their minds, they are always getting the short end of the stick.

I am watching them want what they want when they want it, feeling as if they are never wrong, and when they do not get the immediate gratification of what they desire in the moment, they throw tantrums of all sorts as if rules apply to everyone else aside from them. From up here, it is all so clear, but in my life, when I have been down in the mix with these people I have hardly been able to see them at all and I have continued to get mixed up in relationships with them. I can see that I used all forms of denial to justify their behaviors.

Brick people are motivated by the moment and Palace people are motivated by the journey. I can see as I watch them from up above that Brick people are agenda oriented, they are not relationship oriented. I can see from way up here that I approach all relationships thinking that all people are relationship oriented. It is no wonder I have so often gotten stuck. Brick people are tenacious at holding onto their way regardless of how much resistance they evoke from others. These are destructive people that have been able to seduce me into trying to make them happy and to show them the way to Palace construction. Like a movie playing in front of me, I watch how I was stuck with these people trying to motivate them to examine the journey of the river. From up here, I understand no one can motivate these people. They are dedicated to deception and distortion. They are rigid, unmoving, and unrelenting in pushing their brand of the truth onto people.

I understand now that they have not found a functional way to make their lives work. They are internally frustrated, which makes them egocentric. They get enraged when they see other people's lives going well. They prefer for the world to revolve around them. They want life to be full of fun and excitement and to have others take care of all things boring and difficult. They have an uncanny way of escaping responsibility and placing the blame on those closest to them. It is all about them. What is theirs is theirs, and what is yours is theirs too. Eventually, they will drain you dry.

What I observe as I look down on this lesson in perspective from my Third Floor windows is Brick people are big on problems but short on solutions. They look to their relationships to fix everything, which has been another trap in getting me tangled up with these people. Somehow, I always ended up wrong in these relationships and they made me feel crazy. They try and solve their problems through the use of cut downs, threats, suffering, sarcasm, or being controlling. What happens is the person outside of them ends up solving their problems to get them to stop complaining.

The human journey is about hard work, determination, and endurance. Brick people want all the luxuries of the journey without having to journey. They take a passive approach to their happiness and then blame other people for their misery. In essence, what they do is make excuses for themselves as a way to justify why they have Bricks and other people have Palaces. They will convince you they cannot build a Palace, but they deserve one. I can see from this elevated view that Palace people make mistakes just like anyone else, but Palace people blame themselves and look for understanding. Brick people are those that suffer over their own suffering and are not successful in finding the meaning in their lives. They languish in their personal unhappiness, and I can see I would get stuck in trying to 'save' these types and try to help them grow. I learned over and over they just cannot find people to love them as they want to be loved.

You have Bricks. Bricks are the problems you are here to alchemize to Crystal. Some people want to transform, and others don't. Those driven to have a Crystal Palace are not comfortable with their Bricks. I can see that my misery has always made me miserable and having attention for my misery was humiliating. No one ever felt sorry for me or enabled me to have an excuse to keep my Bricks. Being deeply unsatisfied was not the permanent state in which I wanted to live. You cannot feel entitled to the rights to feel happy and passively wait for happiness to sweep you into a blissful life. Like everything else, I can see from this Third Floor insightful gift, happiness is a byproduct of achieving and hard work.

I can see that when I have gotten lost in the webs of Brick people, I stop focusing on my own work and try to change them by doing the work for them in the hope they would catch on and take responsibility. I have understanding as I stand here my nose pressed against the glass looking down at my Porch, my Yard, and Fence and I see how and where I was getting stuck along the way down the river of transformation. I have to remember *my personal work is my journey*. You cannot journey for another. My journey will always lead me to right places, people, events, and circumstances. I will certainly make mistakes along the way and get hung up in my own Bricks and the Bricks of others, as I navigate my relationship world, but with humility and the ability to stay focused on my journey, I am sure to succeed. Now, I am able to take a deep breath of gratitude for this Third Floor lesson in perspective.

Lost people get us lost. What I can see looking down is Brick people are completely unaware they are lost. This is one of the traps that gets you stuck with them. It takes you time being in relationship with them to see they are lost. You gain this understanding, when you start to feel lost as a result of your relationships with them. When I start veering sharply away from who I am naturally, I have my first clue that I am in a relationship with a Brick Person. If my life becomes consumed with being told I am wrong and I am in a constant state of defending myself, I understand that this is a Brick Person. These people do not have enough of a center to have mutually beneficial relationships.

You will not be able to tell a Brick Person from a Palace person until you are clear about yourself, You must be clear about who you are before you can become clear about the relationships in your life. *The more clear you are about who you are, the better a relationship chooser you will be.* You will learn this lesson through trial and error.

I had to learn that many people do not do their inner work. They walk through life, angry they have a pile of Bricks or feeling it is unfair they have Bricks while others have Crystal Palaces. They boil it down to bad luck and somehow, they always get worked over. I am clear these people do not know the hard work it takes to build a Crystal Palace, or maybe they do, and they do not want to do the work.

The Brick people tend to really like Palace people and they figure out ways to get Palace people to think they have a palace too, and so you let them in as house guests. You soon begin to notice they are not respectful. They leave a mess, use your stuff, act as if you owe them your comforts, and they have no manners. After a while, you begin to ask if you can see their palace which becomes a request that never happens. When You have had a messy house guest, it is like someone came in and defecated in the middle of the living room. You point it out and say "Hey look what you left!!" They say "Well it's your Palace so you clean it up!!" This is when I learned to use my Door. There is also no longer a welcome sign in front of it. I have learned from the Third Floor perspective my Palace is for *me* only. It is my inner world, and something I must always take care of. It is not for the use and abuse of others. *With my door, I have learned never to give my Self away.* What a beautiful lesson.

<u>*The Porch: Our chosen family*</u>

As I look down from the Third Floor to my outside world, I am now focused on my Porch. I love my Porch. My Porch is where all my most treasured people reside in my life. I have a wrap-around deck equipped with cushion chairs, porch swings, ceiling fans, a wood burning stove, rocking chairs, and coffee tables. Out on my Porch, I love to sit and have great conversation with those I love and trust with all my heart. Everyone, who is on my Porch, respects my door and my inner world. They see me. They know me and love coming to visit. Their company is my gift. They also have an idea of how precious a Crystal Palace is because my porch dwellers are either in a Palace or their Palace is under construction. They are committed to their inner worlds.

My Porch people are my *chosen family.* I am deeply vulnerable, honest, and intimate with these people which adds to the growth of who I am. I take what I hear and learn on my Porch into my Palace to assimilate it. My Porch people love me, listen to me and allow me to do the same for them. These relationships teach me. They are mutually beneficial and leave me feeling loved. They are there for me regardless of how ugly or how brilliant my life is. They are my treasures. The most important quality of my Porch people is they are my truth-tellers, whether good and bad. From the truth told to me lovingly and gently, I can understand and grow. I am also able to tell them the truth. What I learned in the Cellar is withholding a truth to keep the peace is the same as being dishonest. It creates the building of the false self. On my Porch, the truth is passed around regularly. It is another place to drink your coffee – the great awakener you learned about in the Kitchen. On the Porch, *truth is the deepest intimacy.*

<u>The Yard: Your social circle</u>

From the Porch, there are three steps down into my Yard. I have a lot of people in my yard. Some close friends, some family, some acquaintances, some friends from work, and some friends of history. The people in my Yard are people I really enjoy. I like to socialize with them on a cordial and superficial level. I do not necessarily possess the trust or closeness with them that I do my Porch people, but I love them nonetheless, and they add much value to my life. They are fun and wonderful people. I have had Porch people become Yard people due to changes in friendship circumstances. When they go to my Yard, I can still love them, but I have learned for whatever reason I have to love them from a greater distance and that is okay. You are here changing and growing, and sometimes as you change, you have to change relationships.. I can see from the Third Floor perspective how important it is to set boundaries and also to let each soul walk their own path. *Differing paths may cause separation, but they do not need to cause a lack of love.*

<u>The Fence: People in your lives who need boundaries</u>

At the edge of my Yard, my Fence is white and wraps around my entire Crystal Palace. The people at my Fence are some of my most loved people and also people – no matter how I love them and they love me – cannot respect my space. I let them on my Porch and they defecated, so they went to the Yard. In the Yard, the same thing happened, and so they had to go and stand behind the Fence. This way the Home Owners Association can clean their mess. I have learned Brick people never clean their own messes. I do not love them any less than anyone else, they just need to have a different location in my life. These people stop at my Fence to say "hi" and want back in, but I have the gates locked. However, I openly enjoy walking down, leaning on my Fence, and having conversations with them.

When I have reached my enough-time with the Fence people, I let them know I have business inside to attend to. *I have learned no matter how much you love someone, they may never know how to respect your inner world*. What I have found with my Fence dwellers is that they are needy people. When I say needy, what I mean is they are so focused on their own needs that it is like an ache. They can only focus on their own ache. If that is the focus, then these people cannot possibly focus enough on the other and the needs of the other to have any kind of respectful or mutually beneficial relationship with them. So, I have learned from the Third Floor perspective and some hard lessons, some people just need to remain at my Fence. There are also people outside my Palace with picket signs marching to the "I hate Sherrie" chant. I have realized their hatred of me is *their* issue to deal with, and so I call in my restraining order of silence and give them no attention.

From the Third Floor, I have learned all people are lovable. I do not have to have rigid definitions of love, family, or friendship. I just have to know the location of every person in my life. I am also aware location is subject to change. Porch people may become Fence people, and Fence people may once again become Porch people. It is about remaining true to my Self and paying attention to how people make me feel and how I feel I impact them. I am not good for everyone, and not everyone is good for me. On the Third Floor, I learned this is okay. Some people have been simply poisonous for me. I have had to get them out to save the love of me and my Crystal Palace.

I do believe you are a reflection of the company you keep. Through your relationships, you are inspired to take a closer look at yourself. I value each and every person in my life for their exact purpose and gift, including my picketers. Sometimes I learn the most from those who have caused me the most pain. So I honor them for the lesson I was able to learn. Each person has helped me to go deeper into my Self. On the Third Floor, I was taught the workings of location. It all began to make sense to me.

Looking Out: Unlimited possibilities

Looking down on my life from above is just one of the great treasures available on the Third Floor. Yet, I have discovered other treasures. Being up so high, I can also look out to the horizon and get a glimpse of how endless my possibilities are. There are mountains, valleys, and ocean as far as the eye can see. Life, from this vantage point is lush, full, wide, open, voluptuous, fruitful, and vast. It is extraordinary to view life from this higher level of consciousness. When I see the Universe out there, I realize the vastness which must live within my Self. There really are no limits.

When you are down in the Cellar, you live in a small world with a detailed focus, but traveling up to the Third Floor you can see each detail healed in the Cellar opens up a larger space in the Universe. Therefore, as you grow, the Universe you live in grows too. It is all connected. As I look out to the horizon, I get snapshots of dreams to dare to live. I see each dream as a real possibility. If I can conjure up a dream as an idea, then the dream must already exist. It is simply waiting for me to make it real. It is hard for my mind to get around the vastness of the endless possibilities. I have learned on the Third Floor how powerful my mind can be if I use faith and belief correctly. I can see that what holds me back on the lower floors is a lack of faith. When I am afraid, I lack faith. I know this to be an area of growth in my life. This will take work on my Ground Floor.

Looking UP: Endings followed by new beginnings

The next treasure I have discovered is the opportunity to look up. My Crystal Palace has a glass ceiling. When I look up, I recognize this life in human form is not forever. There is an ending, when I look up. With this awareness, comes the knowledge that a *well lived life is a well grieved life*. Everything you begin will end, and so you grieve. My life in human form is temporary and will have its end. I know someday, I will pass away and no longer be of this world, but will be of another world. I believe the other world to be even more magnificent than my Third Floor.

When I think about death, I think about the finite time I have in life. The workings of my Crystal Palace are my way to heaven on earth. When I look up and see finality, I realize and appreciate all the things in life I value and am attached to. I am deeply aware of what a precious experience life is. As I become more mature and evolved, I believe I will spend more time on the Third Floor. I imagine in my last years in life, I will come to this place in my Palace with a total sense of readiness for the next part of the journey and the ending of this one.

My visits to the Third Floor at this time in my life are brief but meaningful beyond comprehension. There is much information to take in. At my current level of development, I am not ready to understand all the mysteries of this floor. Much of the Third Floor is beyond my current level of understanding. What I do know is as I continue to work my Palace Formula, the more I evolve, the more I will have Third Floor in-sights. The Third Floor is a gift. The in-sights here are spiritual, extraordinary, non-threatening, higher, peaceful, and purely truthful. *On the Third Floor, I have understanding.*

The process of the Palace is about rising up to the next beautiful level of *you*. You are always in motion as a human being. Movement and touch are essential to you. Change and pain create in you the greatest desire to move. Happiness is the celebrated result of all of your hard work. Happiness and achievement are your times to rest, be content, and enjoy life until the next life class begins. You cannot stop the movement of life or the classes from coming. You are here to be flexible, to grow, and to expand. Movement is always an up and down, ebb and flow process. This is why there is an Elevator and Stairs in the palace, so keep reading!

No Extra Credit Advantage for the Third Floor. Being here is an education all unto itself. Enjoy your stay.

The Elevator and Stairs: The Process of Evolution

On every floor in the Crystal Palace, there is an Elevator door and a set of Stairs. There are three floors, three layers of lessons on each floor, and three processes to the way you move through life. There is one Crystal Palace because there is only one of you.

The Elevator only goes in one direction and to one location. It goes down. The Cellar of my Crystal Palace is where all of my emotions are stored which lock me into old programming. Old programming is automatic, rough, and fast. If I encounter a trigger like a rejection, abandonment, argument, or loss, I am immediately thrust onto the Elevator and down into the Cellar. I usually arrive in the Cellar with an ungraceful thud and a heavy heart. I get out of the Elevator to see that a series of boxes have fallen off the shelf in a heap and are wide open. All the mini-series are exposed and playing at the same time. They are noisy, confusing, and frustrating, but I at least know where I am, and what I need to do.

Each current trigger opens up all other past wounds which are similar in feeling and content I am offered the opportunity to understand why this trigger affected me so deeply. I turn on my light, get on my hands and knees (humility), and put the pieces back together. I organize my emotions, understand why they are so deep, and I write about them to organize myself. I let this current trigger teach me and talk with me. It shares its secrets, and I am able to develop awareness around what this is telling me about my Self. Luckily I love my Cellar. I do not always love the feelings, fears, anxieties and sadness's that come along with dark times, but I do know that each time I am in the Cellar, I am in a new process, and it is time to learn. The feelings and terror of the Cellar never seem to change, and I write a lot about being afraid when I am there. The Third Floor consciousness seems not so real when I am in my Cellar. Nonetheless, I at least have an awareness of the lessons I learned way up there.

I can fall to the Cellar from the Ground, Second, and Third floors. It all depends upon what wound opens and what class is next in line to take. The scariest fall is from the Third Floor to the Cellar because of the complete duality between the top floor and the bottom one. However, life is all about duality, and *sometimes, my greatest falls are my deepest lessons*. I have come to learn life is full of the unexpected. No matter the awareness I have of that, I am still in complete shock when the unexpected occurs. I am thankful I have a place to fall when I am in shock. There is organization and a way to make sense of things no matter how long it takes. That is the very safety of my structure. I have a place in this world. *I have my own place.*

As I mentioned, the Elevator goes in only one direction and one location. The only way out of my Cellar is to evolve my way out one step at a time. Therefore, I must take the Stairs. I have to evolve my way through every learning experience – each step – and this is how I grow. My in-sights light up each step I take so I am guided out of the darkness. Once I am on the Ground Floor, the light can come in. I immediately go to my Kitchen unpack my in-sight basket and figure out all the ingredients I will need to work my new lessons.

Once I have that figured out, I will head to my Office and set measureable goals, live them out in my Living Room, open Windows to let my light of awareness shine and keep my boundaries with my Door! It's a great way for me to be uniquely me. At the end of each Ground Floor day, I will take my hard work up my Stairs to release, cleanse, and rest. Before I slip into my beautiful bed to rest, I will look at myself with satisfaction in the mirror knowing I at least did my best, was of my word, and was honest. I spend most of my time between the Ground and Second Floors because that is simply where I am in my life.

Knowing my emotional location gives me a sense of grounding when life is challenging. It has brought me much peace to know my location. When I am in my Cellar, I am in my *core wounds*. I am in the deepest darkest part of me. The Cellar is the core of the Palace. It is in the bottom-most part of the structure. It is dark, enclosed and furthest down; it is the most *within*. When I need to go within, I go to my Cellar. I choose to go within, when my deepest pain surfaces because of current life challenges and old programming. I am happy to know when I fall apart, I have a safe and private place to go. I used to fall apart and not have any clue of my location. My pain used to make me dizzy with the feeling of being sucked into a void. Now, I have a place to fall when I fall apart.

My Cellar visits are never a result of a failure. Failure really only occurs when you cease to get up and try again. My visits there are always learning and growing experiences. I learn much about my Self, when I am there. Sometimes I am there for extended periods, depending upon what has come up in life to challenge me. When you are in pain, you can feel extremely lost and vulnerable. I still feel that way, but I am reassured by the idea that I know where I am, which means I know the way through. *It is in the Cellar where we find humility.* You are able to see your wrongs and old programs, forgive yourself, and accept that you are exactly where you need to be in your human process.

The Ground Floor is my floor of *hope*. I can rise up from the Cellar and take my time practicing my newly found in-sights. I know what the program looks like on the Ground Floor. On this floor, I have structure, direction and purpose. This is the way through pain and into larger levels of personal expansion. The Ground Floor is the most creative. It is teaching the brain new habits, connecting new neurons, creating new beliefs, and perfecting the idea of the Self you are growing into. *It is on the Ground Floor where maturity is born.* Psychological health and maturity are synonymous. Maturity means grounded within your Self. Remember there is a Living Room on this floor where you can let it all hang out, be loud, laugh without abandon, love like crazy, jump for joy, and simply do nothing but relax. Maturity is about learning to meet your own needs. Maturity is doing the work of love and listening. Maturity is about self-imaging and becoming more and more the *you* you would like to become. Maturity is your essence when you are grounded.

As I rise up to rest each night on my Second Floor, I look forward to seeing the woman in the mirror, who is me at the end of each day. I have come to love her. Whether she is falling or rising, I have come to love her. I love rising up to rest knowing I have done my best. Regardless of how I appear to others or the outside world I do rise to my Second Floor knowing that I have done *my best.* When I have done my best, I more easily put my Self to sleep. My morning and evening cleanses are about releasing. I release expectation each morning, and I cleanse myself of negativity each night. *The Second Floor is about letting go.*

It is here I have the awareness of what is in my control and what needs to fall into place on its own and in its own time. This awareness is something to count on. I can clutch at times by wanting to control what is not in my power, and if I am suffering with that, I will go to my Self-Preservation room and work it out. The greatest lesson I learn in letting go is this: *eventually all things work out.*

My beautiful Third Floor is where Higher Self Consciousness steps in to guide me. I have usually done enough work to rise to this level to receive the gift earned. It works like this: I do my internal work, pass a life class or a series of life classes, and rise up for a Third Floor experience. It is my reward. The work I have done below opens up the Third Floor experience. I get to see on this floor the purpose behind all the work done on my Self. The lower floors are about taking responsibility and making decisions. From the Third Floor view, I can see my decisions are my teachers.

Life breaks down into the simple when I am on Third Floor. Life is the science of decision making. Each decision made is what has made my life's structure. The better and more true my decisions are for my Self, the more visits I have on this mystical floor. I feel faith when I visit here. Faith makes me feel at peace. I feel certain, when I have faith. From the Third Floor, I realize fear and/or worry are unnecessary and often wasteful. When I am here and only when I am here, do I have complete faith in the notion that life is perfect. When I am here, I can see everything. I have no fear. I have understanding. It is a total understanding of the process of life, of what I am doing and why. *On the Third Floor, everything makes sense.* That is what this floor is about. I feel totally connected to my Self when I am here. There are no flaws, no holes, nothing missing. I feel whole.

My Elevator is here to take me to the depths of my growth and my Stairs illuminate my future. The Stairs take me up into the unknown. They take up to the new so there is always anticipation, excitement to get to the new and get started. My Stairs are reflective of my new beliefs about myself and the faith in those new beliefs which inspires me to climb. Going up requires the step by step process, and it requires a certain amount of focused concentration. *If I am not concentrating on the step I am on, I will likely trip and lose my balance.* So as I anticipate the new, I use focus to stay in the step I am in. My Stairs illuminate me from my depths. My Stairs help me to move through my Crystal Palace from the bottom to the top. I use the Stairs for the forward moving progress of my life. When I go back into my depth, I take the Elevator.

The rise and fall of life is the way it is supposed to be. This is what I learn from my Elevator and Stairs. Time is the element of travel. You are traveling in one direction, and that is forward. You have the choice to not travel emotionally and stay with your bricks. The goal is not to get directly to a third floor destination, rather the goal is the process. All the floors are necessary throughout life. The goal is the *process*. It is the journey. Life is in movement and although the goal is always forward, being in the Cellar is not a sign of going backward. It is the start of the next phase of your growth. As you grow, you rise. As you mature, you will certainly have more and more Third Floor experiences, but no floor is more important or meaningful than any other floor. All that matters is forward moving progress.

The in-sights associated with each floor contribute to your overall growth. It is evolution. This is why the Elevator and Stairs are so significant. The Elevator and Stairs are metaphorical for the overall growth process you take on in your uniqueness as human beings. With each floor, you have healings. You leave each floor with the gifts of gratitude; depths of understanding; feelings of accomplishment; increased knowledge; good physical, emotional, mental, and spiritual health; creativity; freedom; joy; and abundance. You begin to understand that all things are designed to lead you to success.

The way you move through life

The Elevator and Stairs are reflective of your movement through life. Any time you enter the Elevator or rise up your Stairs, you are experiencing movement through time. This is your process of evolution. The movement **between** floors and the movement **across** floors offer you the gifts of vertical and horizontal travel in time. Whenever you are on a certain floor in the Crystal Palace, you are living horizontally in the now. Whenever you are on the Stairs or Elevator you are moving either down or up through time vertically. Time is a beautiful thing, as time is motion. There are three floors representing the past, present, future, and these three time periods operate both vertically and horizontally. Let me demonstrate how you can use this to help you know your purpose and location in your healing. Let's look at this horizontal and vertical process.

↕			
Cellar	Past	Beginning	Birth
First/Second Floors	Present	Middle	Life
Third Floor	Future	End	Death
⟶			

When the Elevator takes you to the Cellar, you are traveling back in time (vertically down) into your *past*. As you enter the Cellar, you begin your horizontal movement of growth. Your old wounds or core wounds receive a visit from you with the purpose of gaining another level of understanding and healing. Some current trigger sent you into the core of your Cell and you travel into the past to reach the original pain to heal the current trigger. Each core wound offers you the opportunity to embrace the original pain and heal it further. This healing is the gift or treasure of delving into your singularity because as you heal core wounds, you are essentially deconditioning your old eye-sights.

The Cellar is all about singularity. You have to heal alone. Being alone to face a challenge is big responsibility, but it is what it means to be singular. This is why you have a Cell to go to that is safe. No matter what emotional support you have in life, you essentially have to face your fears on your own. No one can do it for you. You can be encouraged and supported, but the actual *doing* is up to you. The *doing* is orchestrated in your singularity.

As you are in the *past* visiting the core wound, you are essentially in the time of a *birth* into a new phase of life. You are expanding your understanding. You are gathering new information and birthing into a new form of who you are with all this new knowledge. Each birth then takes you into a *new beginning*. So each current trigger takes you on a time travel of personal growth through the number three. In the Cellar, you have the horizontal movement of experiencing the *past*, a *birth* and a *new beginning*. This is the horizontal process of healing as you experience your Cellar lessons. As you connect with your past, you experience a rebirth exhumed out of a core wound linked to a current issue, which leads to a new beginning. The new beginning starts with your vertical movement up the Stairs. The stairs are illuminated with new in-sights to practice.

As you arrive on the Ground and Second Floor phases, you are there in the *present* time learning to be present with your new in-sights. In terms of time, you have now evolved from the time of birth into the time of the activity of giving your in-sights *life*. These two floors are active and alive. They are living organisms of growth, practice, adjusting, resting, cleansing, and changing. It is on these floors where we experiment; we are busy, alert, conscious, and reflecting. We are present. The activity of *Life* is always lived in the present, in the now. The Ground Floor is the activity of the now, and the Second Floor is where we rest and cleanse. The gifts of living and resting help us learn what it takes to have a fulfilling and meaningful life. They help us see the work and commitment it takes to genuinely live and love with understanding. On these floors, you design and live out your individual unique purpose in the world.

When you are on these two floors, you are in the *middle* of all of life. You are living in the middle section of your Crystal Palace. You are no longer at the beginning. All beginnings are Cellar-born. When you are on these two floors, you are in the middle of all the busyness. The middle is also reflective of where and how you find balance in your life. Anything that is in the middle of two ends is the balancer. You learn balance by getting grounded and resting. All things that work in harmony strive to have balance. You cultivate balance on these two floors. The horizontal nature of the Ground and Second floors is being *present* in the activity of *life*. In other worlds, it is about the now or present time; you are no longer in birth, you are in life. You are not at the beginning or the end, you are in the middle, cultivating balance and harmony.

As you illuminate your Stairs with your new life experience, you will travel vertically up to the Third Floor. When you enter the Third Floor, you experience time completely differently. You are essentially in the time of the *future,* seeing the endless possibilities available to you in your future.

The Third Floor is not busy with the activity of living, rather it is imbued with the energy of *being*. It is open with clear, unobstructed vision into the whole purpose of life. It is also here where you have experienced, in terms of time, an *ending*. This could be the ending of a lesson learned, a phase of life successfully passed, a life pop-quiz aced, the ending of a relationship or the end of some other significant experience. Endings sometimes bring us to the Third Floor because it is here that you are allowed to see the big picture. All endings gift you the bigger picture. You come here for this experience to see how your hard work has benefitted your growth, perspective, and maturity. After this bigger picture moment ends, you will again enter the Elevator to end your stay on the Third Floor.

The Third Floor then is also about the time of *death*. It is a very spiritual place the Third Floor. When you come here for a visit, you are always faced with the spiritualizing of your experiences. If you are here, you will inevitably contemplate that life is a process of life and death and life and death. When one thing ends, another begins. Thus, you will experience here the immortality of your individual spirit and the mortality of your human experience. In contemplating death, you more fully appreciate life. You are acutely aware on the Third Floor that all that lives, also dies. You will contemplate life after death, or the afterlife at the close of your human experience. At the close of this humanity experience, you will again be birthed into a completely new beginning. So, the Third Floor's horizontal experience in time is about the *future, endings, and death.*

The Elevator and Stairs are partners in the ascending and descending nature of life's flow in time. Three is the number of the Divine, and the human experience could not be a more Divine process. The Crystal Palace is metaphorical for your Divine Individual Self. You are privileged to be in this experience, if you can see what it is all about. The Crystal Palace metaphor is a way to find the meaning in your suffering and to make sense of how life's process works. If you look at time vertically, you see growth happening in the past (Cellar), the present (Ground and Second Floors) and the Future (Third Floor). You also see growth happening with a Beginning, Middle and an End, and you can also see growth occurring with your Birth, leading into your Life and ending with your Death. All of the floors in the palace offer you horizontal and singular floor learning experiences and vertical or movement learning experiences. This way you are having the Whole Experience of Life.

You live each part of your life vertically in tandem with the horizontal process. For example, each new issue takes you through a beginning and middle and end, each new change has a birth, a life, and a death, and each new phase of your life has a past, a present, and future. You are living all aspects of time at once and within the place of the Self (Crystal Palace). Every process you start will have a forward moving progression because time only travels forward, so even if you visit the past, time is still pushing you forward into your new learning.

Synergy of the Cellar and Third Floor

There are interesting commonalities between the Cellar and the Third Floor. These are significant in reflecting life's dualities and their commonalities. These floors are as similar as they are different. Neither the Cellar nor the Third Floor has rooms. Each is one room, no boundaries. Each is defined by open space. Open space creates an environment of *allowing*. On each of these floors, you have to allow for the births and deaths of life to occur. Both floors encapsulate beginnings and endings simultaneously.

I believe before you enter life, you are in a Third Floor-like space, but even grander. You choose to enter life. You have a mission for your soul, and so you choose to end your in-between life-form and choose birth. *You are a spiritual being before a human being*. You are that single living cell for less than five minutes upon your birth and then you start the process of life. Whenever you have the feeling you have gotten lost, you have had a divine awareness which is Third Floor driven and you return to your Cellar and enter your Chrysalis.

There are no boundaries to your healing objectives in the Cellar, so there is not a need to have walls, rooms, windows, or doors to serve as boundaries. You start in the Cellar to begin your transformation. If you are already in life, you come to your Cellar to face your past and begin a new birth out of an original pain. There are no windows, because when you are in the Cellar, you are only meant to be focusing on yourself. You are cut off from all larger views so as to not get distracted. *In Cellar time, there is no need to see out because you are here only to look within*. You are here to be one with yourself. You are here to start a new process, look at your past, and find your new beginnings in the birth of a new phase of your life. You are in the dark to focus all your energy on your healing process from the most recent death in your life which plunged you into this new birth. The Cellar, like any birth, is dangerous yet illuminated with wonder all at the same time. There are no boundaries on this floor, because there are no limits to how deep within you can go. You are enclosed to be able to undertake the process of birthing out of all past wounds.

The Third Floor is the only other floor in the Crystal Palace that is also one room with no boundaries. It is also a place of being One. Up here we are one with *all*; in the Cellar you are one with *yourself*. The Third Floor is the place of total connection with all of life. Unlike the Cellar, the Third Floor is all windows. It is as expansive as eternity with the totality of understanding that all is happening in its perfect design. You can see life from all directions and angles from up here. From up here, you can see glimpses into all the new beginnings available to you. It is a place of life and death just like the Cellar. All things that begin must end. When you experience endings in life, you ride your Elevator to the Cellar to be birthed into your new beginning through examining your past behaviors. All beginnings are without boundaries which is why the Cellar is without boundaries. You go there to manifest all new beginnings gifted to you from your Third Floor guidance of new opportunities.

The Cellar is also about life and death. In the Cellar you put to rest the parts of you which no longer serve your future endeavors. You take those parts, love them, organize them, understand them, and journal on them until you can place them into an appropriate box with new in-sights to work your Palace formula. In this way, as you travel up to the middle of the activity of the life energy floors, you feel lighter and free to prefect your living experience on your journey through open-ended maturation. The middle floors are equipped with boundaries which serve as practical living strategies for your newly birthed in-sights.

Once on the Third Floor, you have achieved another level of success in life that has now found its ending. Here, you are gifted with a feeling of satisfaction in your growth efforts. You have alchemized yet another part of your Self and you come to review your hard work. You are offered total perspective on what you have achieved. With objective awareness, you can see where adjustments can be made as you look out your windows at the next illuminating task in front of you to strive for.

You end a phase to get reborn yet again. Death tends to be associated with darkness and birth associated with light. The Cellar is dark by metaphor. The light always follows the dark, and in this way, you are biologically connected to your Third Floor. The Cellar and Third Floor are just that way. It is dark when you first enter the Cellar and light when you rise up your stairs of evolvement. It is light when you enter the Third Floor after successfully achieving more Self-love and faith, and it is dark when you leave to start your new process. So the Cellar and the Third Floor are in total working harmony, as partners in the darkness and in the light, in the birth and the death, in the beginning and the end, and in the past and the future. The middle is active, balanced and having the Now.

Each person is like a flower. The roots of who you are reside at the bottom deep underground. You started off as a single seedling. All growth starts with your roots (Cellar). The stem is the vein of life connecting the top to the bottom. Within the vein, is the active life force energy being dispersed throughout the flower (Ground/Middle Floors). If you pick a flower from the middle, there is no way to get the active life force energy up to the top, and the flower will die. The top (Third Floor) is the beauty and blossom of the flower full of color, light, and divinity. It is the focus of the flower, the result of the all the layers below. It all begins with a seedling developing its roots. The roots are the way to a nourished life.

The Cellar is where your most important work is done. The Cellar contains all of your roots. You have to nourish your roots so you can push your experiences up through the Palace and through the vein, so you can blossom into the newer and newer versions of who you would desire to become. The blossom may be the most visually beautiful part of the flower, but it would have no life without the nourishment of your roots. The spirituality of your life involves the whole of the person. This is why no one floor of the Crystal Palace is more important than any other.

Each floor gives you a complete whole which is signified by your Crystal Palace. Your Palace is singular in nature, and it is significant of the Self you have developed and built from the bottom up. The Crystal Palace is your singularity, which will always be in development because you are here to consistently upgrade and remodel, add additions and keep your Palace current and whole. You will always be in Self construction through the duration of your life. When I view my Crystal Palace from a distance I can see it is the most majestic expression of the totality of my individuality. I have a place in this world.

My Palace Address (My Place in the World):

Three Happiness Way
Singularity, Totality
Infinity

You are here to have to the *complete* experience of life in your singularity expressed within the totality. You are here to be in the eternity of your growth. Having the complete experience with awareness solidifies your place in the world. Life wants you to experience all of its angles, edges, and crevices. You will rip and tear, cry and be in crises, you will bleed and fall, you will give it all your blood sweat and tears and still fail, you will succeed beyond your wildest dreams, soar to new and more significant heights, laugh with all your might, love deeply and wildly, and experience times of complete harmony. Life is designed this way. It is supposed to be this way. If it weren't this way you, could not evolve. You develop your singularity through this process, and you alchemize all your bricks to crystal. You build yourself into a whole through having the whole life experience. Your whole is symbolized by your Crystal Palace. Inside that Crystal Palace is each person's unique and individual life process.

Life endlessly provides you with chaos, creating harmony-making experiences, because you cannot fully embrace harmony without knowing chaos. You are here to have the *totality* of life's endless movement. This way, when you pass away, you will pass knowing that you have had the total experience for your soul. It's all about evolution and taking the grand total of the life experience. Before I pass away, I see myself old, wise, well-read, life educated, and glowing with life energy resonating from every cell in my body. I see there is still stuff in my in-box, but I am ready for death and content that I imbibed every bit of this life experience for what it had to offer me. I may have started with holes but I will pass feeling whole. I wish the same for you. The *three* words I will offer your divinity are

Love Your Self.